Rathore on
VALUATION OF ASSETS

Dr. Shailendra Singh Rathore

ISBN
Paperback 979-8-89673-490-1
Hardcase 979-8-89699-389-6

Limits of Liability/Disclaimer of Warranty

The author and publisher have used their best efforts in preparing this book. However, the author makes no representation or warranties with respect to the accuracy or completeness of this book, and specifically declaims any implied warranties, merchantability, or fitness for any particular professional purpose, and shall in no event be liable for any loss of profit or any other professional damage, including but not limited to special, incidental, consequential and other damages.

- Cover Page Designed by Riya Singh Rathore (Gondia) & Ramesh Chhangani (Nagpur).
- Infographic Images designed by Amit Rajendra Singh Chauhan, Gondia, MS.
- Type Setting Assistance by Sandeep Kawade, Gondia, MS.
- Editing Assistance by Aishwarya Singh Rathore.
- Special Assistance from my beloved wife, Shipra Singh Rathore, without the support of whom the book would have been completed in half the time.

This book is dedicated to my mom, whose unwavering love, endless support, and constant belief in me have shaped who I am today. Her strength, wisdom, and kindness have been my guiding lighthouse through every challenge and triumph. I am forever grateful for her sacrifices and encouragement, which have made this journey possible.

...Author

Acknowledgments

This book draws its insight from my ninety-three articles & editorials published in the Indian Valuer Journal since 1991 and the articles published in the Proceedings of many National Conventions of the Institution of Valuers, India. My lectures all across India & UK on this subject add flavor to it.

I am thankful to all those who, knowingly or unknowingly, helped me write this book. References of outside sources have been quoted whenever applicable. Just in case I have missed any, please bring it to my notice. Correction shall surly be applied in the next edition.

...Author

Prologue

In the labyrinthine world of valuation, art and science stand as twin pillars of insight and precision. As the market evolves, so too must our methodologies and understandings. This second volume of my exploration into real estate valuation is both a continuation and a deepening of the journey we embarked on in the first book.

The landscape of valuation is ever-changing, shaped by economic tides, technological advancements, and shifting societal needs. Yet, amidst this flux, the fundamental principles of valuation remain steadfast, guiding investors, developers, and analysts through the complexities of property assessment.

This book differs in many ways from my previous book, published in 2001. It delves into advanced techniques and contemporary challenges in valuation. It addresses the quantitative metrics that form the backbone of our evaluations and the qualitative factors that influence market dynamics and property worth. From the nuances of sustainable building practices to the impact of global economic shifts, we will explore a spectrum of factors that bear upon the true value of real estate.

As you turn these pages, you will find a blend of theoretical and philosophical insights, practical applications, and real-world case studies. Whether you are a seasoned professional seeking to refine your expertise or a newcomer eager to master the intricacies of valuation, this book is designed to be a comprehensive guide.

The path to accurate and insightful valuation is continual learning and adaptation. I hope this volume will serve as both a resource and an inspiration, equipping you with the knowledge and tools to navigate the dynamic terrain of the real estate market with confidence and acuity.

Welcome to the next stage of our exploration.

Dr. Shailendra Singh Rathore

s_s_rathore@rediffmail.com

***

Contents

Chapter 1

Value - A Multifaceted Word

General

In the morning rush hour of 12th January 2007, a mysterious violinist was playing incognito some of the most complex tunes ever written at the L'Enfant Plaza Metro entrance of Washington DC. Most passers-by didn't care; some slowed, and only seven stopped and listened to his tune for any length of time. Over the period of 43 minutes, the violinist performed six classical pieces and collected $52.17.

What commuters didn't realize is that the baseball-capped violinist was none other than Joshua Bell... one of the finest classical violinists in the world. Joshua had performed at a live concert in a Boston theatre only two days ago. 2000 tickets were sold, and each ticket was priced at $100.

What conclusion do you draw from the above story? The story suggests that value is not an absolute concept. The same performance by Joshua Bell, which was highly valued in a concert hall setting with tickets costing $100 each, was largely ignored and undervalued in the context of a metro station. This indicates that the perceived value is heavily influenced by the context and environment in which it is presented, rather than being an inherent and unchanging attribute. This conclusion goes true everywhere.

Meaning of Value

The word 'Value' is difficult to define precisely. The simple definition by Hadley is, "Price is a fact, and value is an estimate of what the price ought to be."

The evaluation of 'values' is very much like Mozart's music. On the one hand, it holds great simplicity; its basic ideas and philosophy can be grasped rather quickly by those who first encounter its rhythmic ripples. On the other hand, below the calm-looking surface, there are fascinating subtleties that remain a formidable challenge - even to those who spend a lifetime in its arduous study.

Sometimes, several meanings of a word develop out of its use over a considerable period. As such, one of the most difficult problems almost all lexicographers might have faced is that many words are used with several meanings. Value (Latin: Valere) is a multifaceted word with several diversified meanings attached to it. "The word value is like water, which is colorless and odorless but can acquire any tinge, odor, or shape of a vessel according to circumstances."... says Justice Brende. The 'Value,' as such, can neither be treated as an absolute concept nor can be assumed as an intrinsic (or inherent) characteristic of property; instead, it depends upon lot many external factors as well.

There exists a fairly large number of definitions of value, but it is quite paradoxical to note that none of them has succeeded in offering its precise, convincing, or all-inclusive definition. Broadly speaking; the term "value" is to be found in social, ethical, political, and religious fields besides having its own importance in business and economic dealings. However, the matter of discussion in this book is solely restricted to economic or monetary values

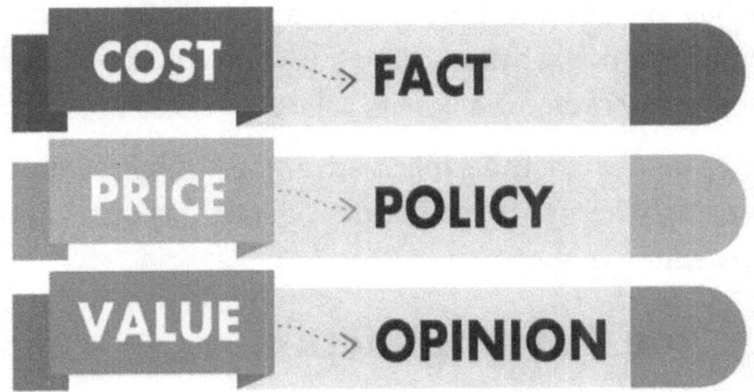

Value, price, and cost do not exist until an exchange of commodities or services occurs. Price, as such, has the following characteristics:

A. It is a special form of value.

B. It is the cost of a commodity plus some additional reward to the producer for his invested capital and labor.

C. It is fixed-up depending upon the demand from consumers compared to their other wants and this adjustment of process brings into existence - value.

Academically speaking, the price of a commodity is the point where the curve offeree of supply of that commodity meets its curve of force of demand. It signifies that the price rises if the demand is more and supply is otherwise. Thus, in a freely operating market at any given time, all other constant factors, such as any decrease in demand or increase in supply, will cause the price to fall. Conversely, any increase in demand or decrease in supply will cause a price hike.

Demand means willing buyers and those who are quite capable of buying. A commodity may be desirable for satisfying wants. But an ability in the form of exchange power is necessary. Demand alone, however, cannot impart price to a commodity. In a competitive market, willing sellers should be ready to part with the commodity for some consideration. Such a price, determined by the market forces of demand and supply, is known as an "equilibrium price."

Cost, on the other hand, is the actual expenditure to produce a commodity having a value. Cost is also a useful concept, especially in depreciation accounting, as depreciation usually works out on the present cost of a commodity rather than on its value.

In brief, value confers the explicit advantage on account of ownership of a given wealth, whereas cost and prices depict the sacrifice required (or expected) to acquire that object.

Value: A Non-Linear Function

Value is a non-linear and oscillating function of so many internal and external parameters (though it is sometimes very difficult to draw a clear-cut demarcating line between them), such as:

1. inherent (or intrinsic) characteristics of the property. (It is to be noted that the word property is used here in a general sense. It includes buildings, machines, goods, and so on):

2. demand and supply conditions prevailing in the market as the Present Market Value (PMV) of any property reflects supply and demand, especially in an environment of full laissez-faire. Also, the ability to pay for a commodity depends, to an extent, on the amount of money in circulation. When money is freely available, prices remain high. When money is scarce, on the other hand, prices nose-dive. When trade is brisk, money circulates rapidly. This affects values. It also increases demand for commodities in general. Effective demand is largely dependent on the purchasing power of the consumer.

However, it is to be noted here that "laissez-faire" is quite an impracticable notion. Several economic theories put forth from time to time by prominent and prodigious economists are based on the assumption of laissez-faire. For example, David Ricardo's "Ricardian Theory" is based on the marginal and surplus principles, Adam Smith's Theory is based on the doctrine of "Natural law," and Mill's Theory" assumes the policy of laissez-faire in economic affairs. No market is free from Government interference and in which perfect competition prevails. No market can grow without state help and protection, either in one form or the other.

What Is Market?

Three women and a goose make a market.

... An Ancient Italian Proverb

One often comes across situations where words commonly used have to be interpreted. The problem gets even more complicated if the statute does not define the term. It is worse still if the same word is defined under any other statute, unquestionably so.

"There is no general market for land in the sense that one speaks of a market for shares, sugar, or any commodity."

...Chemudu case, supra.

The term "market" is invariably and repeatedly used in almost all valuation problems, reports, books, and articles. The whole concept of value revolves around it. The value is determined by the market, and the market's perception, on the other hand, is the only guide for its determination. The odd-looking Italian proverb, as quoted above, involves all the three basic ingredients of value - i.e., scarcity, marketability, and utility.

The term "market" refers to a place in ordinary meaning where buyers and sellers meet for transactions. As per the Concise Oxford Dictionary, the market is "condition as regards, or opportunity for, - buying or selling." Webster's Encyclopedic Unabridged Dictionary of the English Language describes it as, "trade or traffic, especially as regards a particular commodity". The term "market" indicates a place, a region (geographical or otherwise), or a commercial activity where or by which the exchange of commodities between buyers and sellers takes place.

"Market" assumes even broader meanings when it comes to the transaction of real estate. When we discuss the real estate market, it has to be borne in mind that commodities bought and sold are nothing but bundles of rights and interests of land and buildings. The market of real estate does not necessarily mean a place where interests or rights of the real estate property are bought and sold in the open market system where its demand and supply operate freely at a particular point in time. It is more or less an invisible operation where prospective buyers and sellers interact with each other based on utility from the buyer's viewpoint and costs from the sellers' point of view.

Therefore, a more comprehensive definition of the market is required to be invoked, and, as such, the term "Market" should be used in its full generic sense rather than in the customary restrictive way...The market as a switchboard must exist whether the trade is based on some standard medium of exchange or barter. It must exist whether or not profit (in full or in part) is siphoned out of it, whether prices follow supply and demand or are fixed by the state, whether the system is planned or not, and whether the means of production are private and public. It must exist even in a hypothetical economy of self-managed industrial firms in which workers set their own wages high enough to eliminate profit as a category.

Western economists think of the term "market" as a purely capitalist fact of human life and often use the term as though it were synonymous with "profit economy." Yet from all we know of ancient history, the exchange of commodities – and hence a marketplace - sprang up earlier than, and independently of, profit. Market, properly speaking, is nothing more than an exchange network, a switchboard, as it were, through which goods or services, like messages, are routed to their appropriate destinations. It is not inherently capitalist in nature. Such a switchboard is just as essential in a socialist industrial society as in profit-motivated industrialism. Marketplace plays a central role in all societies in which production is divorced from consumption, in which everyone depends upon the marketplace rather than on his productive skills for the necessities of life.

It is also to be noted here that the expression open market does not mean a purely hypothetical "laissez-faire" free from all restrictions imposed by the law. This theory or system of government - that upholds the autonomous character of the economic order, believing that government should intervene as little as possible in the direction of economic affairs - is nothing more than a hypothetical assumption.

In fact, each and every restriction imposed by the Law of the Land, either on the seller or on the buyer, must be taken into account to simulate actual transaction conditions while valuing a property. It would not be inconsequential here to point out that the valuers are nothing more than simulators of the would-be-transaction conditions to arrive at the market value as, in most cases, market value is derived from the viewpoint of a hypothetical buyer.

Gazing the Crystal Ball: Friction-Free Market of the Future

Overall, the implications of the term "market" are quite complex and all-pervasive. The market determines value, and its perception is the only guide for fair determination. Professional valuers are always expected to watch prevailing market trends closely.

Has the process of market-buildings been over by now?... Yes, says Alvin Toffler - a famous writer, renowned social thinker, and recipient of many international awards..." The heroic age of the market building is over - to be replaced by a new phase in which we merely maintain, renovate," he adds. Alvin Toffler correctly assessed the situation while writing his bestseller "Third Wave" in 1980, saying that "the system will increasingly depend on electronics... and new social technologies."

Friction-Free Capitalism

Purchasers get better and better deals as the marketplace becomes more and more efficient. Assessment of the market value of a property assumes the prevalence of ideal market conditions. An ideal marketplace, as such, can be defined as a place in which buyers and sellers have virtually perfect knowledge of the true supply and demand conditions for a particular commodity. Do these ideal conditions ever prevail? The answer is negative.

In 1995, however, Bill Gates (Chairman of Microsoft Corporation) coined a new term and introduced the comprehensive concept of "friction-free capitalism" to describe such a marketplace. The evolution of the concept of Internet cobwebbing the entire globe, at last, is moving us toward an ideal marketplace by encouraging the free and fast flow of information across the globe.

Internet: An Ideal Market-Place

It is quite interesting to observe the drastic renovations in a conventional market, and all such changes are getting reflected in every cranny of our lives. The enormous potential of the Internet surely promises to create nearly friction-free markets in the not-too-distant future. It will lead to revolutionary innovations and accelerate the much-clamored-and-rhapsodized but much-awaited trend towards efficient markets. Prospective purchasers can readily browse - from retailers to retailers while sitting cozily in their drawing rooms (or offices). Over time, powerful software will undoubtedly automate the entire process of comparison shopping, and haggling over prices - more or less - will become drastically efficiently and comfortably effortless, perspicuously so.

As a result, suppliers/retailers/dealers who charge too much will see their profit graphs nose-diving. But sometimes, the opposite will also hold good, and sellers will find their ingenious ways to charge more - at least to certain not-so-price-sensitive purchasers and for certain kinds of commodities. Sellers will undoubtedly use sophisticated technology to extract the highest possible price from a particular purchaser. More so, sellers with something unique to offer will soon discover that the astonishing efficiency of the Internet slavishly works in their favor as well. This, at least in principle if not exactly in tactics, would merely be a logical extension of the conventional market practices that are prevalent today - undoubtedly so. Strategies of flexible prices, as such, could become quite an interesting affair to watch (and a serious affair to frame) in the near future. E-commerce, as such, is going to make drastic changes in our lives.

Would Flexible Prices Prevail in an Ideal Market?

Flexible prices are a typical *characteristic* of the conventional marketplace. As a matter of fact, the very idea of fixing prices according to an individual's ability to pay is as old as the classical concept of progressive taxation itself. Some department stores run so many "discount sales" that there are virtually two prices for most, if not all, of the items - the regular price for the typical purchaser and the discounted price for the patient purchaser. Airline travel agencies and tourist hotels extract as much as they can for seats or rooms booked at the last minute. Two people may encounter different prices simultaneously for identical commodities, possibly because one seems more willing or able to pay than another... and so on. The obvious objective of all these pricing strategies is to capture as much low-margin business of price-sensitive purchasers as possible while reaping somewhat higher margins from those purchasers who are not that diligent.

The conventional trend of flexible prices shall probably continue even in the next millennium as well. Interactive technology allows the sellers to know the identities of those they are selling to in some way or another. Now the websites know that a specific visitor (or client) is revisiting again. From their digital data banks (meticulously maintained and updated regularly), they know what kind of prices one has (or has not) been willing to pay in the past. They may reduce a price to spur him/her to buy, or raise the same if the previous purchasing pattern suggests that the one is not a particularly price-sensitive purchaser.

Essential Features of Value

For a commodity (or asset, or property, etc.) to have value, it must possess three essential qualifications, i.e.

1.   It must be scarce,

2.   It must possess utility,

3.   It must be transferable or marketable.

Human beings need things or commodities for their sustenance and luxuries. This has created wants that need to be satisfied. Man's wants vary from the primary needs that require satisfaction for the imperative sustenance of life to the most extraordinary desires or satisfactions that he may consider necessary for living a fulsome life. "Want" and "Satisfaction" are quite complimentary to each other. One does not exist in the absence of the other and vice versa. Possessing anything that is not wanted will not give any satisfaction at all.

Commodities useful for satisfying wants are liked by human beings who earnestly desire to possess them. This attribute or characteristic of usefulness or, in other words, the quality of power of satisfying wants or needs is termed a utility. This attributes a relative term showing the relation between a consumer and a commodity. Wants provide an impulse or an impetus for producing or procuring commodities.

Utility means the satisfaction a decision-maker receives from given quantities of money (R.T. Ruegg et al.) and, as such, largely depends upon the psychological attitude of an individual decision-maker who may seek a home loan at an interest rate of 15.5%, hire-purchase a car at 27%, use a credit card at 19%, and yet may operate a saving account at 7%.

Every individual prudently employs his capital so that its produce may be of the greatest value to himself. He generally neither intends to promote the public interest nor knows how much he is promoting it. He intends only his own security, only his own gain (Adam Smith, "The Wealth of Nations," 1976). Nor is this behavior trivial. In an obsessive search for beast bargains, farmers optimistically value their agricultural lands not from the viewpoint of fertility but from the salability potential of such lands for prospective non-agricultural uses.

Also, it is necessary that all these three essentials are invariably present in an asset (or commodity) to impart it some value. In the absence of any one of them, the commodity will have no value. For example, oxygen possesses utility but is not scarce; hence, it has no economic value. Rotten apples may be scarce, but since they possess no utility, they have no value. A property has value only because it satisfies all the three requisite requirements. However, it is to be noted that the change in circumstances may increase or decrease the value of a specific commodity. Mountaineers - who have to encounter scarcity of oxygen at high altitudes of mountain ranges - readily pay the price of compressed oxygen they carry in steel cylinders at their backs. Scarcity of oxygen at high altitudes makes it valuable up there.

Moreover, transferability - in no way - should be misunderstood with what it literally implies. Though the land cannot be transferred in the exact physical sense, the owner can transfer his "whole bundle of rights" attached to the land to someone else for some consideration. Patent and Copyright Acts have made it possible to market intangible assets such as knowledge, inventions, computer skills, etc.

Various Definitions of Value

Value, a multilayered, multifaceted word, has been defined in diversified ways. Out of these, some of the dictionary definitions of 'value' are as follows:

Webster's New World Dictionary (Third College Edition) defines, 'value' in the following different ways:

i.   A fair or proper equivalent, in money, commodities, etc., especially for something sold or exchanged; fair price or return.

ii. The worth of a thing in money or goods at a certain time; market price.

iii. That which is desirable or worthy of esteem for its own sake; thing or quality having intrinsic worth.

iv. Estimated or appraised worth or price; valuation.

v.   The quality of a thing according to which it is desirable, useful, estimable, important, etc., worth or the degree or worth.

Probably the best definition of value, in a commercial sense, is that it is the present worth of all the future profits that are to be derived/received by the ownership of a particular property though, either a one-time contractual payment or a stream of regular earnings, in addition to partial/total liquidation at a future point. However, being a future-oriented concept, this excellent definition is quite difficult to apply in actual practice, as we can seldom determine assumed future profits well in advance with a reasonable degree of certainty. Thus, several other value measures are commonly used, some of which are approximations of the foregoing definition.

It can very well be seen from the above definitions that the term 'value' can have different facets and meanings depending upon the prevailing circumstances.

The distinguished quality of acquiring different facets makes it quite a 'mischievous and multifaceted word.' It can also be termed as an unbridled wild horse that obdurately refuses to be trained for a well-defined race track. 'Value' has refused to be tied down to a definite frame or get appended to a particular definition. The definition of 'value' given by Justice Brende at the beginning of this chapter is accurate in all respects, considering the character of 'value.'

Market Value

The most commonly encountered measure of value is 'market value,' which - by representing a momentary consensus of two or more interesting parties to a transaction as per their respective individual assessment of the economic value of the asset -properly refers to the price at which a property could actually be sold. In other words, it is that capital sum that will be paid as of date by a willing buyer to a willing vendor for a given property where each has an equal advantage and is under no compulsion to buy or sell. The buyer is willing to pay the market price because he believes it approximates the present value of what he will receive through the contemplated ownership with some interest or profit rate included therein.

'Willing buyer' and 'willing vendor' are the keywords that can repeatedly be found in several decisions of the Hon. Courts in compensation cases under the Land Acquisition Act (1894) as regards the meaning of the term 'Market value' which has undoubtedly received a definite connotation in the Indian history of valuation. A few interesting citations have been quoted as hereunder:

"The Courts have invoked a mythical willing buyer to justify a valuation higher than any attainable sale price."

... S.L.A.O. Vs P Veerabhandarappa, A.I.R. 1984 S.C. 774 (777).

"The value that a parcel of land would realize if sold in the market, the seller must be willing, a forced sale affords no criterion of market value, and the purchaser must be a prudent purchaser, one who makes his offer after making necessary inquiries as to the value of the land."

...Govt. of Bombay Vs Merwans Moondigar, A.I.R. 1924 Bom. 161.

"(The market price is) the price which that land would fetch when offered for sale, to a seller not obliged to sell and buyer under no necessity of buying it."

.. J.R. Singh Vs. Union of India A.I.R. 1989 Delhi 310.

"The open market price does not contemplate an offer to a limited class only such as the family members."

... Inland Revenue Commissioner Vs. Clay and Buchanan (1914) 3 K.B. 466.

In most matters related to depreciation, market value is used. For new properties, the cost of the open market is used as the original value. However, for certain types of valuation, 'Market Value' is not an appropriate concept.

Although a person normally possesses property so that he may receive benefits from it, some of the benefits frequently are not in the form of money. This fact further complicates the setting of value in monetary terms to place an ordinary commercial value on the property. Hence, the concept of value to a specific owner is very important in property valuation.

Value to the owner may be defined as the amount of money sufficient to compensate the owner if he is deprived of the property.

Generally speaking, this value will not be greater than the monetary amount for which the owner could soon replace the property with its best available substitute, with due allowance for the inferiority or superiority of that substitute. Also, the value to the owner will not be less than the market price for which the property could be sold. The concept of value to the owner may properly be applied to prospective and present owners.

Essential Characteristics of Market Value

In view of all the above discussion, the essential characteristic of the market value can be summarized as hereunder:

i.   The vendor must be willing to sell, and the purchaser must be willing to purchase.

ii. No compulsion, duress, misconception, or bias prevails either to the vendor or to the purchaser, which may deviate the value of the property in question from reality.

iii. The vendor's disinclination to sell his property is absent. Also, there is no urgent necessity or anxiety on the part of the vendor to sell off his property, as is a prominent feature of distress sales.

iv. No sentimental value is attached to the price expected by the vendor.

v.   Vendor must prudently be aware of the potential and price of the land at his disposal for advertisement, and negotiations.

vi. Purchaser must make his offer only after making requisite inquiries, giving proper weightage to the property's potential, and considering the prevailing market conditions.

The transaction must be actuated by business principles. It must be fair, and no consideration must be made from either side in terms other than monetary ones.

Use Value

Next to market value, the most important value is use value. This is what the property is worth to the owner as an operating unit. A property may be worth more to the person who possesses it and has it in operation than it would be to someone else who, if purchased it, might have to spend additional funds to move it and get it into operation. Use value is, of course, very closely akin to the original definition of value that was stated previously. It is difficult to determine for the same reasons.

Use value is often a term used in value engineering (VE) analysis/studies/research/management. From the viewpoint of VE, Donald E. Parker ("Value Engineering Theory." Lawrence D. Miles Foundation, Washington DC) defined use value as the cost of basic function only. As per him, the use value is the monetary measure of the usefulness of the product or service.

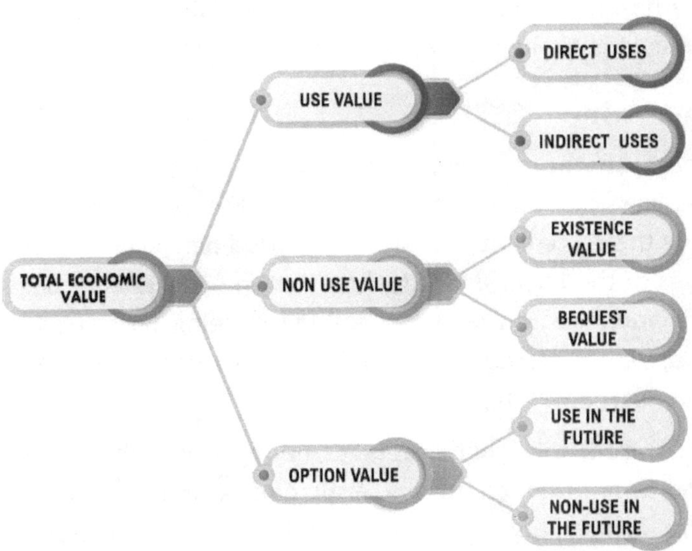

Let's consider the functional analysis of a bridge whose basic function is to allow passage. The bridge deck itself is the only part that does it. Other elements of the bridge are support functions. In analyzing various parts of the bridge, it is found that the structural fill used for embankment from the approach road might be extended to eliminate several of the pile support deck sections. Thus, a part of the bridge deck is now replaced with a road surface, which provides the same function of allowing passage.

A Value Engineering study carried out by Basha et al. (1991) on fourteen selected bridges in Egypt constructed during the past two decades reveals that six of them (i.e., about 43%), including the Cairo Airport Bridge, were not constructed using the best available construction alternative based on economic and engineering considerations. The reinforced concrete system could substitute the prestressed concrete system used in Cairo Bridge. This could likely improve performance in the following criteria: construction cost (by about 30%), maintenance (13%), local resource utilization (56%), ease of construction (25%), and progress rate (41%).

However, Carlos Fallen cautions the value analysts who strive to satisfy only needs while ignoring man's desires. That is the situation that occurs when one arbitrarily strives to provide only use value and categorizes all aesthetic functions as gingerbread or doubtful value.

Aesthetic Value

The reference to the owner's desires is an explicit reminder of the overworked classical statement, "Beauty is in the eye of the beholder." Paraphrasing this statement, it is also recognized perspicuously that value is in the eyes of the buyer. Individual desires and concepts of beauty can be the paramount reason when something is being purchased. Dream, for example, of the corrugated metal manufacturer who envisions all skyscrapers covered with his own product.

Recognize from this, that aesthetics normally is rather a subjective decision and, very often, an individualistic one. Aesthetic function (i.e., a function that contributes esteem value rather than use value) becomes a basic function when desire becomes as strong as need. It is worthwhile to note here that the basic function (also called primary function) is the primary utilitarian characteristic of a product or service to fulfill a user's need.

Fair Value

Fair value is usually determined by a disinterested party to establish a price that is fair to both seller and buyer when both are actuated by business principles prevalent at the time in the locality. Such a buyer would, however, be interested in the enjoyment of the property IN PRASENTI or to obtain a return therefrom on the relevant date, i.e., without waiting to improve the property by the expenditure of money and time. This clearly shows that the property is to be valued REBUS-SIC-STANTIBUS, i.e., as it stands, and could be used on the relevant date.

Nowadays, when unaccounted money plays an important role in property transfer, the concept of fair market price is lost. There are willing sellers and willing purchasers who are willing to transfer property at a higher price than the registered one. In compulsory acquisition cases brought before the court-of-law for compensation wherein the determination of fair market value becomes a hypothetical case, and the valuation depends on comparative method of sale proceeds of similar properties in the vicinity, it may be difficult to satisfy the court about the fair market price based on such pseudo-registration deeds.

Book Value

The word 'value' is also sometimes used in a neutral sense as any money amount associated with specific items of property for some given purpose. An example of this is the use of the phrase ' 'book-value" to describe the unamortized cost of the property as shown by the book of account. As such, "book value" is the worth of a property as shown on the amounting record of the company. It is ordinarily taken to mean the original cost of the property minus the amounts that have been charged as depreciation expense, representing thereby the amount of remaining capital that remains invested in the property and must be recovered in the future through the depreciation accounting process.

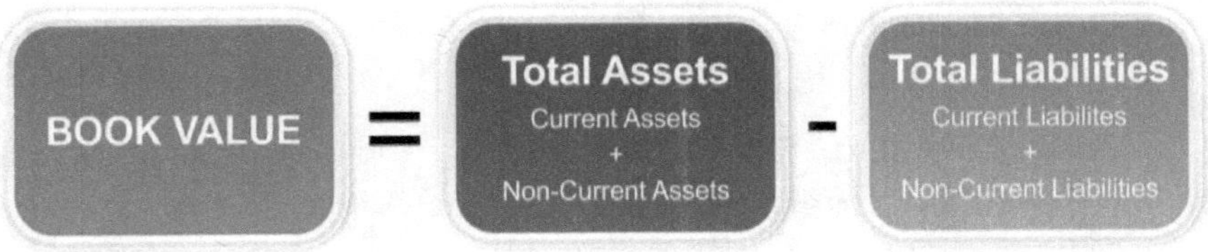

It should be remembered, however, that because companies may use various depreciation accounting methods that produce different results, book value may have little or no relationship to the actual or market value of the property involved.

Why Book Value Differs From Market Value?

It's a matter on record that many famous investors built their fortunes in part by buying assets with market valuations below their book valuations. Book value and market value differ primarily because they are calculated based on different criteria and serve distinct purposes:

1. Calculation Basis: Book Value is based on the historical cost of assets minus depreciation. It reflects the value of an asset or company as recorded on the balance sheet. Market Value is determined by the current price at which an asset or company can be bought or sold in the open market. It reflects the market's perception of the value, influenced by factors such as future growth potential, investor sentiment, and market conditions.

2. Depreciation and Amortization: Book Value takes into account depreciation and amortization, which reduce the recorded value of assets over time. No professional valuer worth his salt undermines the importance of depreciation while carrying out the valuation of assets. Waste Management, the Houston-based publicly traded company, allegedly reported a whopping $1.7 billion in false earnings, falsely increasing the depreciation length for their property, plant, and equipment on the balance sheets. On the other hand, Market Value does not account for depreciation in the same way. It is more influenced by current and future earning potential.

3. Intangible Assets and Goodwill: Book Value may not fully capture the value of intangible assets such as brand reputation, intellectual property, or goodwill. Market Value often incorporates these intangibles, especially if they contribute to a company's competitive advantage and future profitability.

4. Market Conditions: Book Value is static and historical in nature, unaffected by current market conditions. Whereas Market Value is dynamic and highly influenced by current economic conditions, investor sentiment, and market trends.

5. Profitability and Growth Prospects: Book Value does not necessarily reflect a company's profitability or growth prospects. Market Value, on

the other hand, is often influenced by expectations of future earnings and growth.

6. Supply and Demand: Market supply and demand do not affect book value. Whereas Market Value is directly influenced by the supply of and demand for the asset or company's shares.

7. Liquidity: Book Value does not reflect the liquidity of the asset or company. However, market value can be influenced by how easily the asset can be traded in the market.

These differences lead to variations between Book Value and Market Value, with market value often being higher due to growth potential and investor sentiment, or lower during times of market pessimism or financial distress.

Salvage Value

Salvage, or resale value, is the price that can be obtained from selling the property after it has been used. Salvage value which implies that the property has further utility - is affected by several factors. The reason the present owner is selling may influence the salvage value in some way or another. If the owner is selling because there is very little commercial need for the property, this will affect the resale value; a change of ownership will probably not increase the commercial utility of the article.

Salvage value will also be affected by the present cost of reproducing the property; price levels may either increase or decrease the resale value.

A third factor that may affect salvage value is the property's location. It is interesting to note that the salvage value/break-up value/demolition value/ residual value/scrap value of an R.C.C. structure may even be negative (i.e. dismantling charges exceed salvage).

Esteem Value

Esteem value arises from the motivated desire to possess for the sake of possession. It is equal to the monetary sum an owner or user is willing to pay for prestige or appearance. In VE, it can also be defined as the worth of a sell function. Esteem value is no more than the desire of the owner to own it, and it is important to recognize that elements of esteem can serve a useful purpose: the purpose of making an owner desire it.

An excellent example of esteem value is a diamond-studded tie pin. The basic function of a tie pin is to keep the tie in place. Studded diamond only adds to its esteem value.

Another example of Esteem Value is DLF's 'The Camellias,' in Gurugram. Delhi Land & Finance (DLF) is setting new standards for luxury living in India. With apartments priced up to Rs. 100 crores, it has become a top choice for the country's leading businessmen, CEOs, and wealthy individuals. Known for its stunning interiors and world-class facilities, the property impresses everyone who visits. When launched in 2014, the price was Rs. 22,500/- per square foot. Riches, driven by the motivated desire to possess for the sake of possession, have skyrocketed the price to over Rs. 85,000/- per square foot, a massive increase. Apartments that once cost Rs. 25-30 crore now sell for as much as Rs. 100 crores.

Good Value

Good value - a relative economic comparator - is a VE concept and can be defined as the Lowest Life Cycle Cost (LLCC) to accomplish a function reliably. It corresponds to the value index (i.e. the ratio of function cost over function worth) equal to one.

Monopoly Value

Monopoly value usually prevails when the demand is more than that of supply for a specific commodity. For example, as the number of plots prospectively available for sale in a locality decreases, the value of the land increases, and eventually, a time comes when very few plots remain in the market. The fancy price the vendor demands for those remaining plots will be known as monopoly value.

Speculative Value

A certain class of purchasers are interested in purchasing the property and then selling it with some profit after a short period. Such speculators are usually not very interested in taking pains for the real development of the property. Even if it is done, the development process is solely restricted to decorative patch-ups.

The price paid by such speculators is the property's speculative value. In general, the speculative value is less than the market value because the speculator will try to buy the property at a low price and sell it at a high price in the near future. In cases where speculators purchase a property even at the present market value, they obviously have some advanced information (or intuition in some cases) as to which they expect a sharp rise soon. It may be that a highway will pass from that locality, which will cause value hikes.

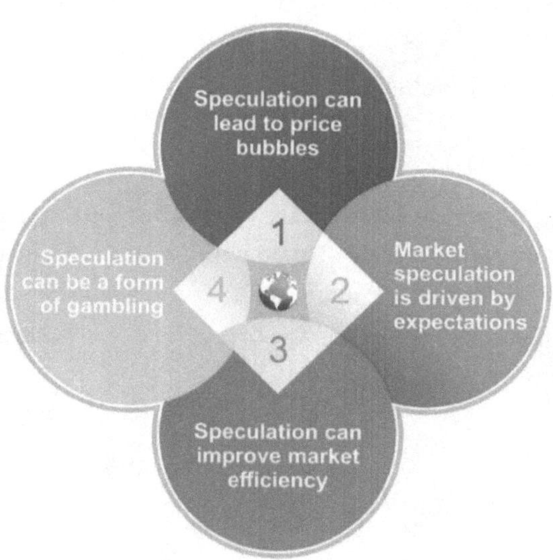

Occupation Value and Investment Value

The main intention of every real estate purchaser is to invest his hard-earned capital to obtain enough return out of it. Thus, a property's investment value indicates the amount offered by a prudent purchaser to possess the property from an investment point of view.

In some cases, however, the purchasers are inclined to own the property for their own occupational uses. The price so offered by such purchasers is termed the Occupation Value of the property.

Investment and speculative values are seen to be one and the same as both have one common aspect: in both of these cases, capital is employed, from the viewpoint of judicious investment, and hence, it is quite difficult to draw a clear-cut demarcating line between the two. However, investments are usually made on a long-term basis. Whereas the speculator's interest is short-termed to set free the invested capital, with some profit, for yet another speculative purchase.

Sentimental Value

Sometimes, due to the owner's emotional or sentimental feelings, he is not ready to part with the property even when a fancy price is offered to it.

In rare cases, a prospective purchaser- due to some sentimental reason or the other- either pays or is ready to pay a relatively higher price than the prevailing market value for a particular property. Such a price is known as sentimental value and bears no relation to nearby properties' market value.

"Disinclination of the vendor to part with the land and urgent necessity of purchases to be disregarded in determining the market value."

... Shamalbhai Lallubhai Patel Vs Addl. S.L.A.O.: A.I.R. 1977 S.C. 899.

Liquidation Value

If one wants to know the actual value of any property it can fetch, it will approximately equal its liquidation value. When the Board of Directors of a company decides - in most cases involuntarily - to liquidate, the company no longer remains a "going concern," and the disposal of its movable & immovable assets becomes a matter of top priority to meet the liabilities thereof.

Liquidation value estimates the sum the holder of the shares would be expected to receive if the company is voluntarily wound up. It is strikingly different from other form values, each based on the continuity of a going concern.

Liquidation value may or may not be equal to fair market value depending upon the circumstances under which the exchange occurs. However, in most cases, it is observed to be somewhat lower than fair market value.

Economic Value

Defining economic value is not an easy task, especially because value is a term with unpredictable whims, and its conceptual boundaries are not defined precisely. The terms "economic value" and "value," though they seem alike at first sight, are not so as they convey the different senses in every respect.

In defining "economic value," an individual's satisfaction must be given due importance. It would be best to define it in terms of the relative satisfaction that individuals and groups obtain from tangible and intangible goods and services.

The problem of the measurement of economic value is also no less important for it enables one to determine the degree of satisfaction one receives by receiving a thing in exchange of another. The scale of measurement of economic value is partly determined by the formal and informal marketplace in which exchanges take place and partly by individual attitudes toward property and wealth.

Appraisal Value

Appraisal value is ordinarily expressed in terms of reproduction cost less accumulated depreciation. It goes without saying that fair value is the end product of appraisal value.

Replacement Value

Replacement value refers to the value of a property, which is determined on the basis of what it would cost on a particular date (at the current price level) to replace the property or its service with an equally satisfactory and comparable property and service.

Replacement value is frequently used synonymously with the reproduction value but, in a more specific sense, is limited to mean the value of equivalent property as distinguished from identical one.

Relative Value

Relative value becomes an issue in company amalgamations and absorptions. Actual Market Value may be relatively unimportant even though it forms the basis of the calculation. The vital question is how to arrive at the relative values of the respective enterprises so that a justifiable settlement between the two parties may be concluded.

Potential Value

The term potential value is used to indicate the intrinsic quality inherently possessed by a property due to its peculiar situations, the extent of area, location (i.e., commercial, industrial, residential, etc.), topography, etc., and similar other factors which may allow its prospective use more advantageously. The potential value must be based on prudent business calculations and not on impractical imagination, or tantalizing speculation, which would otherwise mislead a prospective vendor to make an offer near a fancy price.

Probably the best definition of potential value is what has been given by the American Institute of Real Estate Appraisers (Appraisal Terminology & Hand Book, 1967 ed., pp. 154):

"The value is expected to develop if and when stated probabilities become actualities."

Also;

"The court may consider not only the present purpose to which the land is applied but also any other more beneficial purpose to which it might, within a reasonable period, be applied."

... AIR V 40 C 374.

"In valuing the potentialities, courts should rely on admitted and proved facts."

...1926 Bom 433 (433) [AIR V13].

In addition to the above manifestative variations in the meaning of 'value,' the other value terms that are commonly encountered are - Intrinsic value, Cost value, Capital value, Future Value, Cash value, Rental Value, Tax Value, Warranted Value, True Value, Written-Down Value, Face Value, Condemnation Value, Loss Value, Commercial Value, Fancy Value, Present Value, Guideline Value, Insurance Value, Earning Value, Exchange Value, Utility Value, Capitalized Value, etc.

Summarily, aspects of cost, price, and value can be related to their corresponding important functions, as tabulated in Table 1.

Table 1.1

Sr. No	Aspect	Relates To
1	Cost	Facts
2	Price	Policy
3	Exchange Value	Worth
4	Esteem Value	Want
5	Use/Utility Value	Need/Utility
6	Fancy Value	Desire
7	Book Value	Depreciation
8	Good Value	LLCC
9	Value Index	Cost/Worth
10	Sentimental Value	Sentiments
11	Tax Value	Taxing Statute
12	Commercial Value	Commercial Potential
13	Aesthetic Value	Aesthetics

Value: Does it Differ?

As we all know now, based on the above discussion, the word "value" has several diversified meanings attached to it. Its scope precipitously ranges from Market Value to Monopoly Value, Speculation Value to Investment Value, Sentimental Value to Distress Value, Functional Value to Aesthetic Value, and so on.

In view of so many definitions of value, it becomes abundantly clear that the value of the same property is not at all an absolute affair; rather, it varies quite dramatically with respect to so many factors.

The cardinal factors that may conceivably be responsible - either in isolation or in various possible combinations - for value deviations can be enumerated as hereunder:

i.   time,

ii. purpose,

iii. legal and taxing statutes,

iv. prevailing market conditions,

v.   other relevant circumstances, and so on.

As such, the purpose of valuation - for which the valuation is being carried out - greatly affects the assessed value.

Causes of Value Deviations

Several other pragmatic cases in which the values may be different for different purposes and also under different circumstances have been enumerated as hereunder:

1. "Value" in our country is still a vague and nebulous concept and has been defined from different perspectives, as is apparent from the Gift Tax Act (1958), Income Tax Act (1961), and Wealth Tax Act (1957) read with the corresponding rules thereof. They are being amended quite frequently. The term "Fair Market Value," for example, has been defined in Section 269 A (d) of Chapter XXA of the Income Tax Act (1961) from the perspective of the acquisition of immovable properties in certain cases of transfer to counteract evasion of tax. As per this Section, fair market value:

    (a) in relation to any immovable property transferred by way of sale or exchange, being immovable property of the nature referred to in sub-clause (i) of clause (e), means the price that the immovable property would ordinarily fetch in the open market on the date of execution of the instrument of transfer of such property;

(b) in relation to any immovable property transferred by way of lease, being immovable of the nature referred to in sub-clause (i) of clause (e), means the premium that such transfer would ordinarily fetch on the date of execution of such transfer of such property if the consideration for such transfer had been by way of premium only;

(c) in relation to any immovable property transferred, being the immovable property of the nature referred to in sub-clause (ii) of clause (e), means the consideration in the form of money that such transfer would ordinarily fetch in the open market on the date of transfer if such transfer has been made only for consideration of money.

So far as the valuation for Wealth Tax as per the Wealth Tax Act (1957) is concerned, the fair market value of a property as defined in the I.T. Act (1961) may altogether be different from that of its assessed value as per Schedule III of the W.T. Act and the government, as such, is fully aware of its "concessive value determination process."

Valuation for Wealth Tax, before 01/04/89, was governed by Rule 1BB of the Wealth Tax Rules w.e.f. 01/04/1979. It, now, is carried out based on "Schedule Valuation" modalities given in "Schedule III" of the Act w.e.f. 01/04/1989, which reads as hereunder:

"Section 7(1) subject to the provisions of sub-section (2), the value of any asset, other than cash, for this Act shall be its value as on the valuation date determined in the manner laid down in Schedule III."

However, according to the sub-section (2), the principle prescribed in this Schedule III is limited to the value of a house belonging to the assessee and exclusively used by him for the period of 12 months immediately preceding the valuation date, may, at the option of the assessee, be taken to be the value determined in the manner in the Schedule III as on the date next following the date on which he became the owner of the house or the valuation date relevant to the assessment year commencing on the 1st day of April 1971, whichever valuation date is later:

Provided that where more than one house belonging to the assessee is exclusively used by him for residential purposes, the provisions of this subsection shall apply only in respect of one of such houses, which the assessee may, at his option, specify on this behalf in the return of net wealth. For the purpose of this subsection:

1. where the assessee has constructed the house, he shall be deemed to have become the owner thereof on the date on which the construction of such house was completed;

2. "house" includes a part of the house being an independent residential unit.

It has already been said that the government is very well aware of the "concessive value determination process" as described in Schedule III. Rather, it is wary of the principles prescribed in it. Hence, it has consequently guarded itself by submitting that the residuary cases, which are not covered by the rules 3 to 19 of Schedule III, for the purpose of this Act, shall be estimated to be the price which, the opinion of the Assessing Officer, it would fetch if sold in the open market on the valuation date vide Rule 20(1). Rule 20(2) refers to the valuation matters to the Valuation Officer. Rule 20(3), quite interestingly, reads as hereunder:

"Where the value of any asset cannot be estimated under this rule because it is not saleable in the open market, the value shall be determined in accordance with such guidelines or principles as may be specified by the Board from tune to time by general or special order."

2. Book value is generally lower than the corresponding residual value of plants and machinery in an inflating economy environment as it does not account for inflation. It has already been pointed out that because companies may use various depreciation accounting methods that produce different results, book value may have little or no relationship to the actual or market value of the property involved.

3. A fully tenanted property - when acquired under Maharashtra Housing and Area Development Act (1976) - is valued according to the following formula for the determination of compensation:

Value of the property = Net Average Monthly Rent x 100

However, when the same property is acquired under Land Acquisition Act 1894 (modified to date), assessment of value for the determination of compensation is done rather subjectively as per Section 23(1) of the Act that summarily assumes that the compensation should be given to the owner in the most lucrative manner possible. In addition to this amount, a solatium equal to 30% of the market value is also paid to the person interested. As per the modalities laid down in both of the above acquisition procedures, the worked-out values may differ for the same property in most cases.

4. As often as not, functional values are found to be lesser than corresponding aesthetic values attached thereto. Consider the case of a golden tie-pin with a precious diamond embedded in it; the value of the function it serves is far more trivial than that of its aesthetic value. Even an ordinary safety pin, costing virtually nothing, could have served the same function of securing the tie in its proper position. Admittedly, in such cases, aesthetics dominates the other functions and, hence, becomes the primary function. Similar logic goes with Rolex watches, wherein it would be controversial to say whether the price tag represents the fancy value or esteem value as, quite interestingly, this determination would largely depend upon the financial status of the prospective purchaser. Indeed, it would be a fancy value for a proverbial man on the street. In the Cairo Airport Bridge example, as cited earlier, the functional value is less than the project cost.

5. The Sentimental value of a property to its owner is greater than its fair market value in most cases. This single factor is responsible for so many regular suits challenging the Collector's award to compulsory land acquisition cases under the Land Acquisition Act 1894. Most - if not all -of the disputes regarding the compensation award have arisen only because the person(s) interested considers his property more valuable than its corresponding fair market value.

6. Distress and liquidation values are usually lower than those of their corresponding fair market values due to the urgent necessity of the owner(s) to sell off the property immediately for some compulsive reason.

7. Views of the seller of a property - regarding its envisaged potential and hence its expected value - may differ from that of its actual market value from the viewpoint of a prospective purchaser.

8. As will be discussed later in this book in detail, the valuation of agricultural lands, orange farms, tea & coffee estates, etc., is usually carried out based on the Income Capitalization Method, which consists of capitalizing the Net Annual Income by an appropriate capitalization factor.

   Consider the case of an agricultural land growing a crop, say wheat. Now, consider the following perspective conditions:

   i. If tobacco is grown instead of wheat, or

   ii. if additional irrigational facilities are made available, growing rice and a second crop in addition to wheat becomes possible. The same piece of land will generate different annual incomes in both cases. Hence, based on the Income Capitalization Method, the value arrived at would differ, corresponding to both cases for the same piece of land.

   Another problem with using the income capitalization method is selecting an appropriate capitalization factor. It grants even to adversaries the possibility of partial accuracy and oneself the possibility of error. Obviously, by selecting its lower value, the valuer will mistakenly award lesser value to the property and vice-versa.

9. Speculation values are determined based on the property's short-term value-growth potential. Investment values, on the other hand, are usually determined based on relatively long-term potential. Hence, both of the values may be different in most of the cases.

10. The value of any property for the purpose of fire insurance primarily centers around reinstatement or replacement cost if a fire hazard occurs. This value will be quite different from a valuation carried out for mortgage purposes, which is done with an entirely different perspective in mind.

   In the case of valuation for mortgage purposes, the earning capacity (or net income potential) of the property in question, or its marketability in case of default in mortgage payments, forms the principal feature.

The implications of the above value deviations might seem startling to novice valuers. Nonetheless, the situation gets somewhat simplified by taking a total rather than a fragmentary look at problems, i.e., by adopting a holistic approach. It is to be noted, for instance, that the fair market value of a property at a given time is a gross total of its Potential Value, Aesthetic Value, Use Value, Esteem Value, etc., (excluding the sentimental value, if any). It will remain the same in all circumstances provided that the:

(a) same basic principles are applied with an unbiased attitude;

(b) perspective remains the same, and

(c) the purpose of valuation is completely disregarded.

Can A Property Have Zero Markat-Value?

Market value, as is an established fact by now, refers to the price at which a property could actually be sold. In other words, it is that capital sum that will be paid as of date by a willing buyer to a willing vendor. Dr. R.H. Namavati, in the very opening of his exhaustive treatise entitled "Theory & Practice of Valuation," has unobtrusively cited the classic example of a "bungalow in the desert," which -quite cleverly - depicts the concept of zero market value and would be a matter of academic interest to the perceptive readers.

B.K. Sabapathy also, in his book entitled Practical Valuation (Vol. II, pp. 494-496), has pointed out an interesting example of an immovable property of Mrs. Judi (London) that did not find any market at some point in time.

In this context, it would not be inconsequential to see a very peculiar, strange example of a religious structure that - from the viewpoint of the Court Fees Act 1870 - has zero market value. However, looking into the available citations, it is a somewhat controversial statement. For example:

"An ancient temple devoted absolutely and in perpetuity to religious purposes has no market and therefore no market value."

... AIR 1938 Nag 481 (482) ** AIR 1924 Mad 19 (21, 22) = 46 Mad 782 (FB). [25 Cal 194 = 24 Ind App 177 (PC), Foil.].

"A temple as such has no market value, and a suit for possessing a temple is chargeable with a fixed court fee of Rs. 10/-, under Schedule II, Article 17 (vi)."

... (1938) 40 Pun LR 113 (1155) ** AIR 1924 Mad 19 (22) = 46 Mad 782 (FB).

However, the mere fact that religious structures have no market value was subsequently put rather more appropriately by saying that such properties are incapable of valuation.

"It cannot be said that any property belonging to a temple and sued for as such has no market value. Whether the property is capable of valuation or not depends on the nature of the user to which it is put. Ordinarily, it is the materials and site of the temple and the buildings which are an adjunct to it that will not be capable of valuation."

... AIR 1953 Madh B 40 (Pr. 9) ** AIR 1948 Mad 345 (345).

A property - as a matter of fact - may touch the nadir of its market value or may even register zero market value at a given point in time under extremely adverse circumstances. Theoretically, a particular immovable property will always register at least some value - e.g., the reversionary value of the land at the minimum, if not even the salvage value of the building. However, catastrophic changes - such as war, flood, volcanic activities, epidemic, insurgency, etc. -may inadvertently lead to a peculiar situation in which a particular property may not find a buyer due to the severe disturbance of market forces.

As said earlier, the market is as much a psychological structure as an economic reality. Catastrophic circumstances may sometimes splinter - or even bog down completely - the local market system, at least for the time being until the local civilization absorbs the impact of such changes and market forces passionately attain their equilibrium all over again.

Here, it would be inconsequential to point out that the market value, de facto, is only a complementary concept of the market itself. The whole concept of value revolves around the market, and its perception is the only guide for its determination. The presence of a market system is necessary for the existence of market value.

Value, in other words, will be zero in the absence of a market system. More so, a property may register very little value - or even no buyer at all - if it is not offered for sale in an appropriate market (i.e., if expressed, in other words, to a suitable class of prospective purchasers). This situation may inadvertently crop up at the time of bank/Govt. auctions when the details are not advertised thoroughly among the prospective bidders to create a competitive environment. The author is aware of several instances in which the property at the time of auction received drastically lesser value than its evaluated worth.

Extreme obsolescence may sometimes lead to zero market value of a property/commodity. A manual Xerox machine - very much in use a few years back -would not find any value today if offered for sale. Fast technological advancements may lead to such situations.

***

Chapter 2

Practice of Valuation - A Unique Profession

General

The professional practice of valuation has recently emerged as a highly skilled art (or a consummate science ??, or a jardinière of both ??) and a comprehensive and arduous subject of serious study and systematic pursuit in search (and advancement) of a realistic framework for the development of valuation problems. Valuation, as such, can be defined as:

"An orderly process of expressing economic decisions relevant to the market-value, fair-market-value, compensation, or amount for a specific property at a stated time, place, and based on the definition of the term in the Act."

In developed countries and also in many developing countries, the practice of valuation is now a fully developed field of professional specialization requiring technical competence and requisite academic attainments. The term "profession" eventually takes up new meaning in light of rapid advances taking shape in almost all fields of life, including the field of valuation. Professional specialists, according to Bennis (a social psychologist and a professor of Industrial Management), "seemingly derive their rewards from the inward standard of excellence, from their professional societies, and the intrinsic satisfaction of their task. They are assiduously committed to the task. They are quite uncommitted except to the challenging environments where they can "play with a problem" as assigned to them.

Valuation, as such, is an adventure in "economic research," which in some form or another uses modalities, methods, and techniques of valuation very similar to economic indices and indicators as used in economic analyses and predictions. However, there is no guarantee that these modalities, indices, indicators, etc., will always lead to the correct answers to the relevant problems.

Valuer: A Multidimensional Professional

Valuation leads to an economic decision of a valuer, which indicates the conclusion arrived at after considering all pertinent factors like economic, social, political, physical, and other contingent conditions inherent in the immovable/movable property in question. The practice of valuation emphasizes the feedback relationships among all these factors and the larger "Wholes" formed by these factors. As such, the Professional practice of valuation is now considered a multidisciplinary & multilayered study based on economics, law, engineering etc., and other technical subjects.

The old boundaries between the specialties are collapsing. Professional valuers, at some time or the other, increasingly find that the novel problems thrust at them can be solved only by reaching beyond the fortified boundaries of narrow disciplines and by adopting a wholistic approach. Whereas Cartesian thinkers emphasize the analysis of components, often at the expense of context (i.e., the study of things in isolation from one another), system thinkers stress what Simom Remo, an early advocate of systems theory, called a "total, rather than a fragmentary look at problems."

The professional valuation system emphasizes the holistic approach toward solving valuation problems by taking a total and comprehensive look at the property being valued and considering all the contexts thereof. It should be noted here without any reasonable doubt that, in the real world, an issue is an issue. It is often - or rather invariably - labeled engineering, valuation, economic, social, or legal depending upon an individual's own discipline, experience, expertise, and ways and means of approaching it.

The revolt against narrow specialization also received a boost from the environmental campaigns of the 1970s, as ecologists increasingly discovered the "web" of nature, the interrelatedness of species, and the wholeness of ecosystems. "Non-environmentalists tend to separate things into components and to solve one thing at a time," wrote Berry Lopez in "Environmental Action." Contrastingly, "Environmentalists tend to see things quite differently... Their instinct is to balance the whole, not to solve a single part." The ecological and valuation approaches share the same thrust, in principle, toward the synthesis and integration of knowledge. It would be worthwhile to point out that the conceptual difference between cost estimation and valuation lies here. Cost estimation is a Cartesian process that, contrary to valuation, flows from part to the whole. A "whole" is broken down into modular components, and the cost of each component is worked out to estimate the overall cost of the "whole."

Thus, ideally, valuers should be multidisciplinary people who may specialize in one discipline but are knowledgeable in other disciplines as well. They should be inquisitive, flexible, observant, sensitive, eclectic, and constructive. They should be capable of intermixing freely and questioning inventively to explore the requisite information to arrive at fair, justifiable, accurate, and credible conclusions. Here, the term "credible" has been used in its full generic sense because recognizing that no knowledge can be complete eventually generates the possibility of error. However, such errors must be kept within the permissible limits of tolerances to make a valuation report "credible."

Philosophy of Valuation

No philosophy encompassing the field as startlingly vast and complex as valuation can be described in simple terms. The valuation philosophy is probably as complex and age-old as the philosophy of value itself.

Whenever one encounters a value determination problem, the first and foremost question that invariably crops up in one's mind is the utility of the asset in question, either in functional or psychological terms. Whenever I use a tool, it reminds me of Jean-Paul Sarte's classical statement: "The tool is an idea congealed." In similar tunes, it can be unhesitatingly said that: "The value is a utility congealed." Valuation, as such, is the tool of value determination. Utility, on the other hand, is congealed either voluntarily or involuntarily in some form or the other either by the man by the employment of land and/or labor or by nature itself.

Though there are other ingredients to "value," the utility is the most crucial consideration. The existence of utility is essential to the existence of value. The heart of the utility factor in valuation is the classical law of diminishing utility. The utility theory greatly influences the valuation philosophy, which is primarily an ardent attempt to explain value determination in social or psychological terms. Some traces of the recognition of social and psychological determinants of value can readily be found throughout the value theory.

The utility theory - in its developed form - is playing a prominent role in the exposition of the valuation philosophy, which, in turn, provides information in monetary terms in most of the current value-based decisions in a market-dependent system... "for the price valuers who wish merely to make a first contact between objective price and human psychology, much of the theorizing with respect of utilities, and certainly all the hedonistic and rationalistic elements herein, are irrelevant to his purpose," says S.P. Khanna.

No abstract mathematical model can possibly be simulated for its universal acceptance in the field of valuation. So, to overcome this murk, a generalized valuation philosophy needs to be developed. The modern philosophy of the professional practice of valuation should comprehensively encompass a deeper understanding of the everyday complex field of valuation by accommodating ground realities to have positive accomplishments to its credit and, as such, is now increasingly expected to be characterized by its cardinal orientation to methodology, concept development, and judicious application, therefore. It should be capable of grasping an overview of the ground reality. It should be able to pull aside the curtain to reveal universal value parameters just as a good novelist eloquently reveals the hidden feelings and emotions of the human heart. In a time of exploding change when a new way of life is emerging on the horizon, it should be able to accommodate the fast technological advancements taking place world-wide.

As information is closely related to the overall objective of valuation, a major and primary task of professional valuation comprises collecting useful information. To select all the necessary quality information and relevant evidence, the key informants should be selected carefully to arrive at an acceptable value assessment. As such, it is quite important to identify appropriate economic indicators and building indices and their source as integral elements of adopting a suitable methodology for the requisite purpose thereof. Information about these indicators may be readily available, which has to be applied based on experience, common sense and certain assumptions. In addition to these, extensive first-hand experience with day-to-day real problems reveals that using standard formats is quite useful in the data retrieval process.

These standard formats assist in retrieving all the necessary information and promote understanding by others who wish to verify or review the data. To explore relevant indicators/indices and their sources, "who, how, what, where, and when" can eventually be adopted as the basic questions. In this respect, framing of correct questions undoubtedly assumes utmost importance as no answer can be expected to be correct if the question leading to that answer is incorrect. Considering the interdisciplinary nature of valuation, adopting an interactive approach for information collection becomes necessary rather than rigid statistical data collection methods. The salient features of such an interactive approach to valuation are as follows:

i.   to collect relevant information as an incremental learning process as an indispensable part of the profession;

ii. recognizing the principle of "less is more" (time/information etc.);

iii. to recognize the limitation of optimal ignorance and appropriate imprecision;

iv. to relate information and inputs with reflective observations and conceptualization.

v.   use of indicators and indices to aid information and perceptive understanding. Such indicators and indices are shortcuts to time-consuming data collection and an alternative to unstructured observation.

What is Valuation?

Valuation, as such, is quite an age-old concept. With the passage of time, early human species learned the art of transaction (barter) by mutually exchanging their could-be & should-be-spared commodities in accordance with their adjudged values in terms of quality, strength, ease of availability (or scarcity), etc. - all basic valuation concepts albeit they did not formally have any scientific training for the same. Primitive intuitive solutions were first discovered for their tribal exchange-rate quantification requirements and later improvised to keep pace with fast-growing societal needs. Most of these activities today are classified as valuation, and some of them are considered highly innovative vintage work in the field of valuation.

Neither an exact science nor an absolute art, valuation is indisputably practiced by every individual in his day-to-day life, sparing only those who have solitarily retired in the solitude of Himalayan caves for the singular purpose of spiritual enlightenment of their souls.

No process as vast and complex as valuation can be described simply. However, the Webster's New Collegiate Dictionary describes "Valuation" as:

i.   The act or process of valuing, specifically, appraisal of property;

ii. The estimated or determined market value of a thing; and

iii. Judgement or appreciation of worth or character.

As per Webster's New World Dictionary (Third College Edition), Valuation is:

i.   the act of determining the value or price of anything; evaluation appraisal.

ii. determined or estimated value or price on the market. (iii) estimation of the merit, worth, etc. of anything.

At last but not least, the Concise Oxford Dictionary quotes "valuation" as:

i.   an estimation (especially by a professional valuer) of a thing's worth;

ii. the worth estimated;

iii. the price set on a thing.

Based on the above-cited dictionary meanings & descriptions of "valuation," now a generalized definition of the professional practice of valuation can judiciously be framed as hereunder:

"The professional practice of valuation may be defined as the jardiniere of art & science, of IN PRESANTI value assessment (in monetary terms) of all kinds of immovable/movable properties in exact accordance with the given purpose of valuation attached thereto, by a professional valuer competent in the relevant field of valuation."

The primary objective of valuation is to explicitly establish the value REBUS-SIC-STANTIBUS. Though it appears to be quite a simple concept/ process, it rather holds great complexities in itself due to more than several cardinal reasons. Moreover, what deepens the problem of value assessment is that in today's rapidly changing world, value is observed to be a rapidly changing phenomenon. Given the violent and startling changes now battering our world, there is little wonder to see the values oscillating so wildly that they splinter all previous records.

Role of Professional Valuer

A valuer is a highly skilled professional who - with matured technical expertise & skill - prepares a valuation of the worth of land, buildings, plants, and machinery, or possessions for specific purposes thereof. The primary responsibility of valuers to their clients is to assign, in terms of money, "value" to the movable/immovable property in an independent manner (quite unrelated to the desires, wishes, whims, or needs of the client who engages him to perform the task) with as high degree of accuracy as the particular objectives of the appraisal necessitates.

The scope of his work is very wide and extends from residential property to large estates, factories, offices, shops, plant & machinery, or every kind.

A professional valuer is expected to follow the following code of conduct:

i.   To observe integrity and fair play in the valuation profession.

ii. To refrain from misrepresenting his qualifications to a client,

iii. To treat all information acquired during the course of the business strictly confidential unless released by the client or demanded by the court of law.

iv. To express an opinion only when founded on adequate knowledge and honest conviction if he serves as a witness before a court or commission.

v.   To refrain from associating in work with another valuer who does not conform to ethical practice.

vi. To endeavor to protect the profession of valuation concerning all categories from misrepresentation and misunderstanding.

vii. To give unbiased valuation reports conforming to the objective opinion of the property and not to attempt merely to accommodate the client's interest.

viii. To steer away from the conflict between interest and duty.

The professional valuer is in utmost demand now to cater to this emerging situation, especially in the following two fields:

i.   Valuation of Real Estate

ii. Valuation of Plant and Machinery

Real Estate Valuation

Valuations of Real Estate are required for a variety of purposes, and the following brief outline shows respective considerations:

Mortgage

Buyers need to borrow money in most house purchases to meet present-day prices. Sources of finance are banks and local authorities.

The valuer will make a critical appraisal of the property, taking into account the nature of the location and proximity to amenities. He will estimate the age and consider the character, design, plan decorative and structural condition, and many other factors that may conceivably affect the value of the property in question. He will conduct an academic valuation, where appropriate, by calculating the floor area to arrive at an estimated building cost, allowing for essential repairs and adding the site's value. He will examine his recent sales records to find comparable sale instances and submit his written report to the mortgagee (the Lender), giving his recommendations.

Insurance

In a primitive human society, the variety of risks was small, and initially, the risk was limited only to life. With the sluggish progress from hunting and nomadic stages to the pastoral, there was the added risk to dwellings due to fire, storm, and flood, and hence, the imperative need to protect them with the shield of insurance was felt gradually. Even after the amazing societal and technical advancements from pastoral to mega-city life, these pervasive threats to the dwellings still exist. Interestingly, now, they threaten the existence of dwellings and their sphere of influence, which has enormously expanded to envelope factories, plants, etc.

Human efforts to minimize the effects of loss and damage caused to life and property led to the development of the classical concept of Insurance, which can be defined as a method of sharing the financial losses of a few from a common fund formed by the contributions of many who are equally exposed to the similar risks. It is, therefore, a system of spreading the loss of an individual over a widespread group of individuals, as all of them are not going to face the worst simultaneously.

One of the earliest forms of Insurance, that of reducing risk by taking advantage of numbers, is found in the practices of early Chinese Merchants. They took periodic trips inland to gather merchandise for sale on the coast.

While sailing down the torrential Yangtze River, they would gather above the rapids and distribute their cargoes so that each boat had a small portion of the other merchant's cargo aboard. Thus, if one boat was lost in the rapid, no one merchant would suffer a total loss. This simple co-operative scheme saved many from financial ruin, and increased the profits of all. Thus, Insurance in some form or the other has been known for several centuries.

Modern Insurance Companies do just the same by persuading many individuals to pool their individual risks in a large group by paying some premium and thereby eliminating - or at least minimizing - their risks.

For the purpose of taking an insurance policy on the property, the owner desires to know the replacement value of the property. In all such cases, the value of the land is omitted. The valuer's job in such insurance cases is to estimate the replacement cost of the building or part of it in case of an accident to claim for the settlement of compensation. They may be partially damaged or totally destroyed, but at least the site's value remains. Consequently, the valuer is called upon to advise as to rebuilding and replacement costs, to which he will add a percentage to cover professional fees for the services of architects and surveyors necessary for the rebuilding and site clearance. Thus, the property's market value is irrelevant when it is to be valued for insurance purposes.

Rating

Local bodies levy appropriate taxes on the property and dwelling in return for various infrastructure obligations extended to the locality. This includes education, roads, sewers, and other outgoings necessary to maintain the system. The property tax is based on rateable value. These rateable values are made by the assessor of municipal authority. These values are somewhat hypothetical and are open to criticism and appeal. Therefore, apart from the Civil Servant, valuers in private practice are asked to advise on the accuracy of these assessments, especially considering changing environments and circumstances.

They may be called upon to appear on behalf of their clients at the local appellate Court to argue the case and endeavor to obtain appropriate reductions in rates and taxes.

Also, when the property in question comes under some town planning scheme, its value - as is quite obvious - increases, and consequently, the property owner must pay an additional tax known as a betterment charge. Betterment charges are usually proportional to the increment in the property's value. It becomes, therefore, quite necessary for him to know the increment in the value of his property (i.e., the value of his property before and after the completion of the town planning scheme).

Probate

When people die and leave the property, the estate may be liable to Capital Transfer Tax as per the law of the land. In this event, the deceased's solicitor will seek a valuation of the dwelling and appropriate contents for submission when obtaining probate. Values may be with vacant possession, tenanted, or part possession, and the valuer may consider full or part shares. The valuer in private practice must be prepared to argue his case and go to appeal if at all found necessary.

Sale and Purchase

The valuer must be able to value property on behalf of vendors, and he can also be retained to protect the prospective purchasers' best interests. In the former case, he will explore the potential, seeking the highest possible valuation for his client, while in the latter, there is a natural tendency to be more conservative. However, a judicious balance is necessary in each case.

The basis of valuation under this heading is similar to that outlined under "Mortgage," and at the same time, if the vendor-client purchased the property in recent years, to that purchase price can be added the cost of improvements plus the calculated appreciation as a further addition on current open market value. In addition, the valuer will advise the vendor as to the right price for negotiations.

Compulsory Acquisition for Public Purposes

Quite often, government or local authorities decide to carry out planned city development, including new highways, roads, airports, or improvements to existing facilities, which require the acquisition from private owners of whole or part of the land and buildings that they own and or occupy. The interests of these landowners must be protected, and proper compensation must be assured. The valuer must know the Land Acquisition Acts and how to interpret them in each case.

It will be appreciated that the valuation field is indeed a wide one requiring extensive knowledge, expertise, and experience and is one where sound professional study and involvement are essential. It will be seen that there are two sides of the fence, the government or local authority employee as opposed to the valuer in private practice. The opportunities are considerable, and the qualified valuer is able, if he so chooses, to gain experience in both spheres during his practicing life. A detailed discussion on the role of the professional valuer in Compulsory Land Acquisition cases has been made in Chapter 7.

Direct Tax Acts

Under the Direct Tax Acts, valuations are required under Chapter XXC (Pre-emptive right of purchase) of the Income Tax Act, which is now applicable throughout India when the sale price of Immovable Property exceeds Rupees Ten Lakhs. Even valuations are required for Capital Gains Tax, Wealth Tax, Gift Tax, etc.

Financial Valuations

Financial Valuations are carried out for a variety of reasons, including, amongst others, balance sheet purposes, determination of court fees, bank loans and other funding activities, company takeovers and mergers, compulsory purchases, and taxation. In essence, the valuer is required to assess the true worth of a company's real estate in its present location and role as part of the existing business.

Following a valuation, the specialist valuer may be instructed to negotiate on behalf of his client; therefore, in addition to his technical knowledge and valuation skills, an understanding of company law and other relevant legislation is vital.

Plant and Machinery Valuations

When one pauses momentarily, to reflect a sweeping glance upon the immense variety of P&M producing a vast array of products - widely ranging from miniature cameras to ocean-going cargo ships, mammoth assembly lines to tiny printed circuits, gigantic blast furnaces to domestic electric heaters the gleaming prospect of becoming an efficient P&M valuer on a professional basis surely becomes more and more challenging, overwhelming, and exciting on all counts, unquestionably so.

A wise saying goes, "The wealth of any great industrial nation lies within the boundary walls of its factories and manufacturing plants." And the contemporary notion of this saying, in contextual effect, is true indeed. The primary responsibility of P&M valuers to their clients - so to speak - is to assign "value" to P&M independently with as high a degree of accuracy as the particular objectives of the appraisal specifically necessitate. He critically identifies and examines the tiny shreds of the value-laden parameters cobwebbing the P&M.

How many career prospects offer oneself the unique opportunity of unlatching the doors and inspecting the detailed workings of the P&M contained within those walls, which untiringly produce the Nation's Wealth? It would be worth mentioning here that in the worldwide environment of the "Accelerative Economy," the big industrial corporations, quite paradoxically, are making more profits - or raking up even more losses - from financial and currency manipulations rather than from actual production itself. Nor is this function trivial from the viewpoint of P&M valuers employing the "profit method" for such valuations.

Valuation of P&M is required for insurance, financial, and market purposes, etc. Let us now consider the approach to each of these aspects of plant valuation.

Insurance

Valuations for insurance purposes are undertaken to establish the property's overall value, which is intended to be covered by an insurance policy. The valuation is carried out by compiling an inventory of the plant, machinery, and all other contents (excluding stock and materials-in-trade) which is at risk in the factory and then pricing the items based on either reinstatement with new or indemnity, according to the stipulated requirements of the client.

All the insurance policies have certain stipulations, which must be meticulously studied. Any conditions affecting the valuation must be considered when arriving at the figures shown in the final report to the client.

Preparing an insurance valuation so that both under-insurance and over-insurance are avoided is a complex task, requiring an understanding of P&M in the factory and a thorough knowledge of insurance principles and law.

Many firms of specialist valuers offer a comprehensive loss assessing service, which entails compiling and setting claims in respect of both material damage and consequential loss of profits.

Financial Valuations

As discussed earlier in this chapter, Financial Valuations are carried out for various reasons. Such valuations are undoubtedly the most demanding aspect of plant valuation, utilizing most of the valuer's skills and often resulting in vast sums of money changing hands.

Valuation for Disposal

P&M generally becomes available for disposal following rationalization or modernization programs and in cases of company insolvency. When valuation advice is sought in such cases, the valuer must be fully conversant with price levels and market trends, and a thorough knowledge of the practice and structure of the industry in question is essential.

Plants may be sold by private treaty, tender, or auction sale, and advice on the best disposal method will usually be required.

Following valuation for open market purposes, firms of specialist valuers are often instructed to undertake the disposal of P&M. The plant valuer, in his capacity as auctioneer, will manage the sale, including organizing and conducting the presentation of the machinery, drafting and organizing the advertising program, preparing the sale catalog, fixing the off-set prices, and supervising the delivery of lots.

Auctioneering skills can only be learned from experience, but the auctioneer must be completely conversant with legislation governing the sale of goods.

Deciding Equity at the Time of Foreign Collaboration

Due to the liberalization and globalization of our economic policies in recent years, there has been an appreciable quantum of the inward flow of foreign exchange, and many domestic companies, as such, have entered into technical collaborations with foreign ones. The valuation of the P&M plays an important role in deciding the share(s) of foreign companies in all such instances of foreign collaborations.

Complexities Involved in the Professional Practice of Valuation

As the correct solution to any problem depends primarily on a true understanding of what the problem is, and wherein lies its difficulty, we may profitably pause upon the threshold of our subject to consider first, in a more general way, its fundamental nature, the cause which impedes sound practice; the conditions on which error is most to be feared.

As no metaphor entirely as vast as that of valuation can reasonably be expected to be free from complexities, virtually every valuation eventually grants even to adversaries the possibility of partial accuracy and to oneself the possibility of error. As such, the sweeping synthesis reveals that there are more than several complexities involved in the valuation system, which the valuers frequently encounter.

The professional practice of valuation is not a simple cut-and-paste process of filling in standard formats, as is mistakenly understood in some quarters. Contrary to the wrong notions and convictions among novices in this field, there are still deeper facts about reality. A valuation cannot be manifested by a mere multiplication process (net rental income multiplied by capitalization factor to arrive at the capitalized rental value, for example) but involves interaction and correlation between various compartments of value-laden parameters of a particular system. Every compartment is welded to its own parameters, which have been dealt with in the appropriate place. In fact, the valuation process emphasizes establishing feedback relationships among all such variables/parameters, making it a comprehensive and arduous subject of serious study and systematic pursuit.

Broadly speaking, two main valuation tools are available: the Income Capitalization Technique (Investment Method) and the Physical Method of valuation. These two tools are further classified into different compartments: the Income Capitalization Technique into Rental Method, Profit Method, etc. Physical Method, Land & Building Method, Development Method, Flat-Rate Building Method, Belting, Hypothetical Building Scheme, Average Method, etc. The essence of preparing an acceptable valuation report is to select an appropriate method depending on the peculiarities of the immovable property in question and also on the purpose for which the valuation is being carried out. Courts have also understood this problem, and it was once said that:

"No fixed rules could be laid down to regulate valuation. Each officer must exercise his own discretion."

... 1927 Cal 874 (876) [AIR V 14] (DB)

These different valuation methods are not intended to find alternative values for selecting the highest, lowest, or average values. Still, they are intended to arrive at the most reasonable valuation depending on its purpose. It is to be noted here that some of these methods, such as the hypothetical building scheme, are highly controversial. His Lordship Macleod J. has once fervently commented on this method that:

" I have little doubt that this method originated in the necessity experts found there was to give specific reasons for the high value placed on land which could not be supported by direct evidence."

More or less, all the other physical methods of valuations also have inherent complexities within themselves in one form or another, e.g., determination of the residual life of a building is easier said than done. The valuer has to make a reasonably fair approximation - a more or less scientific prophecy - regarding the residual life of the building based on his professional experience.

So far as Income Capitalization Techniques (either rental or profit) are concerned, they do not involve many problems except for the selection of an appropriate value of capitalization factor, which, in turn, depends upon the following factors:

i. Ease of liquidity of the asset.

ii. Degree of risk involved (or else, the degree of security of the investment)

iii. Income-tax deductions,

iv. Capital appreciation factor,

v. Regularity of return,

vi. Nature of property.

vii. The prevailing "going price of money" as represented by the large banks and the Govt. short and long-term bonds.

As the computation of net income (i.e., rent or profit) is not a difficult task, it comes out that the selection of an appropriate value of capitalization factor is highly vulnerable to criticism and is also the cardinal factor of the success (or failure) of the Income Capitalization Method.

Also, the valuation of leasehold properties is not as simple as it appears because the incumbent valuer is quintessentially required to examine the relevant documents setting forth the rights and obligations of each of the contracted parties (i.e. lessor, and lessee) as the value of a leasehold property is directly related to the rights which are surrendered to the lessee. The greater the number of rights and fewer restrictions existing with respect to the exercise of these vested rights, the more likely the market value will be on the higher side. The leasehold interest is to be valued with reference to the nature of investment in the leasehold. It has to be based on an indirect comparison of various valuation factors, as leasehold properties cannot be valued based on comparative sales. It is more or less a subjective valuation from the lessee's point of view.

Everyone knows that industrial societies produce millions of identical products, including auto transmissions, light bulbs, Pepsi bottles, etc. Nonetheless, the same principle has been applied to so many other things, but not to too much extent, in the case of immovable properties. "One of the problems in the construction industry has been a lack of uniformity, standardization, and coordination because it is a decentralized industry," says Donald E. Parker (1988).

Various factors affect the value of an immovable property, and it is essential for a professional valuer to study these factors at a considerable length. Valuation of immovable properties (including that of their mechanical systems such as elevators, pumps, air conditioners, etc.) has long been a conundrum as more than several inherent complexities, in some way or the other, are startlingly involved with it. Immovable properties are characteristically heterogeneous, i.e., different from one another due to their own discernible, peculiar, and conspicuous character, making their value determination difficult for the incumbent valuers.

Baffling diversities in their functional use to which they are put, locational aspects, different construction methods employed, nature of occupancy (i.e., tenanted or leased, owner occupied, or partly owner-occupied partly tenanted), an astonishingly wide array of construction materials used, degree and quality of maintenance, etc. almost invariably imparts a singular identification (and hence singular monetary value) to immovable property in question. As such, two immovable properties that might have been constructed with the same capital at the same time may have different values at any given time due to either one of the above-stated reasons or the other.

Last but not least, it is very clear that the complexities in the field of valuation cannot be circumvented. Still, they can be boldly faced by the weapons of competence, knowledge, experience, and dedication of the valuers toward their profession.

Conclusions

An obsessive search of best bargains, complex taxing statutes, diversified patterns of immovable/movable properties, etc., has taken the field of professional valuation to new dimensions because it provides a similar level of information to such decisions as estimating or financial accounting information provides to others.

All in all, valuation has now scintillatingly emerged as an autonomous discipline of its own. Those who have acquired the expertise in this field of study and practice, and qualified for this purpose are called "valuers." They may be Valuation Officers under section 12A of the Wealth Tax Act or can be Registered Valuers appointed under section 34A of the same Act. There is no doubt that with the continued trend of materialistic advancements all around, the profession of valuation will become even more important and glorified in the near future.

***

Chapter 3

Depreciation of Assets

Introduction

Depreciation is indicative of the usual, gradual, and inevitable decay of life in each and every living and non-living thing. As a matter of fact, it is a universal phenomenon of the limited span of life. The sun, the mammoth stars, the mother Earth, the charming moon, verdant trees, hills, etc., also have a limited life and are subject to depreciation if viewed from a macroscopic time perspective. While living things can recoup the lost energy, man-made non-living objects like buildings, plants, machinery, etc., cannot do the same, though they can be partly renovated through maintenance, repairs, overhauling, etc.

Depreciation is the decrease in value of physical properties with time generally caused by wear and tear from use, deterioration, obsolescence, or reduced need. It may be tracked during the life of the equipment/property simply by preparing a graph of the market value of the equipment/property with time. Caution should be exercised in selecting the appropriate "market value," For example, most equipment have a wholesale and retail market value dependent upon many factors. Although the fact that depreciation does not occur is easily ascertained and recognized, determining its magnitude in advance is not easy. Investment in a depreciable asset is treated as a prepaid expense deducted over time for income tax purposes. Depreciation is not an actual cash flow but an artificial allocation. However, a cash flow does result from the savings in income taxes generated by depreciation deductions.

The general term depreciation should not be confused with the specific term "depreciation accounting." Depreciation accounting, as such, is the systematic allocation of the cost of a capital investment over some specific number of years.

Purposes of Depreciation

Because property generally decreases in value, it is desirable to consider the effect that this depreciation has on engineering projects. To be depreciable, property

i.   must be used in business or held for the production of income,

ii. have a useful life longer than one year, and

iii. be something that wears out, decays, is used up, becomes obsolete, or loses value from natural causes.

Primarily, it is necessary to consider depreciation for the following reasons:

i.   To provide for the recovery of capital over time that has been invested in physical property.

ii. To enable the cost of depreciation to be charged to the cost of producing products or services that result from the use of property. In other words, consideration of depreciation is necessary so as to provide a systematic method for allocating the depreciation portion of equipment ownership costs over a period of time and to a specific production rate. The term "specific production rate" is important here as the depreciation is largely dependent upon the average daily number of working hours to which the machine is put to use for production. If the machine is being used in extra shifts, for instance, the owner is entitled to claim an Extra-Shift Allowance for depreciation.

iii. Depreciation cost is deductible while computing profits on which income taxes are paid [U/S 32(1) of I.T. Act, 1961). Depreciation accounting is done to allocate the depreciation portion of ownership costs in such a manner that the greatest tax benefits accrue. It should, however, follow strict legal government guidelines, which frequently change as new amendments are enacted.

iv. To provide the plant/machinery owners and/or their project managers with an easily calculated "estimate" of the current market value of the equipment. To accomplish this, the method of depreciation accounting selected should approximate market value.

The Various Meanings of Depreciation

Substantially, all the different technical meanings attached to the word "depreciation" are variants of four basic concepts. These are:

Decrease in Value with Time

This implies that the value of one particular asset is a time-dependent concept and not an absolute one. In other words, values of the same asset would be different if computed on two different dates. If the value, in some specified way, is computed at two different dates, the value at the later date subtracted from the value of the earlier one is nothing but the "depreciation" regardless of what possible causes - either in combination or in isolation - may primarily have been responsible for the value change.

In addition to the wear and tear, the value may also be reduced due to obsolescence as well. A building, for example, may become obsolete in design, planning, and utility, as per time, place, and person. To make the building suitable for one's use, one may have to make some changes, replacements, dismantling, etc. Such extra expenditure will be deducted from the replacement cost of the building and, as such, will go to depreciation.

It would be interesting to note here that the value of a particular asset may sometimes - under special circumstances - be more than its value on some earlier date. In such cases, the term depreciation is replaced with "appreciation." Lands, for example, are not subjected to depreciation. Due to their inelastic availability, increasing population, rapid urbanization, etc., demand goes high with the passage of time. Hence, their value gets appreciated in almost all cases, barring less than a few exceptions.

If the rate of inflation is so high that it compensates for the loss in value due to all the depreciating factors combined together, even the depreciable properties may appreciate.

Amortized Cost

This is the accounting concept of depreciation. This is well described in a report of the Committee and Accounting Terminology [Bulletin No. 1: Review and Resume (para. 56)] of the American Institute of Certified Public Accountants (1953) as follows:

"Depreciation accounting is a system of accounting which aims to distribute the cost of other basic value of tangible capital assets, less salvage (if any), over the estimated useful life of the unit (which may be a group of assets) in a systematic and rational manner. It is a process of allocation, not of valuation. Depreciation for the year is the portion of the total charge under such a system that is allocated to the year. Although the allocation may properly account for occurrences during the year, it is not intended to measure all such occurrences."

Although the common phrase "book value" (as covered in Chapter 1) describes the difference between the cost of an asset and the total depreciation charges made to date against the asset, this difference is more accurately described as "unamortized cost."

Impaired/Decreased Serviceableness

As machines become older, they are often unable to hold as close tolerance as when they were new. Similarly, the strength of structures may be impaired/decreased by the decay of timber members or the corrosion of metallic ones. As a matter of fact, all the structural members are affected - in some way or the other - by the vagaries of weather. Their structural strength goes on reducing due to fatigue and continuous use.

Again, it should be emphasized that this is not a value concept at all. Impaired/decreased serviceableness may result in a decrease in value, but there are many other common reasons for the decrease in value. Assets that are physically as good as new ones are not necessarily as valuable as they were new due to several reasons, such as:

i.   They may have comparatively higher operation and maintenance costs;

ii. they will have shorter life expectancy;

iii. service/production conditions may have changed;

iv. more economical alternative methods may have become available due to technological advancements, etc.

Difference in Value Between an Existing Old Asset and a Hypothetical New Asset Taken as a Standard of Comparison

This is the appraisal concept of depreciation. Many appraisals of old assets are usually based on replacement costs. It is very much of interest to professional valuers engaged in an asset's on-date-value determination.

This concept implies the comparison of two assets. An actual one of the valued, and a hypothetical new one used as the basis of comparison. In order to evaluate an asset by this method, a valuer should answer the question: "What could one afford to pay for this asset in comparison with the most economical new one available in the market?" It would be worth noticing here that the replacement cost of an asset would be different than that of its original purchase price at the time it was actually acquired. Reasons for this difference are obvious, such as:

i. Inflation/Deflation in prices,

ii. Advancement in technology, etc.

Replacement cost is the upper limit of the value of a particular asset to its owner. Such an upper limit of the value of an old asset may be determined by considering the cost of reproducing its service with the most economical new asset available for performing the same one. The most economical new substitute asset may have many advantages over an existing old asset, such as:

i. longer life expectancy,

ii. lower annual disbursements for operation and maintenance,

iii. increased receipts from the sale of products or services.

The deduction from the cost of the hypothetical new substitute asset should be a measure in monetary terms of all of these disadvantages combined together of the existing old asset in question. In the parlance of present value appraisal, such a deduction is called depreciation.

Types of Depreciation

Depreciation, or the decrease in value of an asset, has several causes, some of which are difficult to predict or anticipate. A decrease in value with the passage of time may be classified as follows:

A. Normal depreciation (Fig. 3.1):

B. Physical depreciation

C. Functional depreciation

D. Depreciation due to changes in price level;

E. Depletion.

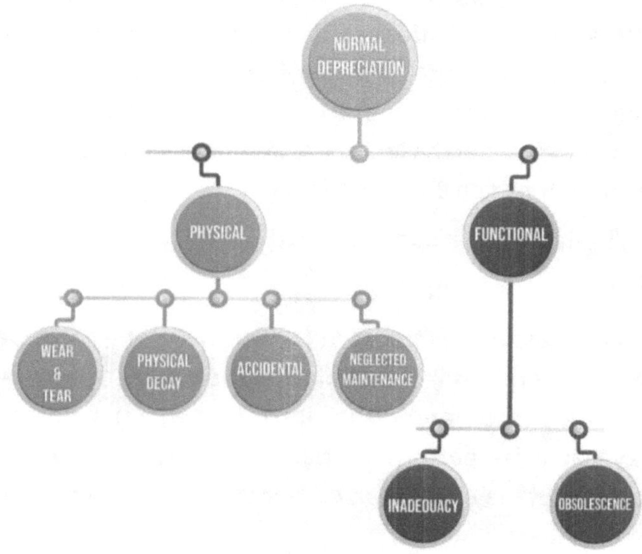

Fig. 3.1 Types of Normal Depreciation

Physical depreciation is due to the lessening of the physical ability of a property to produce results. Its common causes are wear and deterioration. These cause operation and maintenance costs to increase and output to decrease. As a result, the profits may decrease. Physical deterioration is mainly a function of time and use.

Functional depreciation, often called obsolescence, is more difficult to determine than physical depreciation. It is the decrease in value that is due to the lessening in the demand for the function that the property/machinery was designed to render. This lessening may be brought about in many ways. Styles change, population centers shift, more efficient machines are produced, or markets are saturated. Increased demand may mean that an existing machine is no longer able to produce the required volume. Hence, the existing machinery has to be replaced by the new machine to withstand market competition. Thus, inadequacy is a cause of functional depreciation.

Nor is this function trivial. Many a time, the changes in technology have resulted in a reduction of the residual economic life of plants to zero, almost within four or five years of installation. For example, modular compugraphic phototype setting/composition equipment has become almost 100% obsolete with the arrival of modern DTP systems in the market. The recurring expenditure on DTPs is now reduced to almost l/6th, thereby making the preceding technology a scrap within a few years of installation.

Depreciation due to changes in price levels is almost impossible to predict and is seldom accounted for in economic studies. When price levels rise during inflationary periods, even if all the capital invested at the time of purchase has been recovered, this recovered capital will not be sufficient to provide an identical replacement available in the market at current price levels. Although there has been a complete recovery of the invested capital, the capital has decreased in value. Thus, it is the capital, not the property, that has depreciated. It is to be noted here that inflating annual depreciation to compensate for this phenomenon is not permitted when determining profits for income tax purposes.

What is Planned Obsolescence?

Planned obsolescence is a business strategy where manufacturers design products with a limited lifespan, intending them to become outdated, unusable, or less desirable after a certain period. This practice encourages consumers to replace or upgrade their products sooner, driving repeat purchases and sustained demand.

There are several forms of planned obsolescence:

1. Functional Obsolescence: Products are intentionally made with parts that wear out quickly or are hard to repair.

2. Technological Obsolescence: Newer models with improved features or compatibility make older versions seem outdated. Every new mobile handset version with new features makes the former obsolete. David Lewis, an architect and city planner with Urban Design Associates in Pittsburgh, tells of certain apartment houses in Miami that are torn down after only ten years of existence. Improved air conditioning systems and other advanced gadgets in newer buildings hurt the comfort level of these "old" buildings. All things considered, tearing down ten-year-old buildings is cheaper than modifying them.

3. Aesthetic Obsolescence: Frequent design changes make older products look less appealing. Many car manufacturers are changing their cars' looks, making former versions obsolete.

4. Software Obsolescence: Updates are stopped for older devices, rendering them less functional or secure.

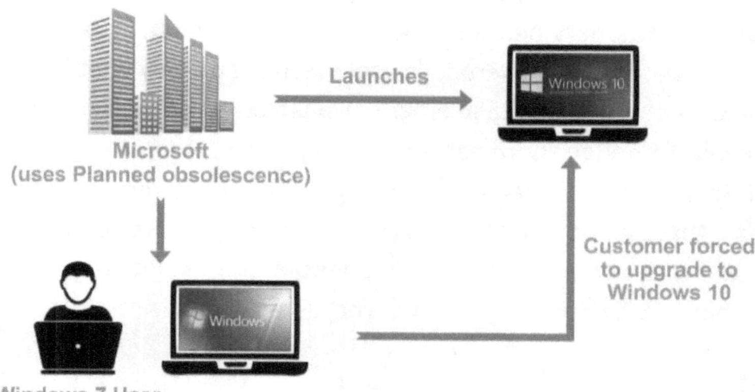

Classical Example of Planned Obsolescence: The Phoebus cartel was a group of light bulb manufacturers that intentionally reduced the lifespan of light bulbs in the 1920s to create planned obsolescence. In 1924, representatives from major light bulb manufacturers, including General Electric, Osram, and Philips, met in Geneva to form the Phoebus cartel. The cartel's name comes from Phoebus, the Greek god of light. The cartel aimed to control the global incandescent light bulb market by dividing the market into national and regional zones. The cartel assigned each zone its own manufacturers and production quotas.

By lowering the useful life of light bulbs to 1,000 hours, the cartel's efforts were successful, with sales increasing by 25% in the four years after 1926. The cartel ceased operations in 1939 with the outbreak of World War II. However, light bulbs continued to be sold with the 1,000-hour lifespan the cartel standardized.

Critics argue that planned obsolescence leads to waste, environmental harm, and increased consumer costs, while proponents say it drives innovation and economic growth.

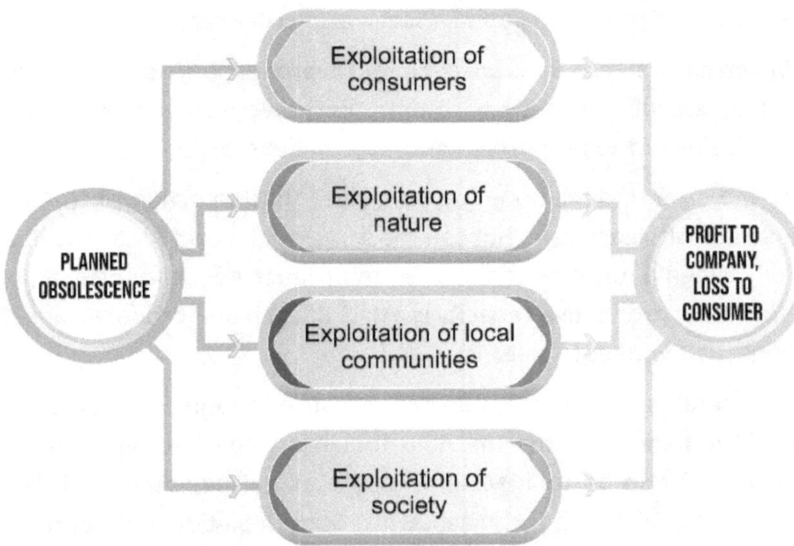

Depreciation Versus Depletion

Depreciation, as we all know very well, is the decrease in value of physical properties with time. While valuing the mining properties and horticultural assets, however, depletion is an appropriate term used to show the attenuation (or decrease) in value of the resource base due to the intentional, piecemeal removal (or exploitation) of certain types of assets. For example, a certain quantity of oil, gas, or ore is available in a given parcel of mineral property. As some of the minerals from the natural deposits are painstakingly mined and sold subsequently, the reserve gradually decreases, and the value of the property normally dwindles as well. Examples of depletions are the removal of coal from a mine, oil from an open quarry, etc. Depletion, as such, refers to an activity that tends to lessen or exhaust a supply, and the word literally means emptying. In this context, it is worthwhile to point out that the Concise Oxford Dictionary appropriately defines 'depletion' as:

i. Reduction in numbers or quality.

ii. Emptying, exhaustion.

Webster's New College Dictionary (Third College Edition) seems to be more closer to its exact meaning as it defines 'depletion' as "the gradual using up or destruction of capital assets, especially natural resources."

When natural resources are exploited in production, depletion indicates a gradual lessening in value with time. With every such exploitation, the residual value of the property in question decreases.

In the case of depletion, it is very clear that a portion of the asset is disposed of with each sale. But can the same not be said for a machine tool as well? When a machine tool is used to produce goods for sale, a portion of its inherent productive capacity is a part of each unit produced and, thus, is disposed of with each sale.

A mineral resource has value only because the mineral may profitably be sold, and similarly, the machine tool has value because what it can produce may also be sold. Mineral resources get depleted, and machine tools get depreciated in technical terms. Both depletion and depreciation, nonetheless, represent a decrease in value through the use up of the asset's value under consideration, either in some way or the other.

There is a difference in the manner in which the capital recovered through depletion and depreciation must be handled. In the case of depreciation, the asset involved usually may be replaced with a similar asset when it is fully depreciated by creating a sinking fund or otherwise.

But in the case of depletion, such replacement is usually neither conceivable nor practically possible. Once the gold has been recovered from the mine, granite has been taken out of an open quarry, or the oil has been pumped out of all oil wells, it cannot be replaced to replenish the mine/quarry/well. In manufacturing, the amounts charged for depreciation are reinvested in new equipment to continue operation. However, in mining, the amounts charged to depletion cannot be used to replace the ore deposit, and the venture may sell itself out of business bit by bit as it carries out its operations of mining and selling. The return in such a case must consist of two portions:

1. The profit that has been earned on the venture.

2. The owner's capital, which was invested.

After the exhaustion of available natural resources, the company would be out of business, and the stockholder would hold stock that would be theoretically worthless but would have received back all his invested capital, including that of cumulative profits therefrom (if there are any).

However, in the actual operation of such ventures dealing with the piecemeal removal of natural resources, the depletion funds are commonly used to acquire new properties, such as new mines and oil-producing properties, thus giving indefinite continuity to the enterprise.

Though there are many valuation methods, including that of classical Hoskold's method, the preferred method for depleting properties (such as mining) is the Discounted Cash Flow (DCF) Method - using an appropriate discount rate -if cash flows can reasonably be estimated or projected with some degree of certainty. It would not be inconsequential here to point out that - in the worldwide environment of accelerative economy - the old concepts of profit-making from a mega venture need to be thoroughly revised and rephrased and this definition is not a matter of choice but a necessary response to the revolutionary changes in the prevailing business environment.

The big corporations are driven almost willy-nilly to invest and borrow in various currencies not on an annual, monthly, or even weekly basis, but literally on an overnight or minute-to-minute basis. Nor is this function trivial. Like farmers who make more from selling land than from growing crops, some major corporations (including mining ones) are making even more profit - or racking up even greater financial losses - from currency and financial manipulations than from actual production.

The theoretical Annual Depletion (A.D.) would be:

$$\text{A.D.} = \frac{\text{Cost of Property}}{\text{No.of Units in the Property}} \times \text{Units Sold during Year}$$

High depletion allowances are often defended as being necessary to encourage the discovery and development of mineral resources, on the basis that such ventures involve a high degree of risk and uncertainty. They have to acquire environmental clearances and must always be ready to face the threat of active environmentalists if they fail to observe stipulated ecological standards, which is 'easier said than done' in most cases. However, the high mortality rate of new businesses, and some even older ones, in the manufacturing and services industries is rather strong proof that they also involve considerable risk and uncertainty. The upheaval in the world economy has threatened the survival of several such industries.

Requirements of A Depreciation Method

A depreciation method should have the following requirements from the standpoint of management & computation:

i.   It should not be too complex, i.e., it should be simple and easily understood by its users. It has been observed that complex methods are not popular among common users, even if they are good.

ii. It should provide for the recovery of invested capital as rapidly as is consistent with the economic facts involved; known and computed salvage should agree, if possible,

iii. It should be accepted by the Govt. Revenue Service, if the method is also to be used for determining Govt. Income Taxes.

iv. It must ensure that the "book value" will be reasonably close to the market value at any time.

These requirements are contradictory and are not easily met. One is to be met with at the sacrifice of the other. If it is too simple, it may not be able to maintain the book value sufficiently close to the present market value at any given time. It may not enjoy popularity among its prospective users if it is too complex. As a result, numerous methods for computing depreciation have been devised. Each is based on some hypothesis regarding the loss of an asset's value versus time and is an attempt to solve the complex depreciation problem reasonably and satisfactorily. Because conflicting factors are involved, and the future is unknown, all the requirements cannot be achieved using any depreciation method.

The requirements of a depreciation method are different for economic study purposes. It should provide for capital recovery and the proper assignment of depreciation cost over the asset's estimated life. The amount of depreciation claimed in a given year is influenced by:

i.   an asset's value,

ii. estimated life,

iii. salvage value and date in service, and

iv. the method of calculating depreciation.

But, equally important, a depreciation method should account properly for the recovered capital funds, thereby reducing the amount of capital remaining invested in a project. The recovered funds, thus, are available to the firm for other uses or investments. Finally, the method used must permit the proper evaluation of an investment's "profitability" in an engineering economy study.

Methods of Depreciation

There are several methods available for the computation of depreciation. Each of all these methods has got its own advantages and disadvantages. To calculate the depreciation by any of the following methods, close estimates of the following must be known:

i.   The purchase price of the equipment/property (P).

ii. The economic life of the equipment/property (the optimum period to keep the equipment), or the recovery period allowed for the income tax purposes (N).

iii. The estimated resale value at the close of the economic life, generally known as the salvage value (S).

Commonly used depreciation methods include the following:

i. Straight-line method (SLD)

ii. Declining balance method

iii. Declining balance method (Matheson formula) with the switchover to a straight line.

iv. Sinking fund method

v. Annuity charging method

vi. Insurance policy method

vii. Machine hour basis method (Service Output Method)

viii. Sum-of-the-year-Digits (SOYD) method

ix. Appraisal method

x. Quantity survey method

xi. Realistic formula

It is to be noted here that the Machine Hour Method is a variation of the service output method.

It has already been pointed out in the previous section that no single method can provide all the conceivable advantages. Hence, it is quite common to utilize at least two, and sometimes even three, different accounting methods on a particular piece of equipment, reporting one value to the estimators for use in construction/ production and another to the Internal Revenue Service to obtain the most favorable tax benefits.

Straight-line Method

This is probably the first ever method developed to compute a property's depreciation. As the name suggests, this method assumes that the loss in value is directly proportional to the age of the asset. Let,

N = depreciable life of the asset in years

P = original cost

S = Salvage value at the end of the useful life of the asset

d_k = annual cost of depreciation in the kth year $(1 < k < N)$

BV_k = book value of the end of Kth year

D_k = Cumulative depreciation through the *kth* year

Then,

$$B_k = \frac{P-S}{N} \qquad \text{...(3.1)}$$

$$d_k = \frac{P-S}{N} \qquad \text{...(3.2)}$$

$$D_k = \frac{k(P-S)}{N} \qquad \text{...(3.3)}$$

$$BV_k = P - \frac{K(P-S)}{N} \qquad \text{...(3.4)}$$

The term *(P - S)* is often referred to as the depreciable value of an asset.

The straight-line method is the most acceptable and widely used method of computing depreciation. It is simple and gives a uniform annual depreciation change throughout the property's service life except when the service life estimate is changed. Proponents of this method hold that inasmuch as other costs, as well as the depreciable life, can be estimated accurately, there is little reason for attempting to use a more complex formula.

This method, however, is the slowest system of depreciation. All other methods of computing depreciation are accelerated methods and should be used under certain conditions only.

Example 1

A new machine in a manufacturing plant has an installed cost of Rs. 40,000/- and an estimated 10-year life. The salvage value of the machine is zero at the end of 10 years. What will be the depreciation cost, or "write-off," during the fifth year, the book value at the end of the fifth year, and the cumulative depreciation cost through the fifth year?

Solution:

Applying the equations (3.1) to (3.4) in this Example, one obtains

$$d_5 = \frac{40,000-0}{10} = Rs.\,4000/-per\ year$$

$$D_5 = \frac{5(40,000-0)}{10} = Rs.\,20,000/-$$

$$BV_5 = 40,000 - \frac{5(40,000-0)}{10} = Rs.\,20,000/-$$

Declining Balance Method

This method provides for even larger portion of the cost of a plant/property to be written off in the early years. Interestingly, this method, in many cases, often more nearly approximates the actual loss in market value with time.

In this method, sometimes called the constant percentage method or the Matheson formula, it is assumed that a property will lose its value by a constant percentage of its value at the beginning of every year. In other words, the annual depreciation cost is a constant percentage of the book value at the beginning of the year. The depreciation ratio in any year to the book value at the beginning of the year is constant throughout the asset's life and is designated by R (0 <R<1).

Declining methods range from 1.25 times the current book value divided by the life to 2.00 times the current book value divided by the life (the latter is termed double declining balance).

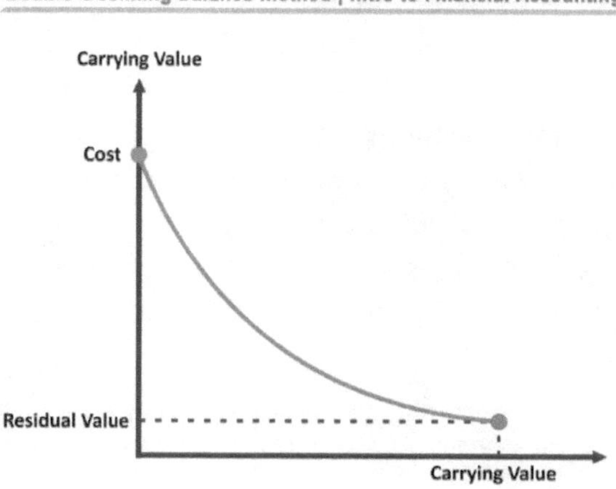

It is also to be noted that although the estimated salvage value (S) is not included in the calculation, the book value cannot go below the salvage value. Thus,

Depreciation during the first year;

$$d_1 = \text{P.R.} \qquad \qquad \text{...(3.5)}$$

Depreciation for the kth year;

$$d_k = \text{P.R.}(1-R)^{k-1} \qquad \qquad \text{... (3.6)}$$

Cumulative depreciation through the kth year;

$$D_k = P[1-(1-R)^k] \qquad \qquad \text{...(3.7)}$$

Book value at the end of the kth year;

$$BV_k = P(1-R)^k \qquad \qquad \text{...(3.8)}$$

Example 2

Solve example 1 using the Double Declining Balance Method.

Solution:

By applying the Declining Balance relationships as given by equations (3.5) and (3. 8), one gets:

$$R = 2/N = 0.2$$
$$= 40{,}000(1 - 0.2)^4(0.2)$$
$$= \text{Rs. } 3{,}276.80/\text{-}$$
$$= 40{,}000([1 - (1 - .02)^5]$$
$$= \text{Rs. } 26{,}892.80/\text{-}$$
$$= 40{,}000(1 - .02)^5$$
$$= \text{Rs. } 13{,}107.20/\text{-}$$

Declining Balance Method with Switchover to Straight Line

The Declining Balance Method as described in the earlier Section, has two disadvantages:

i.   The annual cost of depreciation is not constant every year.

ii. As 'S' is not utilized in equations (3.5) to (3.8), the asset will never get depreciated to zero value.

It is, however, possible to account for the second disadvantage by switching over to some other slower method of depreciation beyond the point where the Declining Balance method undercuts the "Salvage Value." Usually, the depreciation is computed by the straight-line method beyond this point.

Comparison of Straight Line and Declining Balance Methods

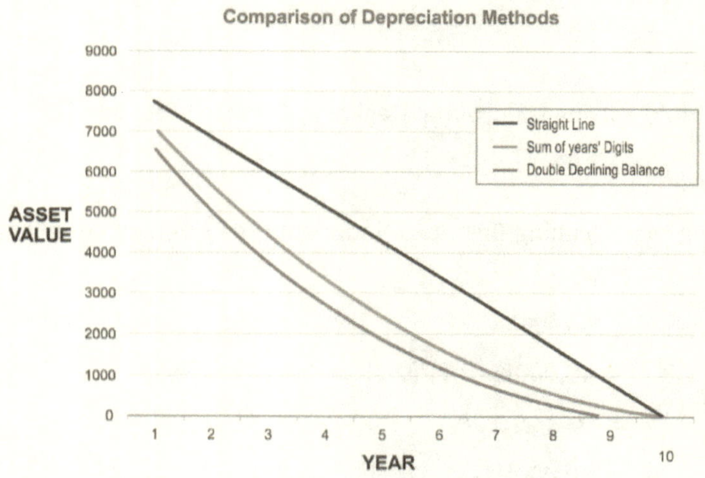

Sinking Fund Method

In this system, a depreciation fund equal to the actual loss in the asset's value is estimated, considering the interest on the so accumulated fund. The rate of depreciation will be constant throughout the life of the machine. Let,

D = Rate of depreciation per year,

R = Rate of interest on the accumulated fund in fraction number,

$$D = \frac{R(P-S)}{(1+R)^N - 1} \qquad \text{...(3.9)}$$

The Annuity Charging Method

In this method, interest is charged on the cost of the machine or asset on the book value every year, but the depreciation is constant every year. If the value of the machine after one year becomes P_1, then

$$D = P.R.+P-P_1 \qquad \text{... (3.10)}$$

Or,

$$D = P\,'(1+R)-P_1 \qquad \text{... (3.11)}$$

In the same way, the value of the machine after two years will be, say, P_2 then,

$$D = P_1.\,R+ P_1 - P_2 \qquad \text{...(3.12)}$$

Or,

$$D=P_{/}(1+R)-P_2 \qquad \text{...(3.13)}$$

Hence, the generalized formula will be

$$D = \frac{[P(1+R)^n - S][1-(1+R)]}{(1-(1+R)^N]} \qquad \text{... (3.14)}$$

Hence, by substituting the different values in the above formula, the depreciation rate can easily be calculated.

The Insurance Policy Method

This method covers the risk of the machine becoming unserviceable before its estimated life. As such, the machine is insured by the insurance company, and premiums are paid according to the insurance policy. Upon the policy's maturity, the insurance company provides a sufficient sum to replace the machine.

Machine Hour Basis Method

This method calculates the depreciation rate considering the total number of hours a machine runs in a year. Therefore, every machine's work-hour chart is maintained to determine the number of hours the machine runs in a year.

The Sum of the Year's Digit Method

In this method, it is assumed that, as the new equipment is installed, the reduction in value will be greater initially and decrease gradually. This fact is taken into account, and, therefore, a greater amount of depreciation is made during the early years of life, and it goes on reducing as the life of equipment decreases. Therefore, for calculating depreciation, the net depreciable amount (i.e., Total Cost - Scrap Value) is spread over the whole life in a decreasing proportion.

The general expressions for d_k, BV_k and D_k would be:

The annual cost of depreciation for any year k:

$$d_k = (P - S)\frac{2(N-k+1)}{N(N+1)} \qquad \text{...(3.15)}$$

Book value at the end of the kth year:

$$BV_k = P - \frac{[2(P-S)].k}{N} + \frac{(P-S)}{N(N+1)} k\,(k+1) \qquad =(3.16)$$

And, cumulative depreciation through the kth year:

$$D_k = P\text{-}BV_k \qquad \text{... (3.17)}$$

Example 6

Solve Example 1 using the Sum of the Years Digits Method.

Solution:

Using equations (3.15) to (3.17), one gets

$$d_5 = 40,000 \frac{[2.(10-5-1)]}{10(11)}$$

$$\Rightarrow \qquad d_5 = Rs.2,909.09/\text{-}$$

and;

$$BV_5 = 40,000 - \frac{2(40,000)\times 5}{10} + \frac{(40,000)}{10(11)} \times 5 \times (6)$$

$$\Rightarrow \qquad BV_5 = Rs.10909.09/\text{-}$$

and also;

$$D_6 = Rs.(40,000-10909.09)/-$$
$$\Rightarrow \qquad D_6 = Rs.29090.91/-$$

Computation of Depreciation: Special Cases

Under Section 28 of the Income-tax Act, 1961, profits and gains of business shall be chargeable to income-tax. Under Section 29 of the I.T. Act, such tax shall be computed in accordance with the provisions contained in sections 30 to 43A. Section 32, amongst others, allows deductions in respect of depreciation on buildings, machinery, plant, or furniture owned by the assessee and used for the purpose of business, which would be subject to the provisions of Section 34. Section 34 lays down the conditions under which depreciation allowance is available. Sub-Section (1) provides that the deductions for depreciation shall be allowed only if the prescribed particulars have been furnished. Rule 5, read with Appendix I, Part I, provides for calculating depreciation.

A plant should not be confused with whirling wheels and smoking chimneys. Under Section 32 of the I.T. Act, a Cinema Theater is also a plant, hence, entitled to depreciation. The Karnataka High Court gave an interesting judgment to this effect. Hon'ble Justice S.A. Hakeem J. (1988) called Cinema Theatre a plant when the question was asked by the Income-tax Appellate Tribunal (Bangalore Bench) with references to Section 256(1) of the Income-tax Act, 1961.

Residual Life of Structures

As is now clear that almost every method used for the computation of depreciation requires the knowledge of the total economic life span of the building. If the residual life can be ascertained fairly accurately, the total span of the economic life will be known. From this, the depreciation rate may be worked out as required by applying different applicable and necessary methods.

It is true for all practical purposes that the building properties deteriorate. After a certain period of discharging useful service, the structures retire, i.e., cease to discharge any useful service. In valuation terminology, this useful period is known as 'Economic Life.' It does not imply in any way that the buildings - by themselves - would collapse automatically after such time. On the contrary, the buildings continue to stand erect till they succumb to natural death due to maximum deterioration, failing important parts, contributing to the final and inevitable collapse. It should not, however, be mixed up with the collapse or damage due to accidents or natural disasters like earthquakes. Insurance companies take care of these losses and have no relation to normal depreciation.

Ordinarily, the Valuer is required to deal with the Economic life of the buildings, i.e., the service life. One of the surest proofs to determine whether the building has not ceased to render requisite service is to examine the yield of the building or improvement. During economic life, the appurtenant land and buildings provide more income than the income from bare land alone if the condition is not otherwise disturbed. Theoretically this might hold good, but these conditions may not be found in reality.

Strategies to Reduce Depreciation

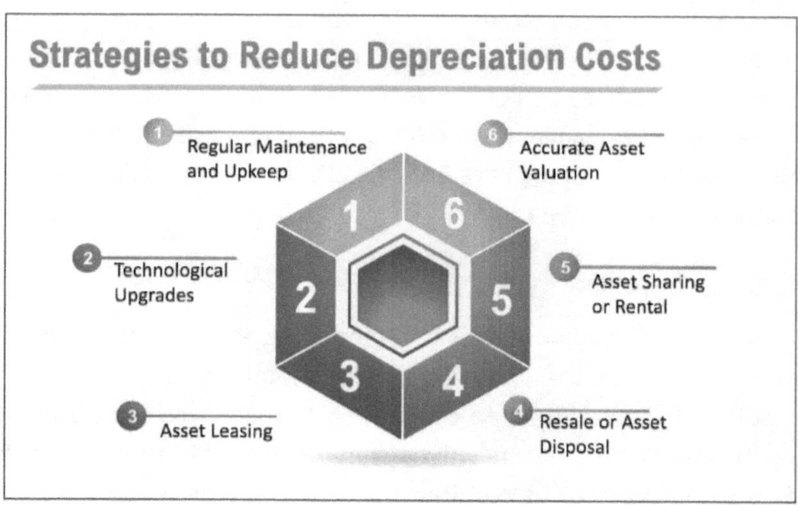

Tangible property subjected to depreciation also involves maintenance. Masonry Buildings with load-bearing walls of yesteryears, mostly found to be constructed with care and by using sound materials, live longer than their presumed life. There are many masonry buildings that have sustained stress and strain for the last 100 years or even more and are still rendering service because of regular maintenance. According to the definition given in the Encyclopedia Britannica, Full Maintenance aims to keep the property intact without deterioration.

But the aim often remains unfulfilled as at the ultimate part of Economic Life, the cost of maintenance and repairs gradually goes on increasing till, at some point, the building itself attains such a condition that it then is found beyond economical repairs when there is no other alternative than to consider its reconstruction, though in most cases with a modified shape, size, and specifications commensurate with the changed circumstances and requirements. The latter part, i.e., life beyond the Economic Life, is said to be the Physical Life of the building. While some buildings may have 60 years of Economic life, they may survive up to 100 years or more during their Physical Life (including, of course, the period of Economic Life).

It is, however, observed, especially in areas affected by the Rent Control Act, that the owner shows the least interest in maintaining the building in the required manner because of the Unremunerative yield. And even though the building is found to have attained a very alarmingly dangerous state for such continuous neglect of maintenance, the tenants would not vacate it but live there till the day of the collapse, as may be evident from a growing number of such News Items in the rainy seasons. The owner is thus deprived of the opportunity of timely and economical repairs/ reconstruction of the building on the one hand. On the other hand, he is liable to compensate all the tenants for losses due to the accidental collapse of the building. Many of the self-occupied buildings and the buildings which do not fall within the area of the Rent Control Act are also found to be lying in neglected condition for being devoid of any maintenance and repairs for a long duration due to apathy and neglect on the part of general house owners. These buildings are also subject to early collapse, i.e., the buildings have reduced life. On the other hand, regular maintenance and capital repair work arrests deterioration and contributes positively towards durability or longer life. Hence, it is essential to determine the future life of structures to find out the amount of depreciation of the structure from which present value may be assessed.

Valuers of immovable properties often encounter the complex problem of ascertaining structures' residual life or future life while evaluating the present worth of old buildings. The question contains too many complexities when the building is very old. There is every chance of misjudgment on the part of the valuer if the building is not meticulously examined in all respects. While doing so, care should be taken to consider the Economic Life span only, i.e., the physical life portion should be left out because depreciation is calculated on the decline of the asset spread over the Economic Life. All confusion in this regard should be cleared.

A very careful survey of the property is necessary after thorough inspection, especially to ascertain the specification of the building, mode and year of construction, settlement of foundation and deflection of load bearing members, signs of all distresses, conditions of the sanitary block, decay due to white ants, termites, dry rots, etc. Capital repairs carried with all details, including money spent and the year in which the work was executed, should also be ascertained. After this, all these points are required to be compared and co-related with such data of other known buildings according to available records and experience gained in previous such data of other known buildings according to available records and experience gained in previous such cases. Capital repairs would increase economic life, which should be considered when finding out the residual or remaining portion of economic life. The valuer's judgment plays a vital role in finding out the residual life and depreciation.

Another point that should be taken care of is to reduce the value of the structure by the cost of capital repairs if not executed but necessary in addition to the depreciated cost. So much judgment, attention, and care are necessary for finding out the residual life of the building as the same cannot be worked out by applying any mathematical formula.

LIC Classification

Life Insurance Corporation (LIC) of India, the premier financial institution sanctioning house-building loans, may be expected to have framed its rules and guidelines to be ideally suited for the purpose. Acceptable age, minimum residual life expected, and period of repayment specified and made effective from 2nd March 1986, for purchasing old buildings under the 'Own Your Home' Scheme are as follows:

Nature of building	Acceptable age	Minimum residual life expected	Period of repayment of loan
(a) Reinforced cement concrete framed & terraced.	35 Years	25 Years	12-1/2 Years
(b) Masonry Walls (Pucca & RCC Roof & Floors)	25 Years	25 Years	12- 1/2 Years
(c) Masonry Walls (Pucca Timber of Joist frame and Pent Roof)	15 Years	20 Years	10 Years

Glancing at the table, the various periods specified above are conservatively on the lower side, but it can be justified if considered in view of ensuring repayment of the loan, which is essential for the success of the scheme. It may appear at first that the Economic Life span may be taken as the sum of the periods mentioned in columns (2) and (3), but it may not be so for any class of structure. The total Economic Life of every building may vary, although classification remains the same, which is very likely.

It may seem odd that no distinction has been made between residential and non-residential buildings. However, the total economic life span of non-residential buildings is generally 70% of residential buildings.

Residual Life: A Few Tips

From the above discussion, it may be concluded in the context of the determination of residual Life of buildings that:

i. Every building needs to be considered individually and should be thoroughly examined with the available data, as there is no mathematical formula or any set procedure and method,

ii. The life span generally specified for different classes of buildings for guidance may not be true in all cases,

iii. It might so happen that the total Economic Life span of a Masonry building may be more than that of RCC framed buildings according to various circumstances,

iv. Quality of the materials used and specification according to which the building has actually been constructed need to be examined, as these are very important,

v. History depicting maintenance and repair works undertaken from time to time with special reference to the capital repairs at least during the past 15/20 years in proper sequence need to be procured, or it may be prepared if none.

vi. Besides the private buildings, RCC buildings and bridges constructed even through the Govt. Agencies collapse at much earlier ages. These have now become common not only in our state but in other states also.

All these data are to be carefully analyzed in the light of experience and compared with similar cases to arrive at a final decision.

***

Chapter 4

Land Use and Land Values

Introduction

Land is a very scarce and inelastic commodity, more so in the case of urban land. Regardless of their use, they comprise imperishable immovable properties wherein the keyword "immovable" gives the idea of their static character. Nevertheless, multiple activities to which the land is contemplatively exposed are essentially dynamic entities revealing whereupon the developed utility potential of the land thereof.

Land use within an agglomeration of human settlement differs drastically depending upon the:

i. location,

ii. situation,

iii. approachability,

iv. future prospects of the site,

v. infrastructural facilities of the area,

vi. environment and availability of lands, etc.

Despite growing hiatus and baffling diversities, the use of land has broadly been classified into nine categories (as per the Master Plan for Delhi, which came in force from 1.8.1990, popularly known as MPD-2001);

i. residential,

ii. commercial,

iii. manufacturing,

iv. recreational,

v. agricultural

vi. transportation,

vii. utility,

viii. Government

ix. public and semi-public, and water body.

However, in several cases, it may not be possible to draw a clear-cut demarcating line between them due to mixed land use activities prevailing thereupon.

Commercial Land Use and Land Values

In any case, the highest land values in a city are always associated with commercial areas and shopping centers. For example, the land rate in Connaught Place (New Delhi) as of 1.4.1974 for residential use was Rs. 200/- per sq. yard as against for commercial purposes Rs. 1000/- per sq. yard, i.e., commercial land was 500% costlier. In the Nizamuddin area, it was nearly 230%, and in an area outside the extended commercial zone on Parliament Street, it was 333% higher during the same period. Most geographers subscribe to this phenomenon by unanimously endorsing a common understanding that Central Business Districts (CBDs) of all cities worldwide are undisputedly characterized by the highest land values prevailing in those cities. Commercial Land Values (CLVs) can always be used as an index indicative of the relative hierarchical importance, i.e. order of stratification, of respective market centers. After the CBD, the regional-level market centers are associated with the highest land values, followed by community and neighborhood market centers.

The nexus between prolific commercialization and transcendent urbanism (i.e. cognitive settlement pattern based on the location of economic activities) is growing stronger and stronger each day as both of them are complementary to each other. The cardinal cause of these pinnacled CLVs, in the CBD or in the commercial core of higher hierarchical order of the agglomeration, is the acute competition among the retailers/

manufacturers for purchasing/renting prime commercial spaces to locate the outlets of their salable commodities/products pursuing thereby the commercial transactions. This has naturally resulted in land shortage, ultimately spiraling their prices and the rental and premium values of shops. In addition, even among professionals who are not businessmen in an exact sense and can carry out their professional activities without occupying prime market locations, it is becoming a growing trend to procure such prime spaces even at substantial premiums as a mark of their astounding professional status.

Assessment of CLVs

As contrasts and diversities of the problem domain make generalization less than meaningful, there is no such abstract mathematical formula by which the market value of the commercial land can be ascertained, and hence, its determination involves a small amount of guesswork, which is a quasi-scientific nature. As such, there is no market for land in the sense that one speaks of a market for shares, gold, silver, or any similar commodity. The value of any such article at a given time can readily be ascertained by the prevailing prices.

In the case of land, its value in general can only be ascertained by a consideration of prices that have been obtained in the past for land of similar quality and positions. However, sometimes it may so happen that the land to be valued possesses some unusual and unique feature(s) as regards to its position or its potentialities in which case the valuer will have no guideline to correlate the market value reflected in the most comparable instance which provides the index of market value.

There is no agency, either private or government, that can supply the official data on CLVs except the sale documents registered with the Registrar of Deeds and the valuation cases dealt with by the Town Planning Department(s). Also, the cognizance of sale deeds between public trusts, government departments, and cooperative societies can be taken. In addition, the rental values of the surroundings can be considered before fixing the CLVs.

Prices as per officially registered sale deeds have been found to be much less than the actual values prevailing in the sale deeds due to legal difficulties with the tax and/or revenue authorities. Hence, comprehensive fieldwork has to be carried out to arrive at the CLV and the rent and premium of the land in question.

Factors Affecting the CLVs

Several prominent factors which may pragmatically affect the CLVs are as follows:

(i) Road Frontage

There is a remarkable difference in land values of commercial belts with road fronts and the land just behind them or in adjacent areas. In the same locality, the land used for shops has a higher value than the adjacent ones used for godowns or residential purposes. Moreover, plots perpendicular to road(s) usually have lesser values due to lesser road frontage. A plot with a larger frontage and smaller depth would be higher in value than a plot with a similar frontage and large depth (i.e., having the same area). "Gomukhi" plots (when the frontage is less than the width at the rear, as shown in Figure 4.1) are generally preferred to "Vyghramukhi" plots (when the frontage is more than the width at the rear, as shown in Figure (4.2) by those who approbate the classical concept of "Vastushastram."

Order of preference for the position of frontage with respect to direction is:

A. West,

B. North,

C. South, and

D. East

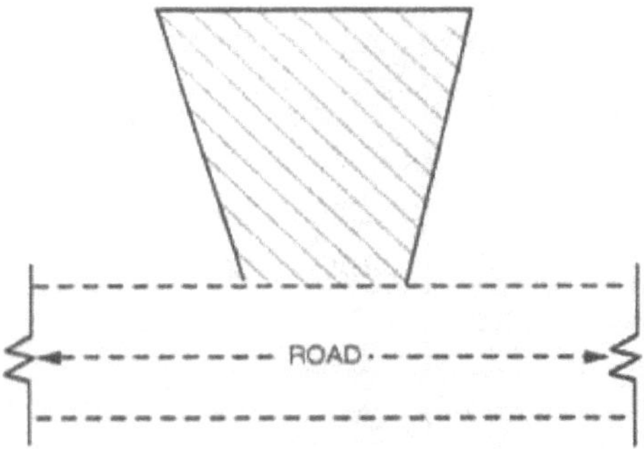

Figure 4.1 Gomukhi Plot

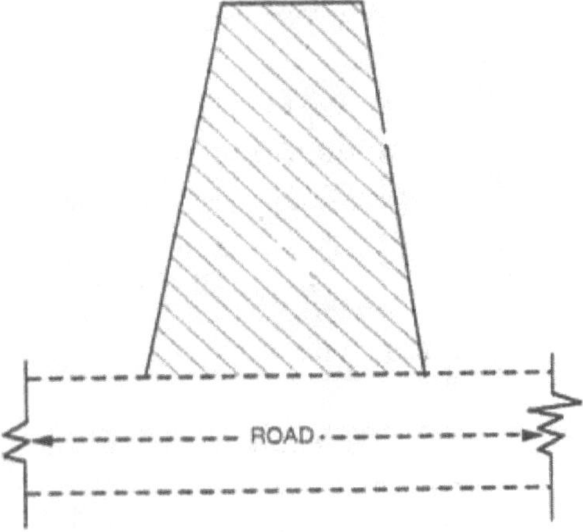

Figure 4.2 Vyghramukhi Plot

Also, commercial plots situated at the junction of two roads (i.e. return frontage as shown in Figure 4.3) are usually valued more than the others in the same area. Such plots are generally valued 25% to 80% more than the similar ones with no return frontage depending upon the location, and supply & demand position. In the context of frontage, it would be interesting to note that there may be lands having no frontage available to them at all. "Land-locked lands" are such lands having no independent means of access (Figure 4.4).

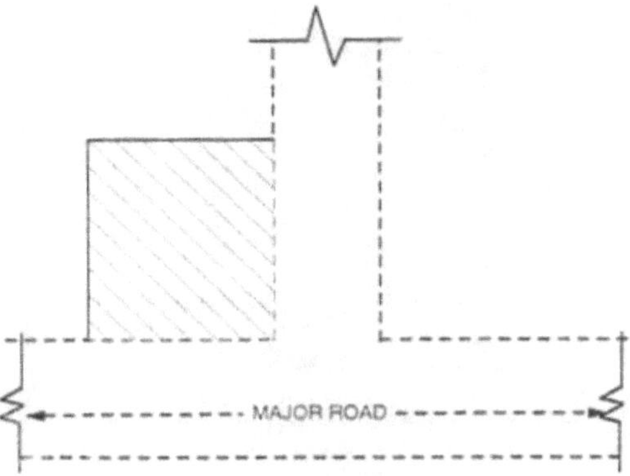

Figure 4.3 Return Frontage

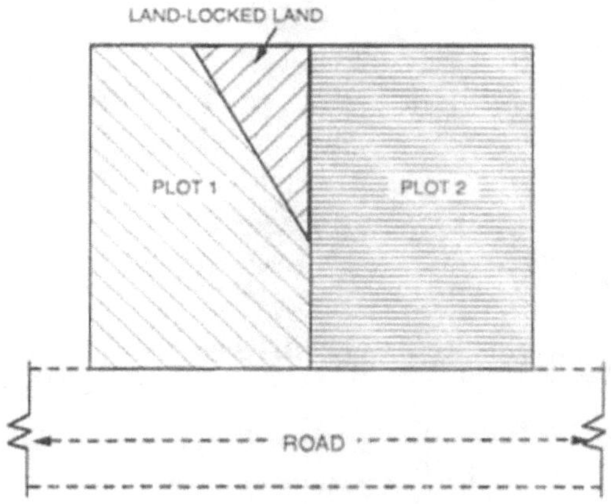

Figure 4.4 Land-Locked Lands

As such, lands are useful only to the adjoining owners, and demand for the same will be limited only to them. Consequently, they will fetch very low prices due to the restricted availability of buyers.

(ii) Development Potential

Development control rules, serving as the prime regulator of an equable built environment, have been a determinant in CLV-matrix and include the following:

A.   Maximum permissible coverage per floor on net plot.

B.   Maximum permissible Floor Area Ratio (FAR) on the net plot.

C.   Maximum permissible height.

D.   Set-backs and parking standards, i.e., a minimum of idle parking on net plot.

The prescribed FAR (FSI) determines the total built space that a plot is allowed to hold with no provision for extra usage in any form and, as such, is used as leverage in processing development policy. As per MPD-2001, Connaught Circus (CBD) and its extensions now have a FAR of 150, whereas FAR values for Nehru Place District Center projects are beyond 125.

In Bombay, the FSI prescribed for all uses is 133 in the island city and 100 elsewhere; however, for industrial use, it is 50. There is also the "Transfer of Development Rights (FOR)" facility from the island to the suburbs as part of the decongestion policy.

(iii) Purpose of Valuation (Taxation/Sale/Purchase/Compulsory Land-Acquisition/Renting/Mortgage etc,

(iv) Business Potential and hierarchical level (CBD/ Regional/ Community/ Neighbourhood) of the market in which the land is situated.

These terms are interrelated as the more significant the business potential, the higher the market stratification order and vice-versa. The higher-order retail nucleations record more value than the lower-order centers due to a higher degree of competition and shortage of shopping space in the former. Also, there is a common practice of charging premium (Pagree) while renting commercial spaces, particularly in higher hierarchical order market centers. Premiums are paid in cash to the landlord on a non-refundable basis when the shop is let out. No receipt of any such amount is ever acknowledged in black and white. The payee, however, manages to recover it, sometimes with profit, when he vacates the premises in favor of another shopkeeper. Similar to CLVs and rent, premiums also increase with the hierarchy of commercial centers.

(v) The land may have some special value for an owner of an adjoining property to whom it may have some very special advantage.

(vi) Size and shape of the land.

(vii) Socio-economic, political, and geographical characteristics; cultural needs and degree of aspiration of the region in its pursuit of economic well-being.

(viii) Legal status of land.

(ix) Some specific disadvantage factors (if there are any) that would deter a prospective purchaser. For example, the plot subjected to easement rights of air, light or passage will fetch less price as the building potentialities in such a case will be reduced considerably.

(x) Future prospects of the site

It has been established by numerous authorities that the land is not to be valued merely with reference to the use to which it is being put at the time of valuation, but also with reference to the uses to which it is reasonably capable of being put in future. However, the land must not be valued as though it had already been put to its contemplative prospective use as it is only the possibility of the land and not its realized possibility that must be considered (U/s 24(5) of L.A. Act).

Conclusively, commercial lands' rent, premium, and values tend to increase with the hierarchical stratification of commercial centers. Uncontrolled settlement patterns and experiential concentration of economic development activities in a particular region, transcendent commercialization, rural development dialectics, rapid industrialization, etc., are some of the factors primarily responsible for the exorbitant CLVs in all the big cities of India.

The quintessential need for evolving a new settlement pattern based on the location of economic activities as a part and parcel of economic policy must be recognized, and it also calls for a comprehensive and effective framework of planning legislation for optimum utilization of our scarce land vis-a-vis Indian economy and its desirable settlement pattern at both macro and micro levels. Instead of forcing rural people to migrate to urban areas, urbanization can be brought to their doorsteps through a sound distribution of economic activities and by evolving a meaningful settlement pattern instead of creating a rural-urban dichotomy.

Social Determinants of Land Use and Land Values

As long as human activity continues to alter the conditions of city (urban) life, and human tastes, prejudices, pastimes, and customs continue to vary, city (urban) structure and values will shift and change.

... RichardM. Hurd

Man, while living in human settlements, whether rural or urban, creates a man-made social environment. Social values lie behind the demand for urban land, and though we usually consider the utility (and hence the value) of urban land in terms of economic advantage, it has also to be recognized beyond any reasonable doubt that under some circumstances, social values may endow urban space with qualities quite extraneous to it.

The identification, analysis, and implication of social determinants as a major force affecting land use activity locations, perhaps, is the most complex part of our urban framework. Ironically, whatever can possibly be stated about this aspect with any degree of assurance is surprisingly and startlingly very little. There is no doubt whatsoever that social and psychological conditions strongly mold many urban locational choices.

There has been an eight-fold increase in India's urban population from 25 million in 1901 to 217 million in 1991. The gigantic urban population of 217 million is spread over 4,689 towns of different sizes. By January 2000, another 64 million dwelling units comprising nearly 31 million in urban areas would have come up. Given the population explosion and the mounting pressure on urban land, land values have soared to an all-time high. Consequently, urban land has gone beyond the reach of the common man and owning even a bit of urban land has become a distant dream of the thriving urban population.

There is a very close relationship between the demand for various social activities and population growth, population characteristics, and the urban way of sustainable living. Urban land development in India has occurred mainly through the long-drawn and time-consuming process of urban accretion on the fringes of existing towns and cities. This has led to a serious imbalance between supply and demand. Also, there are social circumstances that condition the demand and directly influence the pattern of land use, land values, tenure, and the type and design of buildings constructed thereon. In addition, there are catalytic social differences among various urban agglomerations, which give rise to differences both in the quality and quantity of the demand for land for various contemplative uses thereof. These striking differences may be of economic origin but are reflected in the rate of growth and in the social characteristics of the urban population. The gradual expansion of the total urban area (which is met primarily by converting the rural land at the periphery) is accompanied by higher values of the more centrally located sites; their locational advantage is continually increased by their enlarged access to the growing number of people. Higher values, in turn, increase the pressure for economic inland uses, and part of the expanded demand for urban land is met by increasing the density of activities or more high-value lands in the central areas. The basic pressures towards higher land values are due to the increasing demands of a rapidly growing urban population. They are further accentuated by factors constraining the supply of reasonably priced urbanisable land.

Underlying all conceivable relationships in urban areas, the human element is central in the form of behavior patterns, value systems, and a person's psychology. By and large, the final basis of human action is cultural and psychological, which underlines all economic laws. It follows, therefore, that the structure of urban agglomerations, land values, earnings of buildings that house people for diversified activities, and the very growth of such agglomerations are based on the tastes and preferences as reflected in social habits and customs.

Value of Agricultural Lands in India

The term "Land" is not the same as "soil," though they are often used synonymously. A tract of land is defined geographically, as a specific area of the earth's surface. Its characteristics embrace all reasonably stable or predictably cyclic attributes of the biosphere vertically above and below this area, including those of the atmosphere, the soil and underlying geology, the hydrology, the plant(s) thereon, and the results of the past and present human activity.

Ever since the provenance of primitive civilization, agricultural lands have been found to have value for their unique fertility features to provide the elixirs of life of mankind. Even at primitive times, the variance in the value of two agricultural fields was well recognized when people found more produce from one land than from another - either quality and/or quantity. However, the imperative endurance in quantifying various parameters, except on the peril of unrealistic value assessment, was conjectured a little later, and there began adventurous economic research that is still going on.

India is a vast sub-continent in the subtropics, with several agro-climatic regions with distinct rainfall patterns, soil types, topography, cropping patterns, etc. In each region, the variety of crops that can be raised and other allied agricultural activities that can be undertaken thereon have bewildering plurality in contrast to many developed countries raising only a few major crops on a large average. Several diversified natural variables come into play in different combinations in each case at a given period of time.

These external uncontrollable variables may be continuous or discrete, fixed or probabilistic, accurately known, or assigned arbitrary values only by guess. Almost every land has got its own discernible, peculiar, and conspicuous character, making thereby its value determination a conundrum, rather a tough liability on the part of the incumbent valuer who has to be instrumental to the best of his professional competency in the exact interpretation and wise application of the advisory, discretionary, and mandatory rules framed therefor. Every case is to be approached with realistic diversity based on the peculiar facts and circumstances of that case. A valuer, therefore, has to consider all the relevant issues at a given period of time under the situation prevailing thereon. With any change or changes in the situation, various value parameters and influencing spheres may also change accordingly, endeavoring thereby the valuer to have a different look while assessing the value of the same piece of agricultural land.

Value Growth of Agricultural Lands

The extent of cultivable land available in India is decreasing quite steadily. Out of 326.7 Million Hectares (MHA) of the total geographical area, only 153 MHA is cultivable. Factors which have reduced the extent of our cultivable lands are:

i. diversion of land for other human use (due to transcendent urbanization),

ii. erosion of coastal land near the sea, and

iii. The effects of global warming are creating storm surges and cyclones in the coastal areas near the Bay of Bengal, causing land to become inundated with seawater, etc. Moreover, agricultural lands in the non-coastal areas have suffered salinity/alkalinity in Haryana, M.P., and U.P. due to frequent flooding and excessive use of fertilizers.

Nonetheless, enhanced irrigation facilities, the changing cropping pattern, the application of the latest techniques (of science, technology, and management), and the package of Govt. facilities/subsidies offered from time to time opened new vistas in agricultural production and productivity but also created new wealth and increased the value of a fecund variety of verdant agricultural lands including that of several allied activities such as big/small agro-based industries, etc. Despite gradually reducing cultivable areas, an increase in overall productivity clearly indicates the "Reducing Land - Growing Value" dichotomy, which would continue as a major trend for a long time.

Land Value in Reversion

"Reversion" - if one wishes to express it simply - refers to the vested right of the owner(s) to possess the property at the end of the stipulated term granted to the tenant/lessee. As per Webster's New Collegiate Dictionary, "reversion" can appropriately be defined as:

i. a future investment in property in the control of a grantor or his successor,

ii. the right of succession or future possession or enjoyment, or

iii. an act or the process of returning (as to a former condition).

The price of an immovable property comprehensively includes the rights to receive a stream of future income and the reversion to land. The capitalized value of net annual income will be for the estimated future life of the building, and the owner thereafter will have the open plot of land at his disposal without any structure standing thereon, which can subsequently be developed for its prospective potential benefits to realize full value at that time. The full value of land as a matter of fact - can pragmatically be realized only when the structure(s) thereon is demolished. As such, the present consideration of the full value of the vacant land available to the owner after the life of the building is over - in the parlance of professional valuation - is known as "reversionary value" or, in other words, "land value in reversion."

The classical concept of the "reversionary land value" has an important place in the valuation of immovable properties unless it gets either thwarted or diluted and becomes redundant due to some legislative restriction or the other. When a professional valuer eventually uses any valuation concept, it is not permissible to practice its principles and processes blindfold only. On the other hand, it is very much essential on his part to carefully examine whether or not the same concept has become inoperative in one way or another - by any of the restrictions/obligations whatsoever.

Valuation of Reversionary Land Value

The concept of reversionary land value is primarily based on the following basic facts and assumptions:

i.   While working out the reversionary land value, it is always presumed that the building will be demolished after the completion of its span of life,

ii. Land is available to the owner(s) in the open condition left without any encumbrances whatsoever (like tenancy rights, easement obligations, restrictive legislations, and other extraneous factors, etc.) at the end of estimated life of structure though the property(-ies) de facto may be subjected to the contemporary restrictive legislations.

iii. Land value as on the material valuation date is adopted to work out the reversionary land value. Also, the percent rate of interest for calculating the reversionary value should be a "remunerative one" and, such should generally be kept the same or slightly lower than that of the rate adopted for capitalization of net income to compensate for the uncertainty of future land estimate.

To carry out the valuation of land on a yield basis (except for yield in perpetuity), the present value of land is worked out, and also, its reversionary value is obtained. However, if the income is to continue in perpetuity, the problem of reversionary land value does not arise at all. Moreover, for immovable properties occupied by tenants and attracted by the provisions of the Rent Control Act, the question of considering the reversionary land-value does not crop up all the same. While valuing a rent-controlled property for which there will not be any reversion, the valuer should capitalize net income in perpetuity rather than capitalizing for the remaining future life. The concept of land value in reversion gets thwarted even further by the enactment of the Maharashtra Housing and Area Development Board Act (1976), by which the Board will acquire a building - by making a payment equal to 100 times the net monthly rent - after it attains its dilapidated condition.

The valuer is expected to forecast - not as a prophet but based on scientific grounds - as to what the owner will prospectively receive for the open plot in question after the expiry of the expected life of the building. Futuristic projection of the land value, as such, is quite a difficult proposition as professional valuers do not have crystal balls included in their office paraphernalia, and therefore, the present value of vacant comparable open plot per unit area is adopted as the land value for the purpose of reversion.

***

Chapter 5

Valuation of Agriculture Lands and Farms

Introduction

Land, as a whole, irrespective of the use to which it is put to is a precious gift of nature and, as such, can be used for diversified purposes encompassing agriculture, quarrying, transportation, accommodation, etc., or else it may lie as a wasteland for the time being till fortune smiles on it and, subsequently, put to one or the other uses. The land which is capable of being used to raise different crops like cereals, pulses, oilseeds, fruits, sugarcane, fodder for cattle, wheat, rice, etc., is known as "Agricultural Land." The category of land which is capable of being used for raising crops but being kept as fallow for the time being will also be recognized as "Agricultural Land" for its valuation.

Agriculture is the harmonious integration of landscape and people, providing food, shelter, clothing, and other material and non-material needs to men, including health, wealth, and prosperity, in a sustainable way.

As we all know, agriculture is the largest sector in the Indian Economy. Since India is in a transitional stage between old and new systems of agricultural development, both new and old concepts and a combination of old and new concepts are being used in our agricultural sector. The valuation of agricultural lands and farms is a complicated exercise. The diversity of crops raised, the changing cropping pattern, and the varieties of packages offered by the Government from time to time have brought in new vistas in agricultural valuation. There are too many value-laden parameters to be considered for agricultural land valuation, requiring intimate knowledge of agricultural sciences. A valuer must allow for differences such as quality of soil, type of farming, size, extent, quantity, and condition of farm building(s), location of farm house and other accommodation, etc., in his valuation.

Factors Affecting the Value of an Agricultural Land

The various commendatory factors which affect the value of an agricultural land, in one way or the other, can be enumerated as follows:

- Size (in acres) and shape of the land.

- Annual land revenue.

- Type of soil, fertility of land and overall economics of land produce for which the land is most suitable.

- Availability of electricity for running pumps/machines etc.

Is it freehold land or leasehold land? If it is a leasehold land, then:

A. what is the nature of the lease?

B. date of commencement and termination of the lease, and

C. terms of renewal of lease?

- Availability and efficiency of surface and/or subsurface irrigation facilities and the number of crop seasons utilized per year?

- Disposition of land with respect to NH/SH/MDR/ODR/VR,

- Whether the area is wholly or partly waterlogged? (Yes/No). If yes, what is the area of waterlogged patch(es) and the extent of waterlogging?

- Availability of laborers in the nearby vicinity for agricultural work and the economic conditions of neighborhood localities.

- Is the area flood-prone? (Yes/No).

If yes, then what is the frequency of land inundation?

- (Non)Existence of fence, farmhouse, grain storage, and/or livestock/machinery housing facility.

- Distance of nearest market from the field where the land produce can be sold and their available means of transportation to the market.

- Area deduction for the high-tension transmission tower(s), if applicable.

- Is prospective land conversion for orchard/vegetable garden/non-agricultural purposes possible?

- If the land is contemplated to be divided into small plots, it is necessary to find out whether such plots are proposed to be utilized for developing residential colonies or for commercial or industrial purposes, or for any possible combination of the above purposes.

- Does the land fall in an area included in any government development plan? (Yes/No).

- Is the land or its part thereof in adverse possession? (Yes/No).

- If the land is tenanted either wholly or partly, how much time is reasonably expected by the buyer to secure absolute possession after the registry process?

- Details of horticultural assets and natural plantations.

- Any other unique feature(s) of the land.

- Consideration of severance (if any).

Suppose the valuation is being carried out for acquisition (other than compulsory one) from the viewpoint of prospective purchasers. In that case, the following factors in conjunction with the above must also be given due emphasis:

- Is it a distressed sale? (Yes/No).

- Is there any sentimental reason behind the owner's decision to sell?

- Is there any case pending in the court? (Yes/No).

- Is there any other legal problem existing in the title deed? (Yes/No).

- Is there any easement right mentioned in the title deed? (Yes/No).

- Is there any encumbrance? (Yes/No).

- Is the land under joint ownership/co-ownership, what is the share of each owner? Are the shares undivided?

- Is there any minor's share involved in the property? (Yes/No). If yes, then how much?

- Is there any problem in transferring the conveyance of ownership? (Yes/No). If yes, then what are its details.

Although an attempt has been made herein to incorporate all the factors that could reasonably be conceived of in order to fix up the value of agricultural land, the effect of other factors such as the prevailing market trend, change in Govt. policy for a particular land produce, abnormal local circumstances, new agricultural innovations must also be approbated or reprobated by the valuer before arriving at his final opinion.

Methods of Valuation

Each method of agricultural land and farm valuation is based upon a proven element of practice. Valuers need to use their knowledge of the philosophy and professional practice of valuation to estimate the true value of agricultural land and farms.

There are three common approaches to the valuation of agricultural lands and farms, namely:

i.   Market approach,

ii. Cost approach,

iii. Income capitalization approach.

Cost Approach

The need for a "cost approach" to the valuation of agricultural lands arises when buildings and other improvements not directly connected with production/productivity become attractive to prospective purchasers. Examples are residential, storage, and processing/breeding sheds on the land. The nearness of the farm to residual/marketing localities may be yet another factor for the same.

Market Approach

The "market approach" to valuation refers to valuation by comparable sales of lands of the same productivity, amenities, etc. in the vicinity (situated in the same agro-climatic zone), by a well-informed and prudent seller, willing but under no compulsion whatsoever to sell the property to an unbiased buyer who is able, willing, and under no compulsion whatsoever to buy the property in question.

These types of sales transactions rarely occur in practice, at least under prevailing Indian circumstances where the agricultural lands are usually sold to meet extraordinary momentary requirements. In India, agriculture is a way of life, and the inherent ambition of every farmer or even landless laborer is to own land and not sell the land, in view of the innumerable assistance from the Govt. to increase production and productivity. Changes in ownership may occur between relatives, so they are not genuine enough to be used for comparison. Distress sale of land does not give the correct picture of its actual market value. Genuine sales may occur on holdings beyond 10 acres or so since family labor gets fully utilized in holdings below this area. But such transactions cannot not always be used by the valuers due to various other reasons.

The Income Capitalization Approach

While carrying out the valuation of agricultural lands, coffee estates, orange farms, plantations, etc., the income-capitalization method is almost invariably used by the professional valuers. The two main information required for valuation are the farm rent and annual net income of an average owner-operator.

To arrive at the capitalized value of the property, the data to be collected would be:

i. Net income arising from the property after deducting all the outgoings from the gross income.

ii. A justifiably selected highest prevailing interest rate for investment in such type of property by giving due consideration to the nature of the property, type of income, and all other allied factors.

The procedure for valuation by "Income Capitalization Approach" consists of:

i.   mapping of the soil,

ii. determining the crop pattern and estimating yields,

iii. calculating the total production of the holding and the share to the landlord (if the shares are divided),

iv. applying a price to this share,

v.   subtracting estimated landlord expenses to obtain the net income, and

vi. capitalize on this net income to obtain an income value for the farm.

These steps are more easily stated but difficult to accomplish in practice since too many parameters have to be considered and justifiable judgments are to be taken.

While computing after-tax agricultural income, the tax laws concerning agricultural and non-agricultural income have to be kept in view. After arriving at the net income of the farm holding, the value of the holding is determined after dividing the net income by an appropriate rate of capitalization. The rate of capitalization, as such, must be selected quite carefully from economic considerations that are applicable to the nature of farming (see Rate of capitalization).

Some of the observations given hereunder will be useful in valuing agricultural land(s):

i.   If the plot is required to be valued as agricultural land, it has to be valued along with the trees,

ii. Depreciation of agricultural implements can be calculated @ 10% annually for 10 years without reliable data.

iii. The sinking fund for the well is to be calculated at 3/4th of its value.

Rate of Capitalization

Capitalized costs/values have been widely used for many years, particularly by civil engineers/valuers. The widespread use of capitalized costs probably originated in Wellington's Classic work, "The Economic Theory of Railway Location (1887)." This - in a day in which most engineers worked for railways during at least some part of their professional careers - markedly influenced the thinking of the entire engineering profession. In Goldman's "Financial Engineering" (New York: John Wiley & Sons, Inc., 1921), the term "vestance" was coined for capitalized cost.

In Webster's Encyclopedic Unabridged Dictionary of English, "Capitalization" has been defined as an "Art of computing the present value of future periodical payments."

As such, capitalized value can be defined as the amount of money whose annual interest is at the highest prevailing rate of interest commensurate with the type of property under reference, which will be equal to net income arising from the property. In the jargon of economics, the capitalization factor may be referred to as the "discount rate" as it is nothing but the discounted cash flow of all the future EUAPs (Equivalent Uniform Annual Profits), which are not perpetual.

The capitalization factor is the rate of interest that a prudent investor may reasonably expect from any particular property type. Still, such a rate cannot be reduced to a rigid rule or formula. The capitalization rate represents the relationship between annual income and the value of an asset because the annual income from a secure and reliable long-term investment with an unfailing agency like the Govt. is said to be comparable to income from immovable property, which is also permanent in character as an asset. A simple example is a perpetual Govt. bond (one which runs indefinitely) bearing a 10 percent interest rate, paying Rs. 100/- annually on a Rs. 1,000/- bond. This bond will be priced in the market at Rs. 1000/-, as long as the going interest rate of investment is 10%. However, if this interest rate declines to 8%, the bond will sell not for Rs. 1000/- but Rs. 1,250/- (100 divided by 0.08). At this price of Rs. 1,250/- the return of Rs. 100/- will exactly be 8%. Similar is the behavior of stocks and shares and returns therefrom.

Present worth of an income in a future year is given by the formula:

$$\text{Present Value} = \frac{1}{(1 + \text{interest rate})^n} \times \text{Future Income} \quad (5.1)$$

Where,

n = the number of years between the present and when the future income is received.

It is appropriate to adopt a manifestative rate of interest commensurate with other investments of conjunctural nature which may be considered as the nearest substitute in the capital market as the rate of interest to be adopted for the capitalization of annuity is in direct proportion to the:

i.   Degree of Security of the investment,

ii. Ease of convertibility of invested capital,

iii. Nature of property,

iv. Regularity of return,

v.   The prevailing "going price of money" as represented by interest rates paid by large banks, and the government's short-and long-term notes and bonds,

vi. Speculations involved in procuring the income, and other allied factors.

However, there are significant differences between landed agricultural property and other forms of investments with the same capital outlay.

Selecting an appropriate capitalization rate (i.e., "multiplying factor" as is the term sometimes used) is easier said than done. There is an interesting citation in this context:

"Rate of Capitalization for purpose of estimating the value should not be unreal and must have regard to commercial rate of return, after taking into consideration the various constraints and insecurity of property market."

...C.I.T. Vs. V. Patel, 118 I.T.R. 134 Gujarat.

It was once felt that the relevant rate of interest that should be taken into consideration was the interest that gilt-edged securities or Government Bonds would normally fetch. The safety and liquidity of the investment in bonds were relied on as twin factors to take the view that the interest on gilt-edged securities should alone be considered. This was when there were few avenues of safe investment, and investment in private commercial concerns was unreliable. But from 1959-60, circumstances have gradually changed. There are many State and Nationalized Banks in which deposits are quite safe. Even in the share market, we have many "blue chips" that command stability and other attendant benefits, such as the possibility of issuing bonus shares themselves. They are attracting a lot of capital investment.

A 10% per annum return on such safe investments is almost assured. Today, nobody thinks of just 5% to 6% per annum. A higher order rate of 10% is usually anticipated (Union of India Vs. Shanti Devi A.I.R. 1983 S.C. 1190). However, an interest rate even higher than 10% may be adopted if deemed fit by the incumbent valuer. "Rate of capitalization at 12% adopted by the valuer as of the relevant period of 22.5.1973 upheld by the Hon. Tribunal." Says I.T.A.T. Bombay Bench 'A' in I.T. (acq.) Appeal No. 1 (Bombay) of 1974-75 (Sandoz Case).

Valuation of Farm Buildings

The valuation of farm buildings is complicated because farm buildings are rarely sold separately but are sold as a part of the whole farm. It is difficult to reach any clear-cut gross or net income separate from land income.

In horticultural plantations like tea, coffee, teak, cardamom, rubber, orange, etc., one usually finds:

i.   residential farmhouses,

ii. accommodations for processing/packing the produce, and/or

iii. storage/office accommodation, etc.

Valuation of farm buildings independently is necessary in many cases for the:

i.   insurance of fire,

ii. tax purposes,

iii. bookkeeping purposes,

iv. figure out depreciation on building and

v.   preparation of profit/loss statements (i.e., balance sheets) in agro-business.

The general modes of valuation available are:

i.   Land and building method,

ii.   Recent sale value in comparison with one under valuation,

iii. Income capitalization method,

iv.   Replacement cost minus depreciation, (see Chapter 3 for Replacement Cost),

v.   Building values based on whole farm value.

Valuation of Wood Lands

The woodlands comprise two forms of assets, i.e.

i.   the site, and

ii.   the trees growing upon it.

Both of them are separately valued. The value of woodland is based on what it might fetch if let or sold in its natural state.

Timber valuation is a specialized subject. The forest department gives the average cost of plantable land in its annual report and account. The timber and other trees are measured with timber tape, a pole graduate in meters (or some more portable instrument for estimating height), and a book of timber and a table. The volume of standing timber is calculated, and a price is applied per cubic meter depending on its species, age, quality, etc.

On the sale of an agricultural farm, the trees in the hedgerows, standing alone, or in dumps may be treated as separate items altogether. They must be separately measured and priced as they stand. Otherwise, their presence, and not their mere value as timber, is noted as an added amenity to enhance the overall value per hectare of the land in question.

Value of Teak Wood Plantations

Teak *(Tectona grandis)* is one of the most valuable of world timbers known from ancient times - the Sanskrit name is Saka. Teak has been widely used in India for more than 2000 years. The generic name *Tectona* is derived from Malayan word "tekku."

Teak is a large deciduous tree of the Verbena family (Verbenaceae) with a straight but often buttressed stem, a spreading crown, and four-sided branchlets with a large quadrangular pith.

The leaves are opposite or sometimes whorled in very young specimens 1 to 2 ft. long and 6-12" wide. In shape, they resemble tobacco plants, but their substance is hard and surface rough. Small white flowers, very numerous in large, erect, cross-banded panicles, terminate the branches. The fruit is a drupe, two-thirds an inch in diameter, and ripes in November-February. The bark of the stem is about 1/2" thick, gray or brownish gray, the Sapwood white, and the unreasoned heartwood has a pleasant and strongly aromatic fragrance and a beautiful golden yellow color, which on seasoning, soon darkens into brown, mottled with darker streaks. The timber retains its aromatic fragrance to a great age.

During the dry season, the tree is leafless; in hot localities, the leaves fall in January, but in most places, the tree remains green until March. At the end of the dry season, when the first Monsoon falls, the new foliage emerges.

Favorable Locations and Climatic Conditions

Teak thrives best in districts with a mean annual rainfall of more than 1,250 mm. and a mean annual temperature between 12-45 degrees centigrade. However, it grows fast in areas of 3,000 mm of rainfall.

The tree is not usually found in pure forest but mixed with bamboo, which it overtops and which seems necessary for its growth. The most valuable forests are on low hills up to 3,000 ft. Its natural northern limit of growth is about 25th parallel, although plantations have been established as far north as 32nd parallel in Punjab. In early 1960, Burma produced 75% of world teak supply. In India, natural teak forests are found in Maharashtra, Madhya Pradesh, Andhra Pradesh, Gujarat, Tamil-Nadu, Mysore, Kerala, Rajasthan and Manipur. Teak of coastal areas of Kerala and Konkan (MS) grows fast, and therefore, it is soft. The growth rate is slow in the teak grown in Vidarbha and Western Maharashtra; therefore, the wood is hard and dense, beautiful and costly.

Practically speaking, all Indian Teak is utilized within the country itself, and supply falls short of actual requirements. Teak has been cropped in Central America and elsewhere in the New World, but it has never been commercially successful.

Teak grows in a great variety of soils, but there is one indispensable condition: perfect drainage or dry sub-soil. Teak does not always form regularly shaped stems with deep alluvial soil on level ground, probably because the subsoil drainage is imperfect.

Growth Rate of Teak Tree

Although germination is slow in its youth, the tree grows rapidly. Two-year-old seedlings on good soil are 5-10 ft. high, and instances of even more rapid growth are not uncommon. Teak trees may reach a height of between 100 and 150 feet and a circumference of 20 to 25 feet; to attain the latter girth, a tree - grown under natural conditions - must have lived for a period of at least 100 years. In the artificial plantations, teak trees on good soil have obtained a height of 60 ft. in 15 years with a girth breast of 19". In these plantations, it is estimated that a tree, under favorable circumstances, will attain a diameter of 24" (girth of 6 ft.) at the age of 80 years. Normal exploitable girth limits are 7'6" for good and 6'6" for poor teak forests.

Value of Teak Timber

Teak tree furnishes the valuable lumber, yielding a hard, durable, resinous, yellowish-brown wood when first out, but when aged, darkens to the tint of black walnut. Teak wood is used for a large variety of purposes, including ship-building, furniture, doors/windows, wharves, bridges, cooling towers, louvers, flooring, Venetian blinds, etc. The principal value of teak timber in warm countries is its extraordinary durability. In India and Burma, beams of wood in good preservation are often found in several centuries-old buildings. In one of the oldest buildings in the ruins of Vijayanagar, on the banks of Tunghabhadra in Southern India, the superstructure is supported by planks of Teakwood 3/2" thick. These planks examined in 1889 had been in the building for 500 years and were still in a good state of preservation, showing thereby the most peculiar structure of teak in a very marked manner.

The teak is practically imperishable undercover. Another important property of teak, which promotes utilization, is its extremely good dimensional stability. It is of medium weight (45 lb/cubic feet), strong, easily workable, and of average hardness. Termites eat the sapwood but rarely attack the heartwood. However, it is not resistant to marine borers.

The market value of tree depends on the regular cylindrical shape of the log. This should be without knots or other irregularities. Great care is taken in plantations to rid the trees of creepers, which, by their clinging habit, distort the trunks.

Plantation of Saplings

As the seed cover is very hard, the seed has a long life, and it does not germinate easily. The seeds are soaked in water and dried repetitively to become soft for germination. The seeds are ready for germination and sowing in about a month.

The seeds should be sowed in May in a 40'00" x 4'00" x 1'00" deep pit in which the soil is mixed thoroughly with cow dung manure. The seeds should be sown about 2" away from each other. The small plants should be fed with urea and single super phosphate (about 300-400 gms). There is no need for irrigation if there is regular rainfall. The saplings should be watered well and fertilizers used till it grows about 6" long.

Preparation of Stumps

One-year-old sapling, which is 1/2" wide, is ideal for plantation. The ideal time for plantation is the third week of June after some rainfall. If the stumps are planted at 2m x 2m distance, the number of stumps which can be planted in a hectare is 2,500 whereas if they are planted at 1.25 m x 2.5 m about 3,200 stumps can be accommodated in a hectare.

Unfair Practices in Commercial Plantations

The perfect investment market is an economist's dream and plantations are complex affairs and of great variety. Furthermore, the possibility of exploitation gets accentuated by the fact that investors often have imperfect knowledge. Several plantation schemes promise fabulous scale of yield to their investors, "Yes sir, grow money on trees. With a small initial investment, earn lakhs of rupees after 20 years while sitting at home," or in the words to this effect.

Sometimes, these promises, assurances, and guarantees may cause illusion, loss, or injury to the investors due to the deliberate concealment of certain inconvenient terms from advertisements/information brochures/ application forms. As there is no law authorizing any Government agency or apex body to scrutinize and monitor such schemes that are being launched, it is all the more necessary for the investors to ensure that they are not exploited.

Under Section 36-A of the MRTP Act, "Unfair Trade Practices" have been defined very elaborately. Section 36-B Provides for an inquiry into unfair trade practices by the MRTP Commission, whose powers, as per section 36D of the Act, are much the same as in the case of restrictive trade practices inquiry, namely, the passing of a cease-and-desist order.

In the case of "Gold Valley Development Pvt. Ltd. (IA No. 45 of 1987 in UTPE No. 158 of 1987 dt. 20.5-1987), the respondent did not disclose in the publicity material certain material terms such as:

- The land was to be arranged for allotment by the cooperative society, whereas the respondent company was responsible only for carrying out the plantation of trees.

- There would be an arrangement between the respondent and the allottee according to which the allottee would work on the plot with the company's help under its guidance.

- The respondent would not be responsible if the land was acquired.

The commission held that there were material terms and their nondisclosure in the advertisement or brochure misrepresented the scheme's benefits. The respondent was directed not to issue such misleading advertisements in the future.

Similar is the case of Professional Farms Pvt. Ltd. (UTPE No. 195 of 1987; LA No. 55 of 1987 dt. 9.6.1987) in which the company withheld certain inconvenient material terms such as:

- In the event of land acquisition by the government, the allottee will accept the compensation awarded by the government.

- the allottee had satisfied himself about the interest and title of the land and understood all the limitations and obligations. In the event of any dispute, the decision of the chairman or any chairman nominee shall be binding, etc.

The Commission passed an inertia injunction because the nondisclosure of such material information was misleading.

The brochure issued by A.N. Land and Finance Co. promised a yield of Rs. 3,05,000/- after seven years on an initial investment of Rs. 26,930/- made on Eucalyptus trees. The Commission passed a temporary injunction [UTPE No. 114 of 1987 dt. 2.3.1987] on the ground that such a fabulous yield scale shocked one's comprehension and perceptions of realities, and those figures were not supported by any feasible study. The claim that income was tax-free and the investors were secured was false. Therefore, the respondent clearly indulged in the unfair trade practice of making false and misleading promises that were prejudicial to the public interest.

Out of the various plantation schemes announced, several are insured against loss due to fire, flood, lightning, inundation, cyclone, and riots to provide the investor additional security. However, the insured amount is based on the input costs only, which does not go a long way in instilling confidence among prospective investors contemplating investing in schemes that appreciate in value from day one. Moreover, no risk coverage is possible for a change in forest, land, and environmental laws/acts, which is quite likely, considering the span of the maturity period of the scheme.

The need of the hour is the formation of a government or government-aided Apex body to Monitor and regulate the various Agro-based schemes/issues that promise fabulous amounts of returns so as to safeguard the interests of innocent investors.

Valuation of An Orange Farm: A Case Study

Sweet orange is an edible large globose citrus fruit with a bright reddish-yellow tough ring within which are juicy segments. Fragrant white-blossomed, moderately vigorous rutaceous orange tree (Citrus sinensis) having hard yellow wood, ovate unifoliolate leaves, and round, densely foliated top requires plane topography and hot climate. Sweet orange fruit is consumed fresh or as frozen or canned juice. After the juice is extracted, the peel and pulp are used for cattle feed, and citrus molasses is used for livestock feed.

"Nagpuri Santara" is a famous name in this context, and it is mainly cultivated in North-Eastern Vidharbha (Southern Part of Central Plateau), where more than 60% of farmers grow oranges.

The orange soils in India belong to the black cotton soil and loose soil group. As such, the soil should be deep, well-drained, slightly acidic in reactions, rich in organic matter content, and should be located at elevations ranging from 250 m to 350 m from MSL with an annual rainfall of 150 mm to 250 mm and range of temperature 37°C to 45°C. The number of orange trees usually grown per acre area ranges from 120 to 130.

Better production of oranges is controlled more by climatic and environmental factors like rainfall, temperature, and elevation of the place than by soil factors. Soil moisture is a major factor limiting the production thereof. For irrigation, the basin or flooding method is usually adopted.

Due to plane terrains, mechanization of operation in growing oranges is easy. Orange farms are not a highly labor-intensive industry, as labor cost comprises only about 30% of the total cultivation charges.

Approach to Valuation of Orange Farms

Two methods of valuation may be adopted, namely;

Comparative Sales Method

This method is based on the comparative sales instances of similarly placed farms nearby. The valuation based on the income capitalization approach is not well suited for very small housing with a meager income since even a 12% increase in income per acre would alter the land value by 12 to 15%.

Income Capitalization Method

The comparative method may be feasible for small-sized estates and, hence, not worth expediting.

The income capitalization method, as has been explained earlier, consists of arriving at the gross income from the estate, including intercrop and computing the expenses on all accounts and determining "Net Income" therefrom. The net income is multiplied by a suitable capitalization factor to determine the value of the orange farm in question.

Gross Income

Gross income is worked out by the market value of the orange. The average number of such transactions is four years, which covers the fluctuations in market price. In addition, the gross income from intercrops, such as gram, vegetables, etc., is also worked out at prevailing rates in their respective harvest periods as ascertained by the marketing committees or cooperative societies.

Computation of Outgoings

This is the most difficult task for the incumbent valuer, and the relevant information can be gathered from the farm(s) records and discussions with the staff. Another task on the part of the valuer is to determine the "Amortized Establishment Cost" during the initial "non-yielding" (or gestation period) of the initial 4 to 5 years of the plantation. The various groups of activities on which expenses are assessed are given below:

Cost of Production of Orange/Acre

The cost of production of Orange represents all the outgoing growing, processing, storing, and marketing of the land produce, including maintenance and managerial expenses. Cost of production consists of:

i. The amortized establishment charge is the amount incurred on developing land, including the soil conservation measures adopted, water management measures, and raising to the initial non-yielding period of orange trees distributed over twenty years of the economic life span of the plants.

ii. Cultivation cost consisting of cultivation and crop charges: The cultivation charges consist of:

   (a) terking,

(b) digging trenching,

(c) weeding,

(d) pruning,

(e) desuckering,

(f) shade regulation,

(g) gap filling,

(h) manuring,

irrigation

(j) plant protection,

(k) repair of fence, road etc.

The crop charges consist of;

Cost of harvesting,

a. Preparing the produce for the market, such as plucking, measuring, packing and transportation,

b. Watch and Ward.

iii. Expenses for maintenance of farm building(s), road(s), machinery/ equipment, and vehicle(s).

iv. Salaries of staff and labour welfare expenses.

v. nterest charge on capital invested in working capital/land value/ amortized establishment charges for the nonyielding period.

vi. Depreciation of fixed/movable assets.

vii. Office, managerial, and misc. expenses covering postage, stationary, land tax, panchayat tax, etc. The net income per acre multiplied by the capitalization factor gives the value of the land/acre. The value per acre multiplied by the number of acres held will give the market value of the whole estate.

The capitalization factor can appropriately be taken as 10 for the orange farm in question.

Valuation of an Orange Farm at Malegaon (Maharashtra)

(A) General Details

Name of owner(s)	: Ajay Patel
Area of farm	: 25 acres
Total No. of trees	: 3,125 Nos.
No. of trees/acre	: 125 Nos
No. of harvests in a year	: 2 times (at an interval of 6 months)
Average Yield/tree/harvest	: 2,000 oranges
Average price of a pair of orange	: Rs. 0.50/- (last 3 years)
Income of selling woods, etc.	: Rs 20.00/Tree

(B) Establishment cost per acre in five years till steady yield is obtained

(i) Expenditure like Rs. 12.00/- tree digging, basin making, etc. Cost of manure (i.e., for 125 trees) : Rs. 1,500.00/-

(ii) Cost of fertilizer (costing Rs.2/kg) : 1 kg/tree/harvest

: Rs. 500.00/-

(iii) Irrigation charges : Rs. 700.00/- month in 25 acres.

: Rs. 2.70 /tree/year.

(iv) Irrigation charges for five years/acre till a steady yield is obtained : Rs. 1,687.50/- per acre

(v) Orange seed charges : Rs. 0.50/- per tree

(vi) Labour charges for : Rs. 62.50/- per acre

(a) Digging, manure, irrigation

etc. @ Rs 25. per Man day for   : Rs. 3,250.00/- per acre

for 650 man days

(b) Yearly maintenance

(like plant protection, watchman, etc.)   : Rs. 84,000.00/-

(vii) Fencing material (L.S.)   : Rs. 3,000.00/-

(viii) Cost of fertilizer per acre for 5 years   : Rs. (500 x 5)/-

                                        : Rs. 2,500.00/- per acre.

(ix) Inter-crop (gram)

Seed charges @ 10 kg/acre of   : Rs. 80.00/- per acre

rate Rs. 8.00/kg/Yrs   : Rs. 400.00/- per acre

(x) Fertiliser cost 25 kg/   : Rs 2.00/kg

acre @Rs. 250.00/acre

(xi) Charges of cultivation   : Rs. 700.00/- per acre

(like sowing, ploughing main-

tenance, medicine, cutting, etc.)

for five years   : Rs. 3,500.00/- per acre

Cost in five years   : Rs. 97,430/- per acre

Net income from gram for five   : Rs. 3000.00/- per acre

years   : Rs. 15,000.00/- per acre

Net Cost of the establishment (This Rs. 82,430.00/- per acre is to be divided over 20 years or economical life)

Amortize establishment charges in   : Rs. 4,121,50,00/- per
                                          acre

one year

(C) Cost of Cultivation when Steady Yield is Obtained

Irrigation charges	: Rs. 700.00/month in 25 acres
	: Rs. 336.00/acre/year
Cost of fertilizer	: 1 kg/tree/harvest @ Rs 2.00 kg
	: Rs. 500.00/acre/year
Maintenance charges four man working/day @ Rs. 00.25/day	: Rs. 36,500.00/25 acres : Rs. 1,460.00/acre/year
Charges of bamboos for supporting the trees	: Rs. 800.00/acre/year
Watchman charges (two) @Rs. 1,000.00/month	: Rs. 960.00/acre/year
Depreciation of pumps, tool and plants (L.S.)	: Rs. 1,500.00/year/acre
Total Cost of Cultivation	: Rs. 9,677.50/acre/year

(D) Gross Income per Acre

No. of trees	: 125 Nos/acre
No. of oranges/tree/harvest	: 2,000 Nos (Average)
Total No. of oranges/tree/yr.	: 4,000 Nos
Total oranges in 1 acre/yr.	: 5,00,000 Nos
Wholesale rate of orange	: Rs. 250.00/- per thousand
Loss of oranges due to theft and petrification	: 15%
Net Oranges	: 4,25,000 Nos/acre/year
Total gross return	:Rs 1,06,250.00/-

(E) Rate of Transportation

Transportation charges of one box	: Rs 30.00/-
(including the cost of box).	
No. of oranges in one box	: 150 Nos
Total No. of boxes	: 2,834
Charges of transportation	: Rs 85,020,00/-

(F) Valuation of Orange Farm of 25 Acres Growing Orange with Gram Intercrop

(i) Gross Income/acre/year	: Rs 1,06,250/-
(ii) Outgoing/acre/year	: Rs 94,697.50/-
Net income	: Rs 11,552.50/-
(iv) Capitalization factor	: 10
(v) Market value of one acre	: Rs 1,15,525.00/-
(vi) Market value of 25 acres	:Rs 28,66,125.00/-

On the basis of the above case study, it can be said that the valuation of an orange farm requires in-depth knowledge of the relevant horticultural activities involved in addition to the principles of valuation. The productivity and quality of the oranges grown in Vidharbha are the best in India, and hence, the land values are also significantly higher in this region. The value of land obtained by the capitalization method has been compared with the value obtainable from the comparative sales method in the locality. Both of them were found to be tallying.

New Vistas in Agricultural Valuation

Each and every business, including that of agriculture as well, requires an investment of capital. Hence, the widely used appropriate capital investment techniques in evaluation could be adopted for the valuation of agricultural lands and farms. These are:

i. Payback method,

ii. Internal rate of return method,

iii.   Average rate of return method,

iv.   Net terminal surplus method,

v.   Excess present value method,

vi.   Cost-volume-price method (or sensitivity analysis).

Conclusions

The challenges thrown up in agricultural valuation are many due to the variety of crops grown in the vast sub-tropic sub-continent, which can yield innumerable products. The parameters to be considered in agricultural valuation are too many, depending upon the agro-climatic conditions, type of farming, types of power used (bullocks, tractors etc.) crops, cropping, pattern, and fertility management. But, despite the diversity of production/productivity, an array of valuation techniques can be used or developed so as to meet the challenge in valuation in agriculture.

Since a variety of assets are to be evaluated in agriculture other than agricultural land, such as farm buildings, machinery/tools, livestock, and standing crops purchased for supplies and processing of farm produce, different valuations methods are to be adopted as applicable to the class of items. The present-day requirements of the agricultural land valuation procedure demand that valuation done by a competent valuer should be colonnaded by cardinal reasons as he is not expected to act like a prophet prophesying the value not substantiated by quantifiable corroborative facts thereof. Moreover, these facts should be weighed and not counted. No valuation report is consummated by merely expressing an opinion not backed by critical analysis of parsimonious facts until the unique fertility features and land potentialities are visualized from a panoramic perspective.

***

Chapter 6

Valuation of Land by Belting Method

What is Belting?

The word 'belting' in this chapter signifies stripping or zoning a very large area of land for the purpose of its valuation. Belting is done not just for the convenience of its valuation but, in fact, for the simulation of the actual situation thereon so far as its development potential across the entire depth is concerned.

Value distribution in a large tract of land is not uniform throughout the depth, barring only a few exceptions. Consider the following two pieces of land shown in Figures 6.1 and 6.2. Both of them have the same area. Will the market value of both the lands be the same as well? Any professional valuer worth his salt would take only a moment to answer this question in negative.

The land shown in Figure 6.2 is more valuable than that shown in Fig 6.1 as more road frontage is available to it. It can be explained rather more convincingly on the fundamental that front land is more valuable than the back land, and one has to find out the demarcating lines that separate land strips of different values. The concept of belting originates there.

In the U.S.A., this method probably originated from Judge Murry Holfman, who worded this theory in 1886 in the classical "Hoffman Rule." As per this method, the front half (say 15m) of a 30m deep plot is worth 2/3rd of its total value. The remaining rear half of the same plot would be worth only a l/3rd of its total value.

In the year 1973, a very interesting decision was given in Calcutta in the context of belting:

"The method of belts can be resorted only in cases where extensive land having a road only on one side is to be valued. It will not be suitable in cases where the plot acquired has frontage on both sides."

... State Vs. Phanindra Kumar, AIR, 1973, Cal 441.

Also, in another case, it was observed that:

"The value fetched for a small plot of land cannot be applied to lands covering a very large extent."

... 1958 Ker 166 (167) [AIR V 45 C 64]

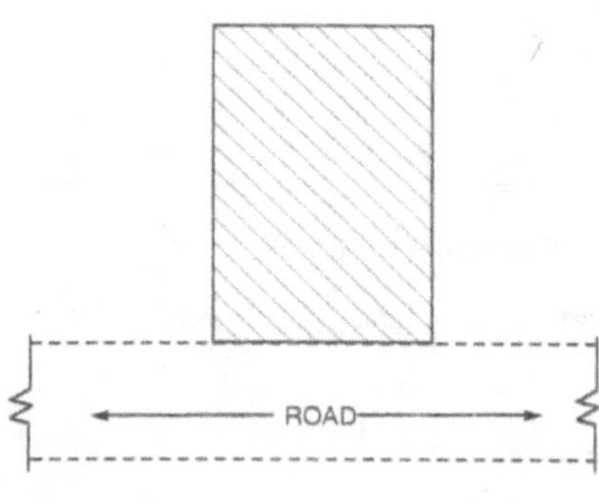

Fig. 6.1

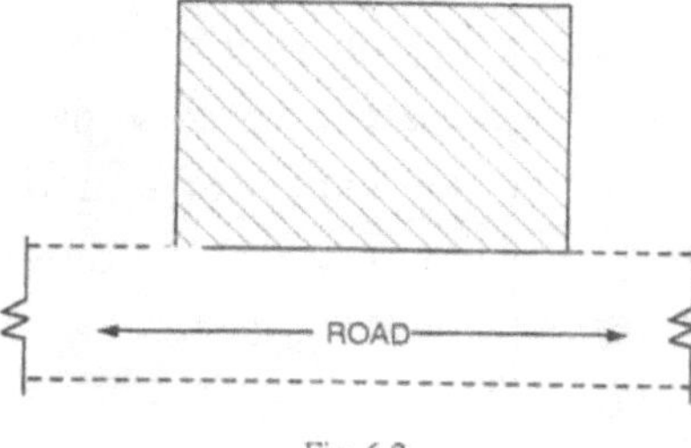

Fig. 6.2

(DB) * 1959 Andh-Pra 52 (57) (AIR V 46 C 21) (DB). (AIR 1923 Mad 332 and AIR 1927) Mad 867, Rel. on) * 1959 Mad 462 (463, 464) [AIR V 46 C 148] (DB) * 1923 Mad 332 (334) [AIR V10] (DB).

Now, it becomes abundantly clear that this land valuation system has specifically been developed to take care of this non-uniform value distribution across the depth of a large land in question. However, in actual practice, it is "easier said than done."

The conceptual methodology behind the method travels from part to whole. "Belting" is to divide a very large area of land into appropriate segments or -what is usually called in the professional field as - strips, and then valuing each strip separately by adopting varying rates for each such artificially segmented piece of the land. Now, values of all the strips are aggregated to arrive at the 'market value' of the whole given area as on the material valuation date.

Need of Belting

A building plot of land of smaller size cannot be compared with a large tract or block of land for the following reasons:

i. Smaller plots are within the reach of many, but a large block of land will have to be developed by preparing a layout plan, carving out roads, leaving open spaces, plotting out smaller plots, advertising, and waiting for purchasers (meanwhile the invested capital will remain blocked) and all the other conceivable hazards of an entrepreneur.

ii. It is undisputedly a matter of common knowledge that small plots command higher market value per unit area than bigger ones. Normally, the reason given for the increased rate of value and prices is that the number of prospective buyers for smaller plots is more than the larger ones. An average common man with limited financial resources cannot afford to purchase a large tract of land, thus limiting the class of purchasers only to those having enough capital to invest speculatively with an expectation to gain. Besides, the yield potential of smaller plots is usually higher in urban areas.

iii. Normally, the local area bylaws prescribe somewhat greater coverage in smaller plots than larger ones. But, in some cases, the belting method may not be feasible, particularly in the fully developed urban plots for commercial use.

iv. Large tracts of land require large and multifarious technicalities, including adherence to the prescribed norms of the planning process on the land and acceptance from various competent authorities.

v. Considerable expenses in developing a large plot, which in the case of smaller plots may not be required or entail only limited expenses like filling the land or cutting up to the requisite formation level.

The classical concept of the Belting Method judiciously covers irregularities in the shape of plots of land. An important point to remember is that making hard and fast rules regarding reducing rates of irregular plots is impossible.

Land value may not be affected considerably if it is slightly irregular in shape. Off-shaped land on the outskirts of a town can be converted into gardens or parks, etc., by judicious employment in residential areas but, on the other hand, is of utmost importance in commercial ones. However, land near or adjoining main roads may prospectively be used for other important business purposes.

The Zoning Concept

The belting method of valuation, as such, makes use of the "zoning concept" to assess the rateable value of hereditaments. This was specifically conceptualized so that the shop assessments should be uniform and comparable; hence, large shops could be assessed based on rentals of small shops. As is obvious, this was not to be applied where comparable rental evidence of large shops was available.

Deriving Values of Larger Plots by Comparative Method from Smaller Ones

It is now well settled that prices fetched for small plots cannot form the basis for large tracts of land as the two are not comparable properties. As such, the size and shape of a plot have a very important bearing on the value. It is, however, surprising that the land rates fixed by the Collectors of their respective districts or different local authorities from time to time in their jurisdiction have no mention regarding the size of the plot to which the said rates pertain to. The valuation cells have adopted the maximum size of such plots as 1,000 sq. meters, and therefore, they consider 60% of the rates for plots above 1,000 sq. meters in size. But, as it seems, there is no hard and fast rule for it, and the valuer's opinion is sometimes not accepted by the taxation authorities despite the justifications given by the valuers.

In the case Rathnanasari v. Secretary of State, A.I.R. 1923, Mad. 332, the ruling was given as hereunder:

"We do not think that the acquisition of such as small plot of land, for which only a small sum of money was paid, can be made the basis of valuation for a larger plot, like the one now in question before us."

"It is impossible to say that such an acquisition stands on the same footing as the present acquisition. Nor can we properly deduce the market value of the land from such an acquisition. For, when very small plots are acquired, they are not very often properly scrutinized, the whole cost of acquisition being small."

But the cardinal question before the valuer is how to determine the value of a large plot of land if the corroborative transactions - that are available near about the same material time and place - are of all small plots only.

The Supreme Court critically examined the question of determination of the market value of a large extent of land with reference to prices fixed for small plots in Administration General of West Bengal Vs. Collector Varanasi, AIR 1988 SC 943 (1988 LAOO 162 SC). In the AIR pages 947-948, Mr. Justice Venkatachalliah of the Bench observed:

"It is the trite proposition that price fetched for small plots cannot form the safe basis for large tracts of land as the two are not comparable properties."

Supreme Court - in the case of Kaushalaya Devi Vs. Land Acquisition Officer, Aurangabad (page 898, AIR 1984 SC 892) - observed that:

"Where large tracts are acquired, the transaction in respect of small properties does not offer a proper guideline. Therefore, transactions

regarding smaller property are not taken as a real basis for determining compensation for large tracts of property. A reduction of 25% was indicated, while there are certain cases where the view is that the reduction should be to the extent of l/3rd."

Does Belting Have Judicial Recognition?

The Hon'ble Courts have expressed different opinions on this system of valuation based upon the prevailing circumstances of the case and evidence on record, and a better line of action will not be to resort to this modality due to the element of arbitrariness influencing the result one way or the other.

In the case of Nityagopal Sen Poddar and others v. The Secretary of State, (1933) A.I.R. Cal. 25, the following observations of the Court are worth pondering:

"Now, as far as the system of belting is concerned, it is a system that is widely used, but its value as a system depends much upon a variety of facts. If data are available showing the proportion at which the value of land diminished, as it is situated at a particular distance from a main road or thoroughfare, the system would be perfectly scientific. In the absence of such data, it may be assumed that in big cities where land is sold by yards or feet there is such a proportion as common experience shows. For instance, in land acquisition or improvement schemes in and near Calcutta, land is generally divided into blocks facing some particular street or road or lane, and each block is divided into three belts, the first to a depth of 60 feet or so on the road frontage, the second to a depth of about 150 feet thereafter and the third consisting of all land behind, and the relative values of the three belts are fixed in the proportion of 100, 66.6 and 50 respectively. But in places and localities where lands are sold by bighas or acres, there is no real evidence of such proportionate diminution in value. The system is based on no sound principle and must be regarded as a method that is not quite satisfactory. Of course, there is almost always a distinction in value between front-land and back-land everywhere. Still, that distinction would not justify recourse to the belting system in every case. It is a highly artificial system and cannot be resorted to as a hard and fast rule." (see Secretary of State Vs. India General Navigation and Railway Co. Ltd. (1909) 36 Cal.

967-36 I.A. 200 (P.C.); Raghunath Das Vs. Collector of Dacca, (1910) 11 C.L.J. 612. The collector Vs. Ramachandra Harishchandra A.I.R. 1926 Bom. 44).

Nor, again, can there be any hard and fast rule that back land must always be of less value than front land or that the proportion should be one to a half or that there must be a certain proportion at a certain distance from the road; see Collector of Poona v. Kashinath Khasgiwall (1886) 10 Bom. 585.

In the case of Mohini Mohan Saha v. State of Bengal, 85 C.L.J. 379, it was observed by Hon'ble Justice R.P. Mukherjee that:

"The unit value of the first belt of the land in question should, therefore, be made dependent on the first belt being the depth similar to those contiguous plots on the valuation of which market value is to be ascertained. When determining the value of a portion of the land having road frontage, the depth must primarily depend on the nature of the plots, the locality where they are situated, and the character of the land. If the area is a commercial one where buildings erected on the roadside fetch a higher rent from shops, let out on the road, such depths as can be utilized for the erection of utilization shops will be regarded as the reasonable depth of the first belt. The character of the business and the nature of shops in a particular area may differ from those of another area. In the Burrabaiar area in Calcutta, the depth of the first belt may differ from that in the Bentick Street area. For residential areas also, the depth of the first belt allowed in Calcutta varies from place to place. It is well known that the building sites in the purely residential areas in North Calcutta differ from those in Ballygunj in the South and both differ from the Chowringhee area. In places which may be deemed to be a factory area, the question of the application of the belting method or of the depth of the first belt may sometimes become either unimportant or even immaterial."

Further, he says that:

"No general or uniform rule can be laid down for all cases where the belting method is applied as to what the depth of the first belt should be. The question has to be decided with reference to the particular area and the nature of the evidence, as may be available in a particular case."

The value of land, in general, depends upon many factors, such as situation, size, shape, frontage and depth, return frontages, width of roadways, vistas, nature of soil, state of development, etc. For a valuer entrusted with the task of assigning 'market value' of land on the crucial date determination has to be made standing on the date line of valuation as if the valuer is a hypothetical purchaser willing to purchase land from the open market and is prepared to pay a reasonable price as on that day. It is also to be assumed that the vendor is willing to sell the land at a reasonable price. In doing so by the instance of sale method, he has to correlate the market value reflected in the most comparable instance, which provides the index of market value.

In Belting method of valuation of land, various considerations are to be kept in mind in deciding whether there should be more than one belt and so, how many, and in determining the comparative valuation of one belt in relation to another. Connected with it is the question as to the depth of the second and third belts, if any, in relation to the first belt. There is no hard and fast rule about it. However, there should not be a wild guess as well.

Method of Valuation

The 'Market Value' of a large plot of land must be determined on the dateline of valuation as if the valuer is a hypothetical purchaser willing to purchase the land from the open market and is prepared to pay a reasonable price as on that date. It is also to be assumed that the vendor is willing to sell at a reasonable price. In doing so, if he adopts the comparable sale instance method, he has to correlate the market value reflected in the most comparable instance, providing the true market value index. There are very positive and negative factors that have to be ascertained, scrutinized, and deduced.

Very often, several comparable sale instances of small plots are available, and very few (or sometimes none) are found for large ones. While using the comparative valuation method in such cases, out of all the comparable instances available, only genuine instances have to be identified on the considerations of time and situation. The market value of the land under appraisal has to be deduced by taking the price reflected in the instance taken as the norm for plus factors and unloading it for minus factors. Plus factors would be,

i.   smallness of size,

ii.   proximity to a road,

iii. frontage on a road,

iv.   nearness to an already developed area,

v.   regularity of the shape,

vi.   level vis-a-vis land under appraisal,

vii. special value for an owner of an adjoining property to whom it may have some special advantage, etc.

Minus factors worth consideration would be:

i.   comparative largeness of area,

ii.   situation in the interior at a distance from the road,

iii. narrow strip of land with very small frontage compared to depth,

iv.   lower level requiring the depressed portion to be filled up,

v.   remoteness from the developed locality,

vi.   some special disadvantageous factors that would deter a purchaser, etc.

The evaluation of these factors would depend on the facts of each case. Common sense is the best guide and is reliable as well.

For example,

"In the case of a large block of agricultural land far in the interior amid blocks of undeveloped land, a deduction of 25% on the ground of largeness of block is justified. Depression of valuation on the premise that development would reach after twelve years- not open to challenge; but further depression not warranted."

... Chimanlal Vs. Spl. L.A.O., Poona A.I.R. 1988 S.C. 1652.

Indeed, the only way in which the market value can be arrived at is to judge from other sales what the whole land would have been likely to realize in the market as favored by Courts also. Still, in the cases of large blocks of land, this system may not be the sound one being highly artificial system. It is well known that large blocks are often sold on an acre basis and not piecemeal unless it is intended to be developed and sold in smaller units.

There is an interesting observation from the Supreme Court is in the case of Mathura Prasad Rajgharia vs. state of West Bengal (AIR 1971 SC 465):

"Where a large area of land in an urban locality is 'sought to be acquired in determining the market value, the 'method of belting' is appropriate. It is common knowledge that lands having frontage on the main roads in urban areas are always more attractive than the lands that have no such frontage. No objection was raised before us against the adoption of the 'method of belting.' It was also accepted that the land under acquisition, the front belt would be 100 feet deep, the second belt would be 150 feet deep and the rest may be included in the third belt. No objection was raised against the opinion of the Tribunal that the price of the second belt should be taken at 75% per cottah of the value of the land per cottah in the first belt, and the price per cottah of the third belt should be taken at 50% of the value of the land per cottah in the first belt."

A plot of land accessible by and abutting a passage from a public street cannot be valued by adopting the belting method from that public street. If it has no frontage on that public street, but only on a passage therefrom, it cannot be said it is in a certain belt on that street.

In a comparative study of land rates for smaller and more significant sized plots (residential), Er. R. Gopal krishnan (Superintending Engineer, Valuation Cell of C.B.D.T.) - as published in Valuation Bulletin (August 1979) - came to the following findings:

While deriving land rates from smaller plots to larger plots based on coverage, the actual auctioned rates were about 5% to 15% lower than the derived rates. This indicates that apart from the adjustment due to coverage, a reduction of about 10% would be needed to arrive at a reasonable market rate for larger plots.

It is also seen that the difference between the derived and the actual rates is higher when the larger plots are two or three stages higher than the smaller plots in the coverage slab, that is to say, if a 66% coverage plot is compared with a 40% coverage plot, the difference between the land rate derived and the actual rate is higher than the land rates from the adjacent coverage plot, that is to say, when 50% coverage plot is compared with 40% coverage plot. Therefore, this also indicates that as far as possible, when it becomes necessary to derive land rates from smaller plots, it would be reasonable to work out the land rates from the next lower or higher coverage slab plots, i.e. to say a 66% coverage slab plots may be compared more reasonably with a 60% coverage slab and so on.

The problem of soaring values of urban property leasing to speculation and hoarding of valuable urban land as a result of rapid urbanization and growth of population in the process led to the 'socialization of urban land' by enacting the Urban Land (Ceiling & Regulation) Act, 1976. No prudent man can now think of purchasing large pieces of land, indeed, transfers of surplus land by act of parties are banned. Every property must be appraised in terms of the 'market' in which it is competitive. Like property should be compared with like one. Since large tracts of urban lands are under threat of being 'taken over' by the government at only the specified nominal rates of acquisition as per the Act, the valuation to be made for determining the compensation payable by the government cannot be identical with the valuation to be made to fetch 'open market' price to the seller. (The Urban Land-Ceiling & Regulation-Act, 1976 has put a ceiling limit of land holding-vacant land situated in an Urban agglomeration).

Land falling within the ambit of U.L.C.R. Act, 1976 should be belted out from the total large plot of land and valued at the rate prescribed in the Act and manner therein.

In the case State of West Bengal Vs. Bibhuti Bhushan Chatterjee and others, A.I.R. 1259 Calcutta 572, the Calcutta High Court ruled:

"We think that for largeness of size, deduction of 10% would be appropriate."

Corner plots fetch higher rates, and hence, the value of such land may be increased by 10% of the rate as an additional amount.

But there are certain interesting exceptions to the rule, and an interesting case is that of a press notification of U.P. Avas Evam Vikas

Parishad for Raibareli Housing Scheme, residential plots measuring up to 400 sq.m. are priced at Rs. 560/-per sq.m. and for land plots larger than 400 sq.m. are to be at 25% higher rate than up to 400 sq.m. rates. This is perhaps because there is more demand for such land, which is scarce in the town. These plots are of fully developed zones.

Guidelines for Valuation

The Supreme Court laid down two important principles in the case of U.P. Government Vs. H.S. Gupta AIR 1857 S.C. 202 in the matter of valuation of a large block of land divided into plots for sale in pursuance of a development scheme:

i.   Where a large block of land was divided into plots for sale in pursuance of a development scheme before the publication of notification for acquisition and the scheme is found to be feasible and workable, the valuation should be plot-wise and not block-wise, and

ii. If there is reliable evidence that there were willing, if not anxious, purchasers for the plots, no deduction should be made for the size. The Chief Justice Macleod of the Supreme Court quoted the following observations (page 949, AIR 1988 SC 943):

"A very simple method of valuing land wholesale from retail prices is to take anything between one and a half to one third, according to circumstances of the expected gross valuation, as the wholesale price."

As a very general rule, land - having a depth not greater than 4.75 times its breadth - can be divided into three belts with values and depths as hereunder:

First Belt = Unit area rate up to the Standard Depth (SD).

Second Belt = 2/3rd of Unit Area Rate for 1.5 SD.

Third Belt = 1/2 of Unit Area Rate up to 2.25 SD.

This method of belts cannot and should not be resorted to where it is feasible to subdivide the land legally into saleable units of small plots or where instances of sales of comparable lands are available. The method of hypothetical layout can justifiably be adopted if it can convincingly be shown that the land question is ripe to be used for building purposes and the smaller building plots, if laid out on that land, would have a good selling proposition and that the valuation based on the method of hypothetical layout could justifiably be adopted. The valuation of comparable small plots nearby would be relevant in valuing such laid-out sites. In urban areas where there is a demand not only for front land but also for back land, which could be laid out in small units of plots with all infrastructure, a development method or plotting scheme is preferred as the same will give more realistic results.

However, it must be noted that where the floor space index controls the development, the depth problem will have little influence on the overall value. Moreover, to value such a plot by adopting the method of belting in preference to the plotting method may lead to an incorrect decision.

Conclusions

Valuation, as has been said and established repeatedly, is not a tailor-made process. Each land has to be treated as a special and specific case and valued appropriately to arrive at an appropriate market value. It is an opinion of a valuation expert and it has to be justifiable as such. Valuation of large-sized land is quite an open problem as no hard and fast rule has been prescribed for a method to be adopted for valuing such lands. In the case of large plots, the belting method has to be adopted carefully, and diversified varieties must be considered. While adopting the belting valuation method, the appraisal should be done judiciously. One may have to even include the value of 'potentiality' on such materials as made available during investigations in the valuation process. One should not merely indulge in making prophecies without having sound backing of the relevant facts. Each case is to be critically appraised based on its individual merit and disposition. Return from investment is the underlying principle in real estate valuation, and this aspect must be considered when valuing land.

Evaluation of each case has to be made in its entire perspective. For example, in Calcutta, one also has to look for rental yield on situation factor: suitable adjustments have to be made if the land is situated on the main road in the price of land, which may be to the extent of:

South-facing plots - rental yield is 20% more.

North-facing plot - rental yield is 20% more.

If the increase in the rental potentiality is only 10%, the value of the north-facing plots has to be discounted by 10% compared to the south-facing plot. It is so because, in Calcutta, the prevailing winds during the hot season are from the south and southeast, and there is very keen demand for south-facing plots. In India, where the temperature rises to high levels during the summer season, there is a great demand for houses that face the prevailing breezes.

The valuer has to look into all the relevant court decisions and take his own decision for considering the valuation of plots of large/small size according to the peculiar circumstances at the site. While adopting the belting method of valuation of a very large size plot for house building activities in such cases, this aspect, besides other vital aspects of the land, will also need consideration.

***

Chapter 7

Valuation For Compulsory Land Acquisition

General Information

Compulsory land acquisition had its prominent role in the pre-independent era, but the conceptual necessity of land acquisition has assumed even greater importance since then. The power of compulsory land acquisition is the sovereign power of the country's government to acquire to achieve the envisaged objectives of Articles 39(b) & 39(c) of the Indian Constitution. For the advancement of any country as a whole, it is natural for the government to have sufficient land at its own disposal where public utility services and public projects like atomic reactors, thermal power plants, oil refineries, mega-dams, etc., are constructed. It is all the more necessary that the land required for the said purpose be had at a very reasonable price to tax the public finance as low as possible.

Under such circumstances, every government expects its subjects to consider their interest in such lands subordinate to the interest of their country as a whole. However, human weakness generally overshadows such national feelings. The individual will only come forward to sell his land to the government provided he gets a fancy price for the same instead of its fair market value to compensate for his involuntary deprivation of the property and the so-called sacrifice he is making for the nation's sake. As often as not, it is also likely that he may not be willing to part with the property at any cost due to the sentimental value attached thereto, which will obstruct the welfare of the citizens of the country as a whole.

Hence, to regularize the procedure, the first land acquisition law appeared in the form of the Land Clause Act of 1845. In the United States of America, the state exercises the sovereign right of compulsory purchase under the powers granted by the classical law of Eminent Domain. On the same principle of Eminent Domain, several other European countries, such as Germany, Italy, France, etc., have framed their systems to serve as guidelines for compulsory acquisition procedures.

Emergence of Land Acquisition Act in India

In India, the first general Land Acquisition Act was passed in 1857, which provided compensation settlement to the person concerned by arbitration. The word "acquisition" was used to signify the overall transfer of the entire bundle of rights vested in the original holder to the acquirer, leaving nothing to the former. Also, the courts have interpreted the word "compensation" as "just equivalent" or "fair recompense," whose terminal point is the market value of the property in question.

The Act of 1870 provided for the abolition of the system under which uncontrolled discretion was entrusted to Arbitrators, and, in lieu thereof, required the Collector, when unable to come to terms with the persons interested in the land which it was desired to take up, to refer the difference for the decision of a Civil Court. In practice, the Act of 1870 was found entirely effective for the protection of either the persons interested or the public purse. The requirement that the Collector shall refer for the decision of the Court every petty difference of opinion as to value, and every case in which any one of perhaps a large number of persons fail to attend before him, has involved in litigation, with all its trouble and delay and expense, a great number of persons whose interest in the land was extremely insignificant.

It has, in fact, frequently been the case that the owners of small pieces of land have had to pay the Court cost to an amount far exceeding the value of the land itself. With the passage of time, several controversies arose - as much as the fixation of compensation is concerned, and so many difficulties are experienced in its implementation.

So as to overcome these difficulties, the Act was amended once again in the year 1894 (Act 1 of 1894) which gives no option to individual if his land is required for a public purpose and thus sale is obligatory on his part. It also makes the Collector's award final, unless altered by a decree in a regular suit. Persons interested in the land will thus still have the opportunity, if they so desire, of preferring an authority quite independent of the Collector to stack their claims of more substantial compensation than the Collector has awarded, and will in all cases have a further right of appeal to the regular appellate court. It is quite interesting here to observe a few rulings that provoke the person interested to file a regular suit in a court of law. These are:

"Court cannot reduce the compensation awarded by the Collector, even if there is an error in calculation."

... 1923 Madras 31 (32) [AIR V 10] (DB).

"Court may decrease market value and award additional compensation for severance provided a total award of the court is not less than Collector's award."

... 1926 Bom 372 (372) [AIR V 13] (DB).

They will no longer, however, be encouraged to litigate by the feeling that they can hardly lose, but may make a great gain by doing so as per the following ruling:

Collector's award will not be easily interfered with unless on a matter of principle."

... ('09) 33 Bom 325 (332).

Apart from the L.A. Act (1894), there are several other acts that have been passed by the state and central governments empowering the various authorities to actually acquire land by observing certain stipulated procedures.

Requisition & Acquisition of Immovable Property Act (Act No. XXX of 1952) received the assent of the President of India on 15th March 1952. It was published in the Extra-Ordinary Gazette of India Part II Section I, Page 133, dated 15.3.1952. This Act extends to the whole of India except the state of Jammu & Kashmir.

The Land Acquisition Act, 1894

The Land Acquisition Act, as such, is a Pre-Constitutional Act. It contains 55 sections, and almost every state has modified either one section or the other to suit its specific requirements. Soon after the year 1950, its provisions were challenged on so many occasions based on the Constitutional fact that the right to hold property is the fundamental right, and as such, the acquisition of land compulsorily by the government is a violation of the fundamental right to hold property by the Bonafide citizens. Supreme Court became an arena of legal warfare until 1978. All these controversies were subsequently subsided by the 44th Amendment of the Constitution, whereby Articles 19(l)(f) and 31 have been repealed and rewritten as:

"Wo *person shall be deprived of his property save by authority of law."*

... Article 300 A of the Indian Constitution

With this Amendment of 1978, the right to property is no longer a fundamental right but only a legal one. By such an Amendment, the government is now empowered to acquire property in the public interest, satisfying Articles 39(b) & (c) of the Sacred Constitution. Provisions of L.A. Act cannot be challenged. Such a challenge would fly in the face of Article 300 A. A few amendments in the L.A. Act have also been made in 1984.

The land can be acquired under two parts, namely part II & part VII of the Act.

Basic Principles of the LA. Act

The following are the basic principles of the Act:

i. The sale by the owner is obligatory on his part, and in this respect, no option whatsoever is given to the owner. No improvement, as such, can be carried out in the property after the date of notification under Section 4 without the permission of the Collector.

ii. Acquisition of land is unambiguously required for a public purpose.

Several prominent rulings have defined the word "Public Purpose," as appeared herein, from time to time such as:

The expression "Public Purpose" is not quite capable of precise and comprehensive definition which may be of universal application. The concept of public purpose is not static. It changes in accordance with the requirements of society from time to time and in accordance with the condition in the country. Broadly speaking, its object is to promote public health and general welfare. 1959 Punj 5238 (542) [AIR V 46 C 167]: ILR (1958) Punj 1451. (Acquisition for establishing an Institute of Technology to give technical education held for a public purpose).

Right to Fair Compensation and Transparency in Land Acquisition, Rehabilitation and Resettlement Act, 2013 (LARR Act)

The Right to Fair Compensation and Transparency in Land Acquisition, Rehabilitation and Resettlement Act, 2013 (also Land Acquisition Act, 2013 or LARR Act or RFCTLARR Act is an Act of the Indian Parliament that regulates the land acquisition and lays down the procedure and rules for granting compensation, rehabilitation and resettlement to the affected persons in India. The Act has provisions to provide fair compensation to those whose land is taken away, brings transparency to the acquisition process of land to set up factories or buildings and infrastructural projects, and assures rehabilitation of those affected. The Act replaced the Land Acquisition Act of 1894, enacted during British rule.

Section 26. Determination of market value of land by Collector

(1) The Collector shall adopt the following criteria in assessing and determining the market value of the land, namely:

(a) the market value, if any, specified in the Indian Stamp Act, 1899 (2 of 1899) for the registration of sale deeds or agreements to sell, as the case may be, in the area, where the land is situated; or

(b) the average sale price for a similar type of land situated in the nearest village or nearest vicinity area, or

(c) consented amount of compensation as agreed upon under sub-section (2) of section 2 in case of the acquisition of lands for private companies or for public-private partnership projects, whichever is higher:

Provided that the date for determination of market value shall be the date on which the notification has been issued under section 11.

Explanation 1: The average sale price referred to in clause *(b)* shall be determined taking into account the sale deeds or the agreements to sell registered for a similar type of area in the near village or near vicinity area during the immediately preceding three years of the year in which such acquisition of land is proposed to be made.

Explanation 2: For determining the average sale price referred to *m Explanation I,* one-half of the total number of sale deeds or the agreements to sell in which the highest sale price has been mentioned shall be taken into account.

Explanation 3: While determining the market value under this section and the average sale price referred to in *Explanation 1* or *2*, any price paid as compensation for land acquired under the provisions of this Act on an earlier occasion in the district shall not be considered.

Explanation 4: While determining the market value under this section and the average sale price referred to in *Explanation 1* or *Explanation 2,* any price paid, which in the opinion of the Collector is not indicative of actual prevailing market value, may be discounted to calculate market value.

(2) The market value calculated as per sub-section (1) shall be multiplied by a factor to be specified in the First Schedule.

(3) Where the market value under sub-section (1) or sub-section (2) cannot be determined for the reason that:

(a) the land is situated in such area where the transactions in the land are restricted by or under any other law for the time being in force in that area, or

(b) the registered sale deeds or agreements to sell for similar land are not available for the immediately preceding three years, or,

(c) the market value has not been specified under the Indian Stamp Act, 1899 (2 of 1899) by the appropriate authority, the State Government concerned shall specify the floor price or minimum price per unit area of the said land based on the price calculated in the manner specified in sub-section (1) in respect of similar types of land situated in the immediate adjoining areas:

Provided that in a case where the Requiring Body offers its shares to the owners of the lands (whose lands have been acquired) as a part compensation, for the acquisition of land, such shares in no case shall exceed twenty-five percent, of the value so calculated under sub-section (1) or sub-section (2) or sub-section (3) as the case may be:

Provided further that the Requiring Body shall in no case compel any owner of the land (whose land has been acquired) to take its shares, the value of which is deductible in the value of the land calculated under sub-section (1):

Provided also that the Collector shall, before initiation of any land acquisition proceedings in any area, take all necessary steps to revise and update the market value of the land based on the prevalent market rate in that area:

Provided also that the appropriate Government shall ensure that the market value determined for acquiring any land or property of an educational institution established and administered by a religious or linguistic minority shall be such as would not restrict or abrogate the right to establish and administer educational institutions of their choice.

This clause seeks to provide criteria for assessing and determining the market value of the land by Collector.

Section 27. Determination of Amount of Compensation

The Collector, having determined the market value of the land to be acquired, shall calculate the total compensation to be paid to the land owner (whose land has been acquired) by including all assets attached to the land. This clause seeks to determine the amount of compensation by the Collector after determining the market value of the land to be acquired.

Section 28. Parameters to be Considered by Collector in the Determination of Award

In determining the amount of compensation to be awarded for land acquired under this Act, the Collector shall take into consideration:

firstly, the market value as determined under section 26, and the award amount in accordance with the First and Second Schedules;

secondly, the damage sustained by the person interested, because of the crops and trees which may be on the land at the time of possession thereof;

thirdly, the damage (if any) sustained by the person interested, at the time of the Collector's taking possession of the land, because of severing such land from his other land;

fourthly, the damage (if any) sustained by the person interested, at the time of the Collector's taking possession of the land, because of the acquisition injuriously affecting his other property, movable or immovable, in any other manner, or his earnings;

fifthly, in consequence of the acquisition of the land by the Collector, the person interested is compelled to change his residence or place of business, the reasonable expenses (if any) incidental to such change;

sixthly, the damage (if any) *bona fide* resulting from diminution of the profits of the land between the time of the publication of the declaration under section 19 and the time of the Collector's taking possession of the land; and *seventhly,* any other ground which may be in the interest of equity, justice and beneficial to the affected families.

Section 29. Determination of Value of Things Attached to Land or Buildings

(1) The Collector, in determining the market value of the building and other immovable property or assets attached to the land or building which are to be acquired, uses the services of a competent engineer or any other specialist in the relevant field, as he may consider necessary.

(2) The Collector, for the purpose of determining the value of trees and plants attached to the land acquired, uses the services of experienced persons in the field of agriculture, forestry, horticulture, sericulture, or any other field, as may be considered necessary by him.

(3) The Collector, for the purpose of assessing the value of the standing crops damaged during the land acquisition process, may use the services of experienced persons in the field of agriculture as he may consider necessary. This clause seeks to determine the value of things attached to land or buildings.

Section 30. Award of Solatium

(1) The Collector, having determined the total compensation to be paid, shall impose a "Solatium" amount equivalent to one hundred percent of the compensation amount to arrive at the final award.

Explanation: For the removal of doubts, it is hereby declared that the solatium amount shall be in addition to the compensation payable to any person whose land has been acquired.

(2) The Collector shall issue individual awards detailing the particulars of compensation payable and the details of payment of the compensation as specified in the First Schedule.

(3) In addition to the market value of the land provided under section 26, the Collector shall, in every case, award an amount calculated at the rate of twelve per cent, per annum on such market value for the period commencing on and from the date of the publication of the notification of the Social Impact Assessment study under sub-section (2) of section 4, in respect of such land, till the date of the award of the Collector or the

date of taking possession of the land, whichever is earlier. This clause seeks to provide award of solatium by the Collector after having determined the total compensation to be paid to arrive at the final award.

Eco System of Land Acquisition

Role of a Valuer in Land Acquisition Cases

A professional valuer, while determining the fair market value of properties either acquired or to be acquired under the Act, should thoroughly consider the following stages:

i.   The survey sheet mentioning dimensions.

ii. Structural details, number, and names of tenants (if any), and the prevailing land use.

iii. The date of notification in the official gazette as per Section (4) of the Act, the date of order of acquisition, and the award issued by the competent authority. In case the date of acquisition is lapsed, whether fresh notification is issued or not.

iv. Any additions and alterations done after the date of notification should be disregarded. However, any improvements made with the prior permission of the competent authority after the notification shall be considered.

v. Rent of five years received or receivable as prevailing rent in the vicinity should be taken into account. In the case of unoccupied areas or areas free of rent given to nearest relatives, it should be considered on the basis of prevailing rents in the vicinity.

vi. An average or gross rents thus obtained from records for five years should be considered and I/5th (i.e.) of such gross rent should be deducted for the purpose of municipal taxes, insurance, collection charges, and repairs and maintenance, expenses are not known. However, if proper accounts are maintained then actual expenses should only be considered to arrive at actual net rent.

vii. In case of any fruit/timber tree(s), if at all standing on the land, a fair assessment thereof depending upon its life, yield, and future life shall be added to the value of the property.

viii. Note down the actual land use and adopt an appropriate capitalization rate to capitalize the value.

ix. In the case of rental valuation, the reversionary value of land is to be disregarded. However, in the land and building method, the land values should also be added to the appropriately depreciated values of structure(s). The purpose of valuation also plays an important role. If a valuer is asked to advise on the fair and reasonable market value of the properties to be acquired then his course of action should be as laid down above. However, suppose the property is already in process or acquired. In that case, the value should be determined from the award of compensation (received or receivable) after deducting the interest payable for the period from the date of notification and the date of payment of compensation. Obviously, solatium on the market value as on the day of notification should also be added as per Section 23(2) of the LARR Act. The awards issued normally take into account the various incidental expenses such as court fees, documentation charges etc. These charges should be deducted from the award. In the absence of such account, a reasonable amount between 15% to 20% may be deducted from the awarded compensation.

It is generally observed that the valuation for taxation differs from the valuation for acquisition purposes. The tax laws are constantly amended, and various directives and sometimes steps and methods are issued (like in rule 1BB in the Income Tax Act). Such amendments have been made to simplify the procedures and avoid probable litigation and loss of time. Therefore, several aspects could be ignored. A valuer should make a judicious decision in adopting the course of valuation by narrating them very clearly while working out valuation for taxation purposes. Suppose he observes a difference (not more than 15%) between the two values adopted by different methods. In that case, the average value should be certified as fair and reasonable.

It is important to note here that a person aggrieved may ask for a high valuation for compensation purposes for land acquisition. He may need such valuation reports to be recorded in court proceedings. At the same time, the same person may ask the valuer to produce a report indicating far less value, taking advantage of the subjudice matter for taxation purposes. The judiciary stands above all, and therefore, the valuer should be careful in finding out the market value since he may be blamed for unethical professional practice.

The courts (if observations are recorded) may initiate lawful proceedings against the valuer. A valuer, as such, should not solely depend upon the data produced by the land owner (i.e., the person interested) but should take all precautions and efforts to collect and verify the requisite data. Obtaining such clarification from an advocate is wise if any legal matter warrants clarification.

The Land Compensation Acts of India and UK: A Comparative Study

There are key differences between the land compensation acts of India and the UK, which govern government acquisition of private land for public purposes and the compensation process for landowners. The comparison is particularly relevant since, until 2013, India followed the Land Acquisition Act of 1894, a relic from British colonial rule.

The most important difference that drew my attention is mentioned in Part 1 of Land Compensation Act 1973 (LCA 1973), which says: "Responsible authorities may be liable to pay compensation for depreciation in the value of an interest in land which is attributable to the use of public works where the 'relevant date' is on or after 17 October 1969, and where no land has been taken from the claimant." No such clause is present in the Indian Act; compensation is given only to those whose land is acquired. Here are some other comparisons of the two:

1. Legal Framework

India: The primary legislation is the Right to Fair Compensation and Transparency in Land Acquisition, Rehabilitation and Resettlement Act, 2013 (LARR Act). It replaced the Land Acquisition Act of 1894 and aims to provide fair compensation and transparent processes for land acquisition. The Act also mandates rehabilitation and resettlement for affected families.

UK: The Land Compensation Act of 1973, along with the Compulsory Purchase Act of 1965 and the Planning and Compulsory Purchase Act of 2004, primarily govern land acquisition and compensation. The framework focuses on compensation based on the market value of the land and aims to ensure fairness in compulsory purchase.

2. Compensation Calculation

India: Compensation under the LARR Act is determined based on the market value of the land, multiplied by a factor as explained in Section 30 of the Act. Along with solatium, there is a provision for additional compensation for livelihood loss, resettlement, and rehabilitation.

UK: Compensation is based on the "open market value" of the land, which is what a willing buyer would pay to a willing seller. In addition to market value, the landowner may receive compensation for any loss or disturbance caused by the acquisition, such as the cost of relocation or loss of business profits.

3. Public Purpose and Justification

India: The LARR Act requires that land acquisition be justified as serving a "public purpose," such as infrastructure projects, development, or government programs. It mandates a Social Impact Assessment (SIA) for certain acquisitions to evaluate the impact on affected families.

UK: The concept of "public purpose" is broader and includes infrastructure development, urban regeneration, and environmental projects. The acquiring authority must demonstrate that the acquisition is in the public interest, and alternatives must be considered to minimize displacement.

4. Process and Transparency

India: The LARR Act emphasizes a transparent process, including public consultations, hearings, and the requirement of consent from affected families in some cases (70-80% consent, depending on the type of project). The Act mandates a preliminary notification, publication of the intent to acquire, and opportunities for objections.

UK: The process involves serving a notice to the landowner and the right to object and appeal the decision. There is less emphasis on public consent but a strong focus on judicial oversight. The law requires the acquiring authority to justify the necessity of the acquisition in a public inquiry if there are objections.

5. Rehabilitation and Resettlement

India: The LARR Act includes provisions for mandatory rehabilitation and resettlement of affected families, including providing alternative land, employment, or financial assistance.

UK: There is no statutory obligation for rehabilitation and resettlement, but compensation for loss or disturbance may cover some of these costs. The focus is mainly on financial compensation rather than social support.

6. Right to Appeal

India: Affected parties have the right to appeal to the Land Acquisition, Rehabilitation, and Resettlement Authority, a quasi-judicial body created to address grievances.

UK: Landowners can challenge the acquisition through public inquiries or judicial reviews, ensuring a legal recourse for contesting the acquisition.

Summary: The key differences lie in the approach to compensation (fixed multipliers in India vs. open market value in the UK), the requirement for public consent and social assessments in India, and the UK's emphasis on judicial oversight and financial compensation rather than resettlement.

Conclusions

The professional real estate valuer is sometimes called upon by his clients - affected by the acquisition process - to prepare a report for the property's market value as of the date of notification. It is in this context that a valuer is supposed to have comprehensive knowledge of the contents and provisions of the LARR Act, which will not only guide but will also assist him a great deal while preparing his report, of the property to be compulsorily acquired by the law, in a convincing manner containing documentary evidences and corroborative references of appropriate court judgments.

*** *** ***

Chapter 8

Valuation for Mortgage of Properties

Introduction

An etymological study of the word "mortgage" reveals that it is a combination of two words (i.e., "Mort" & "Gage"). The former was derived in old French from classical Latin and means "dead," and the latter means "pledge" in Middle English, and this form derives itself from old French. As such, the literal meaning of mortgage is "dead pledge". Simply put, a mortgage can be defined as advancing money against any form of security like cattle, gold, property, etc. As per AIR 1955 Bom 419 (425):

"If it appears from the deed that it was the intention of the parties to create the security on the land, it is sufficient to create a mortgage."

A "Security," generally speaking, is anything that makes the money more assured in its payment or more readily recoverable, as distinguished from, e.g., a mere I.O.U., which is only evidence of a debt. Therefore, the assurance in its payment or ready recoverability constitutes a particular thing as a security for debt.

A mortgage is a transfer of an interest in immovable property. Such interest is capable of transfer by way of assignment, mortgage, etc., and is heritable. As immovable properties are the best form of security, the number of real estate valuations carried out for mortgages far exceeds that of valuations for other purposes. Several financial institutions, like Banks, Public and Private Limited Companies, Life Insurance Corporations, etc., advance loans to individuals and organizations after obtaining mortgages in real estate and, hence, are the major employers of valuers for this purpose. Real estate developers, brokers, and Semi-Public Institutions also often need this service.

Valuation for a mortgage requires fundamental knowledge of the various types of mortgages, their implications and effects on market values, legal ramifications, redemption, etc. This chapter deals briefly with the various aspects of this subject. Sections 58 to 104 of the Transfer of Property Act (1882) deal with this subject.

What is a Mortgage?

The author does not need to phrase his own definition to define mortgage. As per Section 58 of the Transfer of Property Act, a mortgage is:

"The transfer of an interest in specific immovable property to secure the payment of money advanced or to be advanced by way of loan, an existing or future debt or the performance of an engagement which may give rise to a pecuniary liability."

Also,

"The transferor is called the mortgagor, the transferee a mortgagee; the principal money and interest of which payment is secured for the time being are called the mortgage money, and the instrument (if any) by which the transfer is effected is called a mortgage deed."

The mortgage deed contains the covenants for the repayment of principal debt and stipulated interest to be paid by the mortgagee by the mortgagor.

It is to be interestingly noted that a mortgage:

"may be executed for the interest alone on a loan without the principal itself being secured."

...AIR 1940 Pat 512 (DB).

From the definition of the mortgage itself, it appears that there is a debt or some pecuniary liability, the payment of which is secured by this transaction. The test for seeing whether a transaction is a mortgage or not:

"... is to see whether the property comprised in it is made security for a loan or debt or the performance of an agreement.

... AIR 1915 Mad 382 (383) (DB)

Pledge And Hypothecation

The mortgage of movable property is to be distinguished from the pledge. In the former case, ownership of goods passes. In the latter case, the pledgee gets possession but no right to goods beyond what is necessary to secure debts.

In a hypothecation, the possession of the property is retained by the owner. Only certain rights in that movable property are transferred to the person in whose favor the property is hypothecated. Where the goods themselves are handed over to the bank in whose favor a document is executed by way of security, the goods in respect of which the document is executed become pledged within the definition of "pledge" as per Section 172 of the Contract Act.

As per AIR 1939 Lah 15 (16) (DB):

"While there can be a hypothecation of movables without delivery of possession, there can be no pledge of movable property without an actual delivery of movables." Also;

"The hypothecation of property to secure a future liability to pay the mortgage money in case the mortgagee should be deprived of the mortgaged property is a mortgage to secure a contingent liability."

... AIR 1925 Pat 288 (290) (DB).

Kinds of Mortgages

Following are the types of mortgages as per the Transfer of Property Act. However, it has also been held that:

"it is possible to create a mortgage apart from what is provided for in the Act."

... AIR 1955 Trav-Co 130 (132) (DB).

Simple Mortgage

As per Section 58 of the Act:

"Where, without delivering possession of the mortgaged property, the mortgagor binds himself personally to pay the mortgage-money, and agrees, expressly or impliedly, that in the event of his failing to pay according to his contract, the mortgagee shall have a right to cause the mortgaged property to be sold and proceeds of sale to be applied, so far as may be necessary, in payment of the mortgage-money the transaction is called a simple mortgage and the mortgagee a simple mortgagee."

Characteristics of a Simple Mortgage

The basic characteristics of the simple mortgage are:

i.   There must be a loan,

ii. There is a personal liability to pay.

As per AIR 1961 Punj 477 (480):

"The definition of simple mortgage does not by itself exclude personal liability of the debtor and, indeed, the very act of taking a loan or incurring a debt would... imply a liability to pay and unless this liability in some permissible manner excludes the personal liability the debtor or the obligee can scarcely be heard to say that he is not personally liable."

Also,

"A personal covenant to repay the mortgage money must be presumed to exist unless there is something in the nature of the mortgage to negative it."

... AIR 1959 Madh Pra 178 (179, 181).

iii. Possession of the mortgaged property is not delivered to the mortgagee. The mortgagor himself retains possession and agrees that in default of his non-payment of the loan, the mortgagee shall have the right to sell the property. However, "The mere fact that possession was given to the mortgagee over the mortgaged property will not necessarily show that the mortgage was a usufructuary one."...AIR 1944 All 198 (199) = ILR (1944) All 588 ** ILR (1953) Patiala 570 (576, 577) (DB).

iv.   There is no foreclosure clause.

v.   The mortgagee cannot sell the mortgaged property privately to recover the principal loan or interest. Such a sale can take place only through Court. The words "cause the mortgaged property to be sold" imply that the property has to be sold only through the intervention of the Court. This right of the mortgagee is inherent in the simple mortgage itself, so this power of sale needs not be expressed. However, it should be exercised only through the Court.

Mortgage by Conditional Sale

As per Section 58(c) of the T.P. Act, the characteristics of a "mortgage by conditional sale" are the following:

i.   The mortgagor ostensibly sells the mortgaged property. The transaction has the appearance of a sale, but is really not a sale,

ii.   The condition is that the sale shall be absolute in default of payment on a particular date or the sale shall be void on such payment and the property re-transferred.

iii. The remedy of the mortgagee is by foreclosure and not by sale,

iv.   It must be created by one document and not by two documents, i.e., one for sale and the other for repurchase, (proviso to Section 58(c))

v.   It must be by a registered instrument if the consideration is above Rs. 100/- and if it is below Rs. 100/- either by delivery or registered instrument (Section 59).

Remedy for the Mortgage

It is foreclosure under Section 67 of the T.P. Act. When repayment is not made within the stipulated time, the contract exhausts itself, closing the transaction. It becomes an absolute sale to be enforced by foreclosure. From that it follows that the creditor can look to the land pledged to him for the satisfaction of his debt. As the decree for foreclosure is the only remedy to which the creditor is entitled, he takes the land in satisfaction, and if it is worth more or less than what is due, the benefit or the burden of it is that of the mortgagee, who sues for foreclosure. But until a final decree for foreclosure is passed, the mortgagor can redeem.

Usufructuary Mortgage

As per Section 58(d) of the Act:

"When the mortgagor delivers possession (or expressly or by implication binds himself to deliver possession) of the mortgaged property to the mortgagee, and authorizes him to retain such possession until payment of the mortgage money, and to receive the rents and profits accruing from the property (or any part of such rents and profits and to appropriate the same) in lieu of interest, or in payment of the mortgage-money, or partly in lieu of interest, or partly in payment or mortgage-money, the transaction is called ~r> usufructuary mortgage."

Here, "delivers" does not necessarily mean delivering immediately. Where the mortgagor cannot give immediate possession, it is sufficient if he gives the right to possession.

The words "or expressly or by implication binds himself to deliver possession" were inserted in the Section by the amending Act of 1929 to negative the view that the mortgage was not a usufructuary one in the absence of actual delivery of possession.

When we carefully analyze the clause dealing with this kind of mortgage, we find that the essential feature of a pure usufructuary mortgage is that:

i. There is a delivery of possession of the hypotheca to the mortgagee. However,

"A usufructuary mortgagee empowered to take possession and appropriate the rents and profits in lieu of his debt is not bound to take possession. He has merely a power to do so, and if he chooses to forgo the benefit, it would have no effect as between him and the mortgagor to recover his debt."

... (1909) 32 Mad 281 (283) (DB).

ii. The mortgagee cannot sue for the payment of his debt, but is only entitled to remain in possession of the mortgaged property till the principal and interest are defrayed according to the terms of the agreement. It should be understood that the mortgagor, in some cases, may: *"instead of giving actual possession, direct the tenants of the mortgaged property to pay rent to the mortgagee."*

... AIR 1943 Sind 59 (61) = ILR (1942) Kar 452 (DB) ** AIR 1915 Mad 382 (383) (DB) ** Pun, L R 566 (567).

iii. There is redemption when the amount due is personally paid or discharged by rents and profits received. There being no personal liability to repay, there is no forfeiture, and hence, no remedy is open to the mortgagee by way of sale or foreclosure.

iv. If the consideration is Rs. 100/- or above, it must be registered; if it is below Rs. 100/- either by a registered deed or by delivery of property.

As an usufructuary, the mortgagee has the right to the exclusive possession of the property he can exclude even the mortgagor; if he does not get possession, his remedies are:

(a) to sue for possession, or

(b) for damages for the breach of the contract to give possession, or

(c) for damages for the money lent under Section 68.

Difference Between Usufructuary and Simple Mortgage

The main difference between a usufructuary mortgage and an ordinary mortgage is that in the former, it is part of the initial agreement by which the security is created that the mortgagee shall at once go into possession of the mortgaged property and apply the proceeds he may derive from the use and occupation of it to discharge the mortgaged debt. In contrast, in the case of an ordinary mortgage of the usual sort, it is, in general, not the initial intention of the parties that the mortgagee should go into possession of the property pledged immediately or at all. However, he is empowered to do so if the interest on the mortgage money is not paid.

However, it is to be noted on the other hand that the mere possession of the property does not make the mortgage a usufructuary one unless it is shown that the income of the land was to be appropriated towards payment of interest or partly towards payment of the principal and partly towards interest.

English Mortgage

As per Section 58(e) of the Act, such mortgage is said to take place where:

"The mortgagor binds himself to repay the mortgage money on a certain date and transfers the mortgaged property absolutely to the mortgagee, but subject to the proviso that he will retransfer it to the mortgagor upon payment of the mortgage money as agreed."

An analysis of this clause shows that the mortgage called English mortgage has the following characteristics:

i.   It is accompanied by delivery of possession,

ii. There is a personal covenant to pay the amount,

iii. It is affected by absolute transfer of property with a provision for re-transfer in case of repayment of the amount,

iv. The remedy is by way of sale (Section 69 of T.P. Act) and not by foreclosure,

v.   The power of sale out of court (viz. private sale) is conferred on certain persons under certain circumstances. Three essentials of an English mortgage are as follows:

i.   The mortgagor should bind himself to repay the mortgage money on a certain day (personal liability) as,

"In an English mortgage, the debtor remains personally liable to pay the debt."

... (1906) 4 Cal L Jour 510 (513) (DB).

ii. The property mortgaged should be transferred "absolutely" to the mortgagee (absolute transfer).

iii. The "absolute" transfer should be made subject to a proviso that the mortgagee will reconvey the property to the mortgagor upon repayment of the mortgage money on the date on which the mortgagor bounds himself to repay the same (Proviso for reconveyance).

All the three following essentials should invariably be present to constitute an English mortgage because:

"Where on the construction of the document it is found that one or other of the essentials of an English mortgage is absent, the mortgage is not an English mortgage."

... AIR 1935 Cal 659 (662, 663) (DB).

Equitable Mortgage or Mortgage by Deposit of Title Deeds

As per Section 50(f) of the Act, an equitable mortgage is as much a legal mortgage as any other mortgage having received statutory recognition under clause (f). Its characteristics are:

i. It is created in the towns of Madras, Bombay, and Calcutta and in those notified by the State Government from time to time.

ii. It is affected by the deposit of documents retaining the title. There is no delivery of possession of the property.

iii. The deposit is by way of security for existing or future debt,

iv. No registration is necessary (Section 59 of T.P. Act),

v. Remedy is by sale and not foreclosure.

vi. All the provisions that apply to a simple mortgage will apply to an equitable mortgage.

If an equitable mortgage is executed outside those towns specified, it is invalid and gives no right to the mortgagee to proceed against the properties comprised in the mortgage. However, the property mortgaged may be situated outside those towns.

It is essential that there is a delivery of title documents and that such delivery be made to the creditor, intending to create security thereon. The deposit of the title deeds should be in one of the commercial towns specified. What is deposited must be the title deeds and are material evidence of title. So it follows patta of lands and share certificates are title deeds, but a map of the property or tax receipts are not documents of title.

It must also be noted that if the parties intended the bargain to be reduced to writing and the consideration is Rs. 100/- and upwards, then there must be registration, not if the document is merely evidential of the deposit of title deeds.

Anomalous Mortgage

As per Section 58(g) of the Act:

"A mortgage which is not a simple mortgage, a mortgage by conditional sale, a usufructuary mortgage, an English mortgage or a mortgage by the deposition of title deeds within the meaning of this Section is called an anomalous mortgage."

The following four forms will be anomalous mortgages:

i.   a combination of simple and usufructuary,

ii.   combination of conditional sale and usufructuary,

iii.   local mortgages such as qtti, Kanom,

iv.   other miscellaneous forms.

In all these cases, the mortgagor's remedy will either be sale or foreclosure as the terms permit. If the value is over Rs. 100/-, it must be registered. If below Rs. 100/-, it should be done either by registered instrument or delivery of possession.

Salient Features of Mortgages

Salient features of the mortgage are as follows:

(i) Redemption

In the mortgage deed, the mortgagor agrees to repay the loan, and when the loan is fully repaid, he has the power to recover his property from the mortgagee. This is termed as the equity of redemption. It is to be noted here that a suit for redemption of the mortgage before the amount has become due on the mortgage is not maintainable even if the mortgagor has tendered the amount due with interest up to the expiry of the specified period. However,

"Where the mortgagor covenants that he will pay the mortgage money "by" a particular date, he is entitled to redeem at any time before the date."

...AIR 1941 Mad 484 (485) = ILR (1941) Mad 767 (DB).

(ii) Mortgage of Leasehold Property

It is possible to have a mortgage deed for a leasehold property. However, in such cases, care should be taken to revalue the property periodically to ensure the remaining loan amount does not exceed the property's value.

(iii) Insurance

It is desirable to have property insurance in the name of both - the mortgagor and the mortgagee. The insurance policy is kept with the mortgagee, and the mortgagor is required to pay the premium regularly and show the receipts for such payments to the mortgagee.

(iv) Amount of Loan

Usually, 50 to 60 percent will be a safe advance limit on its capitalized value.

(v) Period of Loan

The loan repayment period is generally longer; hence, the property must stand as security for the loan over a longer period. The valuation of the property is so framed that it serves as a sound lendable basis accommodating the future benefits and services as well as the detriments and dis-services that will flow from the ownership of the property over the period for which the loan is made. Thus, the value for mortgage purposes must reflect the risks involved in the secured property over a long period into the future.

Subsequent Mortgages

A property can be mortgaged more than once. In such cases, the first registered mortgage deed will have a first claim compared to the subsequent mortgage deeds. Hence, the mortgagee of the subsequent mortgages should be careful when deciding the loan amount against the property. In the case of a usufructuary mortgage, however, it is to be noted that:

"There cannot be two different usufructuary mortgages on the same land at the same time."

... AIR 1950 Pat 79 (80).

A mortgage by the mortgagee of his rights is called a sub-mortgage. A sub-mortgagee has no privity of estate or privity of contract with the original mortgagor. So far as the sub-mortgagee is concerned, the privity of estate and privity of the contract is between the mortgagee and the sub-mortgagee, and as such, the sub-mortgage can be put an end to by redemption or by release only by the original mortgagee. Also,

"In a suit by the mortgagor for redemption against the mortgagee and his sub-mortgagee, the judgment should direct an account of what is due to the original mortgagee and then of what is due to the sub-mortgagee and upon payment to the latter of the sum due to him not exceeding the sum due to the original mortgagee and upon payment of the residue, if any of what is due to the original mortgagee, both shall reconvey the property to the mortgagor."

... AIR 1956 Madh-B 118(110).

Third-Party Guarantee

Normally, the mortgagee is more interested in recovering his loan rather than possessing the mortgagor's property. Sometimes, a personal guarantee from a reputable party is included in the mortgage deed. In an emergency, the mortgagee may request such party to repay the loan advanced to the mortgagor.

Valuation for Mortgage

The property's value for the purpose of mortgage should be worked out so that the same can be sold for the value so ascertained at the most unfavorable time. Valuation, as such, should be performed on a rental basis, and proper care should be taken to use an appropriate value of capitalization factor. The net income should be carefully worked out to see that it at least covers the interest of the loan that is granted. Also, the value of the materials not specifically included in the mortgage deed, which the mortgagor can remove, should be included in the valuation. In the case of leasehold property, if the unexpired lease period is short, the loan amount to be advanced should also be reduced proportionately. The valuer should insist on having a copy of the legal opinion, the latest encumbrance certificate, and the Sale Deed and Mortgage Deed if possible. He should go through them carefully before valuing the property. The knowledge about

Leases, Mortgages, Easement Rights, etc., will be quite essential for the valuer to do justice to his professional responsibility.

Example

A commercial building is leased for 20 years at Rs. 40,000/- per annum. All expenses are to be borne by the lessor.

Period expired - 10 years

The present rental value is Rs. 1.5 Lakhs per annum.

Value the property for mortgage purposes for the freeholder's interest. Advise the amount that he can expect as mortgage money.

Solution

The unexpired period of the lease is 10 years. Given the steady escalation in rental values, it can reasonably be assumed that the same trend will be maintained for the unexpired period.

Lease Rent net = Rs. 40,000/- per annum.

Assuming yield @ 6% per annum and no sinking fund.

Years purchase for 10 years at 6% is 6.14.

Value is Rs. 40,000 x 6.14 = Rs. 2,45,600.

Reversion to full rental value

Present rent = Rs. 1,50,000/-

Years purchase in perpetuity at 6% per annum deferred for 10 years is 9.3%

Reversionary value   = Rs. 1,50,000 x 9.31

                       = Rs. 13,96,500/-

Total freehold value = Lease Term + Reversion

                       = Rs. 2,45,600/- + Rs. 13,96,500/- = Rs. 16,42,100/-

If the mortgage amount is limited to 60% of the value, the maximum amount he can avail of will be Rs. 9,85,260/-. However, if the mortgage amount is restricted only to 50%, the loan that can be secured on the property in question would be limited to Rs. 8,21,050/-.

***

Chapter 9

Valuation of Ownership Apartments

Growth of Apartments

With the development of city-kingdoms by the Sumerians of Assyria, to the redevelopment of today's central cities, there has been an evolution of thought and practice. From the evolution has come a rich set of lessons, experiences, traditions, and growth trends. As such, growth is not proceeding in a balanced way in India, and the curious growth-decline dichotomy will remain a major trend in Indian urban development for a long time to come, unacceptably so. So, rapid is the growth of cities and the problems of industrialization that the social ramifications of this revolution are being manifested by the phenomenally protuberant growth of cities in the form of multistoried apartments, which seem to be in the rapid phase of their insatiable expansion due to manifold prominent reasons such as:

i.   Transcendent urbanization,

ii. Unbalanced growth of industries.

iii. Restrictions under various rent legislations,

iv. Price hike in building materials in preceding years,

v.   Exorbitant prices of urban land due to its scarcity.

vi. Overgrowing needs of urban communities necessitating their accommodation close to cities and towns.

vii. Tiresome bureaucratic rigmarole to comply with and so are several disincentives generated by tax and other laws for embarking upon house constructed on an individual basis.

viii. Short-term investments in ownership flats are extremely profitable.

What is an Apartment?

An apartment is part of a property having a direct exit to a road, street, or highway, which, together with its undivided interest in the unit common area and faculties, form an independent residential unit. The expression "residence" implies some sort of permanency and habitable position of the property. According to the Kerala High Court in CIT V. Mrs. Elizabeth Varghese (132 ITR 605), the expression "building comprising one or more residential units occurring in clause (b) of section 23 (1) of Income Tax Act, 1961 has to be understood as signifying composite structures containing a plurality of residential and dwelling units, such as apartments. The mere fact that a building has several rooms with an attached bathroom facility will not render it a building comprising as many residential units as there are rooms. Clauses (a) and (b) of the proviso to clause (b) of Section 23(1) will take within their ambit only buildings comprising a plurality of dwelling units like apartments, which by themselves will constitute houses or homes.

Several people use common facilities as a basic philosophy behind the development of apartments. The owners of the apartment have to make use of various common areas and service facilities like passages, elevator(s) and/or staircase(s) with lobby(ies), pump-house(s) including the water distribution system, store(s), parking space(s), fire escapes, compound wall(s), etc. As the definition goes, a habitable residential unit, together with the undivided interest in such common areas and facilities, constitutes an apartment which is a heritable and transferable immovable property within the meaning of the law in force provided that no such apartment and the percentage of individual interest in the common areas and facilities appurtenance thereto shall be partitioned or subdivided for any purpose whatsoever.

Legal Status

The social necessities are well in advance of law, as is the case with multistoried apartments. The private builders and other groups of societies exploited and extorted innocent needy people through malpractices in promoting construction, sale, and even in transferring the apartment in an illegal manner. Once the allottees paid a few installments, the price of apartments and the handing-over period increased. Here, it would be worthwhile to cite an example of Nagpur (M.S.), where a private builder launched a multistoried apartment scheme on a site moderately away from the heart of the city.

The agglomeration of received responses revealed that the offered prices from the prospective owners were low due to the facts that:

1. Every now and then, some builder, hypnotized by the promising exorbitant profits, comes up with his apartment scheme without having requisite financial, technical, and artisan backup, and the scheme backfires even before the deck is cleared for its execution due to restricted allocation of resources. Hence, the needy prospective owners generally do not have faith in such newcomers in this field unless they prove themselves worthy to be relied upon.

2. Most prospective apartment owners find it challenging to visualize the forthcoming construction just by going through the drawings. Moreover, they do not know what construction quality they will ultimately get. Therefore, they want to purchase the ownership rights of the apartments already completed or on the verge of completion (as the competitive market enables them to be selective). It also cut down the waiting period for the possession of duly completed apartments. Due to the above-stated reasons, the builder had to compromise with the prospective buyers at their terms and offered rates. He did it and started constructing the apartments after receiving sufficient advance payments.

The situation started reverting as the construction started growing up. Inspired by the feasibility of getting appreciated rates offered by the approaching needy buyer who wanted to get early possession by paying more, he decided to get rid of the allottees who had paid up initially.

So, the builder ceased playing squarely and, after stopping the construction, started using every technique in the world to corner the allottees by developing the fear that they would lose their advance deposit. Last but not least, allottees were depressed to the extent that they were compromising and ready to part with their ownership rights if their initial investments were refunded. That passed the way for the builder to sell off the ownership rights to the needy buyers at appreciated rates.

The citizens of Delhi residing in the apartments united, which led to the passing of the Delhi "Apartment Ownership Act of 1986." Subsequently, other states also enacted similar laws.

To calculate the length of "Capital Gain Tax," the period would commence from the date the possession has been taken of the apartment and not from the date of becoming a member of the society, and it would not depend on the type of construction scheme. Only when possession has been taken that we could assess it as "Income from housing property." In November 1992, the Maharashtra government served demolition notices to over 100,000 flat owners in the far-flung suburbs of Bombay, stretching from Virar in the west to Bhiwandi in the east. Many of them were occupied, while some of them were still under construction. Nearly 60 percent of the multistoried apartments in this suburban belt have violated numerous state government acts and by-laws on housing, including the three acts that deal with the conversion of agricultural land for building purposes, the Maharashtra Land Revenue Code, the prevention of consolidation & Holding Act and the Bombay Tenancy & Agricultural Act.

Ironically, although the demolitions are aimed at punishing the erring builders/promoters, it is the apartment owners who gets penalized ultimately. Once a building is demolished, the apartment owners cease to have any rights at all. They also have no claim on the land on which the building stood, as the builder often continues to own the land. A housing society can have the property transferred to itself from the builder. However, to avoid the 10 percent stamp duty that must be paid for the transfer, many societies do not bother with the name on title deeds under the Transfer of Property Act. Few are foresighted enough to anticipate any problems ahead.

Although, laws have been enacted in Delhi and other states such as the Delhi Apartment Ownership Act (1986), West Bengal Apartment (Regulation of Construction & Transfer) Act (Act XVII of 1972), U.P. Ownership of Flats Act (1975) and the U.P. Ownership of Flat Rules, 1984 (amended to date) etc., it is feared for want of suitable sale deeds, stamp duty including registration fees etc. are bound to create confusion. Even maintenance of flats would suffer, leading to the dilapidation of the building if left to individual apartment owners. A similar situation has already been experienced in multistoried buildings under the "Rent Control Act."

The immediate need for stronger legal protection for flat owners is seen as imperative.

"Flat owners should statutorily receive a duly signed certificate from the advocate and architect of the builder, stating that all the legalities and formalities have been complied with. These certificates should also indicate the respective registration numbers of the advocate and architect. This will go a long way in safeguarding flat owners," suggested advocate A.D. Sabnis.

The Real Estate (Regulation and Development) Act of 2016

Keeping all this in view, the Government of India passed the Real Estate (Regulation and Development) Act of 2016. It is an Act of the Parliament of India that seeks to protect home-buyers and help boost investments in the real estate industry. The Act establishes a Real Estate Regulatory Authority (RERA) in each state to regulate the real estate sector and acts as an adjudicating body for speedy dispute resolution. The bill was passed by the Rajya Sabha on 10 March 2016 and by the Lok Sabha on 15 March 2016. The Act came into force on 1 May 2016, with 61 of 92 sections notified. The remaining provisions came into force on 1st May 2017.

Despite all the stringent regulations in place, the frauds continue. In December 2024, the Central Crime Branch (CCB) of Bengaluru registered a case against Ozone Urbana Infra Developers Private Limited and several banks and financial institutions for allegedly defrauding homebuyers of Rs 3,300 crore. The complaint was filed by Errol John Noronha, president of the Ozone Urbana Buyers Welfare Association.

Errol accused the developer and financiers of obtaining loans in buyers' names without project completion, diverting funds to other entities, and defrauding customers. The developer reportedly secured Rs 1,500 crore in mortgage loans and Rs 1,800 crore through other transactions, totaling Rs 3,300 crore in misappropriated funds.

Factors Affecting the Value

The various commendatory factors which affect the value of an ownership apartment in one way or the other can be enumerated as follows:

i.   Purpose of valuation

ii. Initial Direct Cost: There is a progressive increase in the indirect cost component, which may be as high as 30% of the selling price of the flats. Some of the factors contributing to it are:

(a) Brokerage for purchase of land.

(b) Advocate, architect, and structural engineer's fees.

(c) Stamp duty, registration, and other legal charges.

(d) Interest on working capital (for construction) and capital blocked in land.

(e) Expenditures incurred for obtaining demarcations, N.O.C.S. approvals etc.

(f) Project publicity expenses.

(g) Site/Head office management overheads,

(h) Municipal tax on the land up to the date of project completion,

i.   Watch and ward,

ii. Builder/Developer's profit,

iii. Direct Initial Cost:

It comprises of the following:

(a) Cost of land (apportioned equally) for every apartment.

(b) Appropriately apportioned cost of the foundation (up to plinth level), common areas, and common service facilities to each apartment based on their plinth areas worked out as per 18:3861-1975 (First Revision).

(c) Cost of individual apartments from plinth level or bottom of floor to bottom of floor of next higher floor or roof. There is a common fallacy in estimating the cost of upper floors at a lower rate than that of the lower ones. This, of course, would have been true had the cost of the foundation been added to that of the ground floor only, which is not true as the foundation cost is equally apportioned to all the floors of the building thereof. The upper floor(s) construction cost is slightly higher due to higher material lifts and other construction difficulties. Moreover, there is an appropriate apportionment to the upper floors to the cost of the extra thickness of structural members at their lower stages.

(d) Extra costs are incurred for any apartment outside the plinth area, such as an open verandah, balcony, etc.

Based on the apportioned indirect cost and direct initial cost of an apartment, in proportion to its saleable area, its final value can be recommended, giving due regard to the following factors:

iv. Location of the apartment in the building.

v. Value of extra items (ornamental or otherwise).

vi. Nature of the building and its expected life.

vii. Regard for aesthetics and environment.

viii. Adequacy of functional performance.

ix. Saleability.

x. Safety considerations (Flood/Fire/Earthquake/Tides/Structural, etc.)

xi. Energy considerations, such as apartment orientation with respect to the sun, etc.

xii. Legal status of the apartment,

xiii. Apportioned common liabilities (recurring or otherwise) to the apartment, such as annual maintenance.

xiv. Other unique feature(s) affecting the value of the apartment (if any).

Conclusion

The apartment owners have to make use of various common areas and service facilities. Things are not so under individual ownership buildings, thereby making the regulation of individual ownership apartments in a multistoried building a tough liability on the part of the incumbent valuer. It is a conundrum since the interest keeps on varying. And so working out "market value" is difficult.

***

Chapter 10

Valuation of Leasehold Properties

Introduction

The valuation of leasehold properties is not as simple as it appears due to the obvious fact that the incumbent valuer is quintessentially required to examine the relevant documents setting forth the rights and obligation of each of the concerned parties (i.e., lessor, and lessee) as the value of a leasehold property is directly related to the rights which are surrendered to the lessee. The greater the number of rights and the fewer restrictions existing for the exercise of these vested rights, there will be more likelihood of the market value being higher.

The leasehold interest is to be evaluated with reference to the nature of investment in the leasehold. It has to be based on an indirect comparison of various valuation factors, as leasehold properties cannot be valued based on comparative sale instances. The professional valuer should also closely specify in his valuation report what particular interest he values in the property.

This chapter briefly discusses in sequence the definition of leasehold properties, types of leases, factors affecting lease and buy decisions, including the pragmatic advantages of leasing a property, and the valuation of leasehold properties. So many important decisions of the Hon'ble Judges have also been quoted where felt appropriate.

Definition of Leasehold

As per Webster's New World Dictionary (Third College Edition), the lease is:

"a contract by which one party (landlord, or lessor) gives to another (tenant, or lessee) the use and possession of lands, building, property, etc. for a specified time and for fixed payments."

In the McGraw-Hill Dictionary of Engineering, the lease has been defined as a:

"Contract between land owners and another granting the later the right to use the land, usually upon payments of an agreed rental, bonus, or royalty."

Based on the above-cited definitions, a generalized definition of the lease has judiciously been framed by the author as hereunder:

"Lease is a right to occupy and use a property for a specified period of time on the condition of payment of periodical rent, etc., as per terms and conditions (covenants) stipulated beforehand and mutually agreed upon by the lessor and lessee in respect of the property in question thereof."

As per the definition given by the McGraw-Hill Dictionary of Engineering, it appears that only lands can be leased by setting forth the rights and obligations of the lessor and lessee. However, it is to be unambiguously noted here that the buildings, lands, machines, plants, etc. can be leased out.

Types of Leases

The full ' 'bundle of rights" inherent in the property with freehold tenure may further be divided by a lease or leases to create two or more interests in the property like lessor's interest, lessee's interest, sub-lessee's interest, etc. The lessor - in some consideration -surrenders part of such a "bundle of rights" vested with him to the lessee, retaining the right to repossess the property at the end of the lease term called "reversion." After the expiry of the stipulated lease, it is obligatory for the lessee to let the lessor hold over the property, failing which, the lessee will be treated as sufferance.

As such, there are five principal forms of lease:

i.   Building lease

ii.   Occupation lease

iii. Perpetual lease

iv.   Sublease

v.   Life lease

Building or land lease

Open ground is given on lease on payment of what is called ground rent. Lessee can erect buildings and develop the property as per his own requirements. The lessee keeps buildings in repair, and he pays outgoings. The other terms and conditions may be specified and mutually agreed upon by both parties. Such kind of ground rent is known as "Secured Ground Rent." Ground rent of a piece of land without any requirement of improvement - on the other hand - without any requirement of improvement is known as "Unsecured Ground Rent." Building leases are generally granted for 99 years or different periods. Usually, the period is long enough to recover the capital invested in land improvement. The essential characteristics of the long-term lease are:

Ground rent is well secured by means of improvement of land, and the lessor is not subjected to capital Gain Tax except with a lease with a premium.

In respect of carrying out the improvement, the alternative provisions may be that the lessee to remove the building at his own cost after the expiry of the lease resting the land to its original position to the lessor free of cost or on payment of the value of the relevant time, the value to be fixed by the mutually agreed method.

In some cases, the lessor sells the freehold right to the lessee after or before the expiry of the lease. However, in the case of the land lease, it should unambiguously be noted that the corpus of lease does not entitle the lessee to fell or sell timber standing thereon or to excavate mines and utilize minerals therein unless he is permitted to do so in specific words in his lease document. Several citations are available on this aspect which have been made by Hon'ble Judges. A few of them have been listed hereunder:

"Lease of land granted by A to B whether permanently or temporarily - Corpus of lease does not include "timber" standing thereon."

... AIR 1923 Pat 95 (95) = 6 Pat Jour 127 (DB).

"Lease of land granted by A to B whether permanently or temporarily - Corpus of lease does not include minerals found in subsoil in the absence of specific words transferring them also.

...AIR 1941 Pat 31 (31, 32) (DB).

"A zamidar is presumed to be the owner of the underground rights in the tenancies created by him in the absence of evidence that he ever parted with them."

... AIR 1951 SC 288 (293) = S C R 534.

Occupational lease

Under this kind of lease both land and building are given out on lease. The term of the lease varies according to the type of property. The residential buildings are usually leased out for 3 to 5 years if it is a short-duration lease or 20 to 30 years. If the property is to be leased out for 14 to 21 years, there may be a clause for revision.

If the lease rent is equal to the full rent of the land and building together, then the rent is called "Rack Rent." On the other hand, if it is less than the full rental value, it is called "Head Rent."

Sometimes the term Head Rent is also used to distinguish the rent paid to the free holder from the other rents paid in respect of the same property by another sub-lessee. Though the lease period in the case of the occupational lease is a short one, the chance of the property reverting to the lessor is difficult due to the Rent Control Act, under which eviction is difficult. While ascertaining the fair market value of such properties, it should be noted that an intending purchaser can purchase only the rights the lessor has in the property that are readily available.

Sublease

Depending upon the terms and conditions mentioned in the original lease, a lessee may grant a lease to another person for a shorter time than his own lease period. In all such cases, the original leaseholder becomes the lessor for the sublease holder. It is to be noted that a sublease can be granted only for a period longer than the original lease period. Such a gap of a few days is essential between the original lease and the sublease periods to facilitate the property's reversion. If both the periods are the same, it becomes an "Assignment" and, as such, is not called a sublease. The new ground rent, reserved under the sublease, is called ' 'Improved Ground Rent."

"Covenant between landlord and tenant which runs with the land can be enforced against sub-lessee if it is restrictive one."

...(1845) 41 E R 1143 (1144) ** AIR 1952 Pat 409 (416) (DB).

(Covenant in the head lease for payment of a profit share is an affirmative covenant and not a negative one. Hence, it cannot be enforced against the sub-lessee.) ** AIR 1936 Cal 727 (736) (DB).

Perpetual lease

In the case of a perpetual lease, the lease is granted for a specified number of years. It is, however, renewable from time to time at the discretion, will, or desire of the leaseholder in perpetuity. The lessee is, however, obligatorily required to respect the covenants and terms of the lease document. As long as there is no violation of lease conditions, the lessor cannot terminate the lease.

Life lease

In a life lease, the lease is granted for the life or lives of one or more persons. The lease ends on the death of such person or persons as specified in the lease document.

The lease documents framed to form any type of lease as described above are unique in themselves, and it is absolutely necessary to critically examine each and every lease document thoroughly to evaluate the impact of its contents on the value of the property. As such, the value of a property is directly related to the rights in the property. The greater the number of rights and fewer covenants existing for the exercise of these rights, there will be more likelihood of the value being higher. A very interesting decision of the Court - given in the favour of a Hindu widow - in the context of Life-Lease is:

"A *lease of land executed by a Hindu widow cannot, in the absence of any words creating a heritable estate, be construed to create a perpetual lease merely because the lands are given forever for cultivation. The words always or forever (Hamesha) in a grant are not inconsistent with limiting the interest given. Since the widow held only a life estate, she must have intended for the grant to operate for her life.*"

... AIR 1959 Madh Pra 52 (57).

Covenants of Lease

Covenants are of vital importance and can be defined as a clause in a lease document under seal covering the liberties and restrictions offered by the lessor(s) to the lessee(s).

"*To decide the term of the lease, the lease deed must be read as a whole, keeping in view the real intention of parties. The intention has to be judged at the time of execution of a document and not what parties think about it earlier or later on; secondly, various clauses of the document must be read in harmony with one another to avoid conflict and contradiction as far as possible. If there is a provision that runs counter to the main theme and object of the deed, the same should be overlooked.*"

... (1968) 2 Comp. L.J. 46 (52) (All) (DB).

The following citation wisely expresses the essential characteristics for the effective annexation of a covenant to a land:

"What is essential for the effective annexation of a covenant to a land is the intention of the original parties to the covenant. (As per Section 40 of T.P. Act) In deciding whether a covenant in a lease is an affirmative or negative covenant, the Court must look to the substance and not to the form."

...AIR 1945 Cal 89 (92) (DB).

(Covenant in head lease implying an obligation to pay specified rent - Covenant bind

sub-lessee.)

"(Under the same section) contract to grant a lease has been held not to be a covenant that runs with the land, and not enforceable against the representatives of the covenantor."

...AIR 1925 All 427 (429) = 47 All 582 (DB).

"The expression "Covenants run with land" has been taken from the English law of real property. It is an exception to the general rule that all covenants are personal."

... AIR 1970 SC 1872 (1875) = (1970) 2 SCR 40.

"If... the covenant binds the land in its inception or it affects the nature, quality, or value of the land, it will go to the transferee as being annexed to it."

... AIR 1959 Pat 463 (472) = 38 Pat 443 (DB).

The following covenants have been held to run with the land:

i. A covenant by the lessee to pay rent.

    ... (1823) 107 E R 152 (154) * AIR 1935 Cal 368 (388) = 62 Cal 346 (DB).

ii. A covenant by the lessor to renew a lease at the option of the lessee.

    ...AIR 1921 Mad 541 (541) = 44 Mad 230 (DB) ** AIR 1959 Assam 22 (24) (DB) ** AIR 1954 Orissa 1 10 (112) = LR (1954) Cut 1 (DB).

iii. A covenant by the lessee not to transfer the land without the landlord's consent.

    ... AIR 1923 Cal 679 (680) (DB).

iv. A covenant by the landlord to renew a lease at the option of the tenant.

    ... AIR 1921 Mad 541 (541) = 44 Mad 230 (DB) ** AIR 1959 Assam 22 (24) (DB) ** AIR 1954 Orissa 110 (112) = ILR (1954) Cut 1 (DB). (Leasehold interest served by agreement of parties - Each of the assignees was entitled to enforce the term prevailing for the renewal so far as his separated part was concerned, irrespective of the other.) ** 1927 Mad 513 (516) = 50 Mad 595 (DB) ** (1912) 16 Cal L Jour 217 (223) (DB).

v. A covenant by the landlord to allow the tenant to erect a structure on the demised premises.

... AIR 1923 Oudh 114(116) = 27 Oudh Cas 64.

vi. A covenant by the lessor to pay the lessee cost of construction of a building on the determination of the lease.

...AIR (1953) 1 Cal 34 (38) (DB).

vii. A covenant requiring a tenant to put up a building.

...AIR 1954 Orissa 110 (112) = ILR (1954) Cut 1 (DB).

The usual and common covenants that usually can be found in a lease deed are:

i. To pay the lease rent specifying the lease rent and mode of payment

This covenant specifies the amount of lease rent and also the mode of payment of the same,

ii. To repair or renew the building

This covenant makes the lessee responsible for repairing the leased property, which may or may not include structural repairs. The lessor may demand damages if the lessee does not honor this covenant. A lease forfeiture clause may even be annexed to it, empowering the lessor to reenter in case this covenant is breached.

iii. Not to assign/sub-let/re-let

The lease document usually contains a covenant prohibiting sub-letting or assignment. It may also prohibit re-letting as well in some cases. This covenant may be either conditional or unconditional. In conditional prohibitions, the lessor usually stipulates some specific conditions under which permission to this effect can be granted, such as:

a. payment of premium,

b. payment of extra ground rent, or

c. such terms and conditions as may be mutually agreed upon as and when needed,

iv. Lease renewal

The lease renewal clause is also an important part of the lease document, which specifies the conditions of lease renewal after the expiry of the lease period. As is obvious, the lessor may clearly specify not to extend the lease after the expiry of the lease period. There is an interesting citation in the context of lease renewal:

"Covenant to renew a lease at the option of the lessee at the time when the lessor himself would have ceased any interest in the property was held to be a personal one and not the one running with the land."

...AIR 1929 Cal 50 (54) = 55 Cal 841 (DB).

v. Lease-forfeiture clause

The purpose of this clause is to ensure that the lessee fulfills all his obligations as stipulated in the instrument of lease, failing which the lessor has the legal right to cancel the lease and take possession of the property. In other words, the lessor has the right to "re-enter." Several interesting variations - in this context - have been cited as hereunder:

"'Certain persons jointly leased property to X and subsequently became divided by partition decree - The Section 37 (T.P. Act, 1882) held would enable one of the persons so divided to enforce against lessee forfeiture clause in lease so for as his share was concerned."

... (1905) 29 Mad 29 (35, 36) (DB)**AIR 1915 Mad 813 (814, 815) = 38 Mad 445 (DB).

Section 12 of the Transfer of Property Act (1882) clearly says that:

"Where property is transferred subject to a condition or limitation making any interest therein, reserved or given to or for the benefit of the person, to cease, on his becoming insolvent or endeavoring to transfer or dispose of the same, such condition or limitation is void."

Here, an interesting and contextual citation is:

"Lease contained clause of forfeiture on lessee's bankruptcy and permission to assign lease with the consent of lessor - lessee assigned lease, with lessor's consent and became bankrupt - Held that there was no forfeiture of lease and that it was not affected by the bankruptcy of first tenant."

... (1891) 60 L J Q B 776 (778).

vi. For or against a particular use

The lessor(s) - under this clause of the covenant - can restrict the lessee(s) from using the leased-out property in a restrictive way.

"Where a lease does not permit the premises to be used for any purpose other than business premises, the tenant, by living in a small portion of the premises, does not contravene the condition of the lease."

Several other self-explanatory covenants have been listed as hereunder:

vii. To pay the taxes,

viii. To surrender the "bundle of rights" back to the lessor after the expiry of lease period if the lease is not renewed,

ix. To insure,

x. For quiet enjoyment.

Lease or Buy Decisions

When an organization (or a person) requires a building, land, plant, or equipment, the first and foremost question crops up in his mind as to whether to lease it or buy it. Some factors that primarily influence the choice of leasing or buying affect cash flow directly. One approach may offer advantages over the other. Freehold tenure assures better maintenance and care. Although the freehold tenure entitles the freeholder the right to utilize and deal with his property as he pleases (subject to applicable rules and regulations of local authority and the Government), leasing of the property has its distinguished advantages, such as:

i. The owner has been in possession of the property for a pretty long time, and he is not quite prepared sentimentally to transfer his freehold ownership to someone else.

ii. A lease may give a firm the ability to cancel quickly and avoid losses. Equipment ownership may influence a contractor to continue using obsolete equipment after superior equipment has been introduced in the market. It may also influence the contractor to continue using the equipment beyond its economic life, increasing the cost of production. The equipment purchased primarily for a given type of work may induce the owner to continue doing that type of work. In contrast, other works requiring different types of equipment might be available at a higher profit.

Purchased assets may take longer to liquidate; meanwhile, loan repayment obligations mount. Convenience is another factor that may be important to the decisions but may not be reflected in cash flow.

iii. Leasing can increase the financial leverage of a firm in two ways:

a. It enables a firm to use more assets than it could under a secured loan agreement. This is due to the fact that the purchase may require a substantial investment of money or credit that may be needed for other purposes. Companies may find it better to lease unproductive assets (such as furniture, cars, delivery vans, etc.) so that the same capital can effectively be utilized to purchase higher productive profit-making plants and machinery. Also, a lessor tends to have less risk than a creditor who finances the purchase of an asset because legal ownership remains with the lessor. This often makes a lessor willing to provide leasing arrangements to a firm that cannot obtain a loan for purchasing assets due to a low credit rating.

b. It tends to have less impact on the future borrowing capacity of a firm than borrowing to purchase.

iv. As the property develops or the locality gains more prominence with the passage of time due to economic growth or otherwise, the leaseholder's vested interest increases with the lease period's advancement.

v. Relative tax positions may make it advantageous for another firm to own assets and for the user to obtain them through leasing.

vi. Leasing may facilitate an organization's administrative success in securing regular replacements of assets within the lease terms rather than through purchase. Regular replacements may be important to avoid the costs of obsolescence,

vii. As the inflation rate is reflected in future resale value, a lower inflation rate will tend to benefit leasing over owning and vice-versa. Conclusively, after all is said and done, by far, the most influential factor in deciding whether to purchase or lease an asset is dependent on its expected long-term utilization. Leasing is usually the less costly alternative if the expected use is short-term or sporadic.

Before making the final leasing or buying decision, reviewing other relevant factors that have potential importance in such a decision-making process is a good idea. One out of all these is whether the company's existing capital resources of cash/credit are short and if leasing would conserve existing credit/cash for other prospective and productive uses. Another factor is whether the difference in cash flows between leasing and buying is sufficiently large to be of any practical consequence to the company's solvency. The firm's capability to utilize depreciation write-offs and other deductions (if available) should also be considered.

Valuation of Leasehold Properties

The difference in the value of properties on leasehold and freehold land had already been accepted by the authorities concerned, and the same is not disputed. A heavily encumbered leasehold property with more than several restrictions has less value than that of a similar property without these encumbrances. Hence, before proceeding with the valuation, it will be essential to analyze the relevant terms of the lease.

While valuing a leasehold land, it is necessary to ascertain its fair market value for all the vested interests combined together. Then the appropriate apportionment should be done between the lessor and lessee to evaluate their respective shares of apportioned interests. In other words, it should be a "whole to part" process as evaluating the lessor's and lessee's interest in a property separately and adding them together will not give the correct result so far as the market value is concerned.

i.   Capitalized value of the lease rent for the unexpired period of the lease, and

ii. Present value of reversion to the property at the expiry of the lease period.

Lessee's interest in the leased-out property consists of the following:

i.   "Profit rental" for the unexpired period of the lease, and

ii. Interest on the cost of improvement, if any, as per the covenants of the lease agreement.

The capitalized value of the net Income (also known as "profit rental") for the unexpired period of the lease will be the lessee's interest in the property.

Illustrative Examples

A plot of land has been given on building lease on a ground rent of Rs. 3000/-p.a. The lease is for a period of 99 years, and the unexpired period of the lease is 20 years, after which the building will revert to the lessor. If the freehold present market value of the above-said property (lessor's interest + lessee's interest) is Rs. 5,00,000/-, what is the present value of the lessor's interest in the property?

Solution:

As per the given lease conditions,

1.   The lessor will receive a net income of Rs. 3000/- per annum for 20 years.

2.   The lease will be terminated after 20 years, and the lessor will get possession of the property, which has a PMV equal to Rs. 5,00,000/-.

PV of Rs. 3000/- p.a. @6% for 20 years = $A(1+i)n-1 \dfrac{(1+i)n-1}{i(1+i)n}$

(Using Uniform Series Present Worth Factor)

where, $i = 0.06$

$A = 3000$

$n = 20$

=> PV = Rs. 34409.76/-

PV of Rs. 5,00,000/- @ 6.5% receivable for 20 years $= F\dfrac{1}{(1+i)n}$

(Using Single Payment Present Worth Factor)

where, $i = 0.065$

$A = 500000$

$n = 20$

=>PV = Rs. 141898.50/-

PV of the lessor's interest in the property

= Rs. 34409.76 + Rs. 141898.50

= Rs. 176308/-

Classical Example

A plot of land has been given on a building lease on a ground rent of Rs. 1.00/- p.a. to the Shivanand Cultural Education Society (Gondia). The lease is for a period of 99 years, and the unexpired period of the lease is 77 years, after which the building will revert to the lessor. Calculate the present value of the lessee's interest in the property.

Solution:

PART I

General:

1.   Purpose for which valuation is made. Legal Dispute of possession

2.   Date on which valuation is made. 07/12/1998

3.   Name of the owner/owners.

Shivanand Cultural Education Society (Gondia)

4.   If the property is under joint ownership/co-owner ship, share of each such owner. Are the shares undivided?

The land in question is under the leasehold ownership of the Shivanand Cultural Education Society (GONDIA). The lease was granted by the Govt. of Maharashtra for a period of 99 years, as per the letter dated 04/08/1966 (no. Ws/22/08/66) signed by the undersecretary.

5.   Brief description of the property.

(5.1) No. of floors.

Block A – Ground Floor only

Block B – Ground Floor & First Floor

(5.2) Plinth area floor-wise. As per IS: 3861-1966).

Ground Floor (Block A) – 1466.37 Sq. Ft.

Ground Floor (Block B) – 1240.25 Sq. Ft.

First Floor (Block B) – 1240.25 Sq. Ft.

(5.3) Year of construction.

1966 (Based on inference drawn by the undersigned as the lease was granted in August 1966 and Block B was inaugurated in the same year (i.e. on 19th December 1966) by the Hon'ble Chief Minister of M.S. Shri Vasant Rao Naik)

(5.4) Estimated future life: 43 years (Approx. & conditional)

JUSTIFICATION

Although it would always be a difficult task to ascertain the future life of the building for even the most competent valuer, it seems reasonable to assume – based on available construction data and degree of maintenance – that the overall economic and severcieable life of the building should be around 75 years or so (i.e., the building is going to survive economically for another 43 years or so). This estimate assumes that the building is regularly looked after and properly maintained and that no catastrophic event (such as an earthquake, etc.) occurs.

(5.5) Type of flooring: I.P.S. flooring

(5.6) Special architectural or decorative features, if any: None whatsoever worth mentioning

(5.7)

(i) Electrical wiring – surface or conduit. Surface

(ii) Class of fitting superior/ordinary/poor. Ordinary

(5.8) Sanitary installations: No. of water closets: Block A – One Block B – One

(5.9) No. of lifts and capacity of each lift: Not Applicable

(5.10) Underground pump capacity and type of construction: Not Applicable

(5.11) Pumps – Types, Nos., and their horsepower: Not Applicable

6.   Location, Street, Ward No., Village, etc.

Village   - Kudwa

Tehsil   - Gondia

District   - Bhandara (M.S.)

PIN Code - 441 614

[Blocks A & B are situated on the eastern side of Tirora (Hiwra) - Gondia P.W.D. Road. Block A, as such, is around 51.00 m away from the C/L of it. Block B, on the other hand, is approximately 36.00 m away from the C/L of the same.]

7.   Survey/Plot No of land.

Khasra No. (Block A) – 109/3 Khasra No. (Block B) – 111/1

8.   Is the property situated in a residential/commercial/mixed/industrial area?

The property is situated in the residential (i.e., hostel) area of M.I.E.T. for students (boys), warden(s), and principal thereof.

9.   Classification of locality – high class/middle class/poor class.

Mostly Poor class (in view of village Kudwa residents only and disregarding the status of hostel boys who come from various social and income classes).

10. Proximity to civic amenities, like schools, hospitals, offices, markets, cinemas, etc.:

Punjab National Bank - Adjacent

Ashoka Video   - 0.75 Km. (Approx.)

Railway Station   - 3.00 Km. (Approx.)

Noble Hospital   - 3.00 Km. (Approx.)

11. Means and proximity to surface communication by which the locality is served: (Broad & narrow-gauge) rail & road transport

Land;

12. Area of land supported by documentary proof. Shape dimensions and physical features.

Area of land (Block A) = 17 x 30 sq. m. = 510 sq. m.

(17 m is in the N-S direction & 30 m is in the E-W direction).

Area of land (Block B) = 24 x 15 sq. m. = 360 sq. m.

(24 m is in the E-W direction & 15 m is in the N-S direction).

The plan is enclosed herewith.

13. Is it freehold or leasehold land? The land in question is a leasehold land. Ground rent payable per annum is Rs. 1/-. For more lease details, please see Page #1 of this report (i.e. Section # 4).

14. Are there any agreements of easements? If so, attach copies: Not Applicable.

15. Does the land fall in an area in any Town Planning Plan of the Government or any statutory body? If so, give particulars: Not Applicable

16. Has the whole or part of the land been notified for acquisition by the government or statutory body? Give the date of notification: Not Applicable:

17. Attach a dimensioned site plan: Enclosed herewith Improvements:

18. Attach the plans of all structures standing on the land and a lay-out plan: Enclosed Herewith Sales:

19. Give instances of sales of immovable property in the locality on a separate sheet, indicating the name and address of the property, registration No., sale price, and area of land sold.

Parallel sales instances are not available for comparison. The leasehold interest is to be evaluated with reference to the nature of investment in the leasehold. It has to be based on an indirect comparison of various valuation factors, as leasehold properties cannot be valued appropriately based on comparative sale instances.

20. Prevailing Land rates.

Rate of land under Block A = Rs. 14.77/- per sq. m.

Rate of land under Block B = Rs. 14.56/- per sq. m.

21. If sale instances are not available or not relied on, the basis of arriving at the land rate would be the Guideline Rates for the current year.

Cost of Construction:

22. Year of commencement of construction and year of completion.

   1966 (Section #5.3 of this report has already justified this inference.)

23. What was the construction method – by contract, by employing labor directly/both?

   Reliable details regarding the method of construction adopted are not available to the undersigned valuer. Hence, it isn't easy to stipulate as to whether the building(s) in question were constructed by employing labor directly or by assigning the construction on a contract basis.

Part II – Valuation

The object of the valuation of leasehold properties is to fairly determine the compensation that a lessee is entitled to if deprived of the otherwise available opportunities under the lease agreement. It is, therefore, more or less a subjective valuation from the lessee's point of view.

Computation of the Present Value of the "Net Profit Rental" for the Unexpired Period of Lease:

The valuation of leasehold properties is not as simple as it appears due to the obvious fact that the incumbent valuer is quintessentially required to examine the relevant documents setting forth the rights and obligation of each of the concerned parties (i.e., lessor, and lessee) as the value of a leasehold) property is directly related to the rights that are surrendered to the lessee. The greater the number of rights and the fewer restrictions existing with respect to the exercise of these vested rights, there will be more likelihood of the market value being higher.

Lessee's interest in the leased-out property consists of the following:

1. "Profit rental" for the unexpired period of the lease, and

2. Cost of construction(s), maintenance, and improvement(s)

The capitalized value of the net Income (also known as "profit rental" for the unexpired period of the lease will be the lessee's interest in the property.

M.I.E.T. (Manoharbhai Patel College of Engineering & Technology), as of today, is charging Rs. 4,000/- (Gross rental) per student per annum for providing hostel facilities to those residing in its hostels.

Around 23 students can conveniently be accommodated after slightly modifying the buildings (i.e., Block A & B).

Expected expenditure for such modification = Rs. 65,000/- (Cost)

Expected gross return per annum = Rs. 92,000.00/-

Expected expenses for providing electricity, security, and other requisite facilities to these students and also to maintain the building = 25% of the gross return

$$= 0.25 \times 92,000.00$$

$$= \text{Rs. } 23,000.00/-$$

Expected net return per annum = Rs. 69,000.00/-

PV of Rs. 69,000.007- p.a. @ 6% for 43 years $= A \dfrac{(1+i)n-1}{i(1+i)n}$

(Using Uniform Series Present Worth Factor)   =   69,000   x 15.306173

  =>PV   = Rs. 10,56,125.90/-   ... (Earning)

where, $i = 0.06$

$A = 69,000.00$

$N = 43$

It would not be economically advantageous to reconstruct the building after the expiry of this economic life (i.e., after 43 years this day approx.) to utilize the residual unexpired period of the lease (i.e. 24 years) to the fullest extent possible. The reason is obvious. The huge investment on the building will not be recovered in just 24 years. Here, the undersigned valuer reasonably assumes that the lease will not be extended.

Computation of the Present Worth of the Investment Made by the Lessee for the Erection of Block A & B

Replacement-Cost-New-Less-Depreciation method has been adopted for the valuation of the property in question.

i. Total Ground Floor Area: (Block A + B) – (1466.37 + 1240.25) Sq. Ft. (i.e. 2706.62 Sq. Ft.).

The replacement cost of the new & similar G.F. Structure based on prevailing material & labor rates is around Rs. 270/- per sq. Ft.

Hence, the Total Replacement Cost of the

$$G.F. = Rs. (270.00 \times 2706.62)/-.$$

$$(i.e. Rs. 7,30,787.40/-).$$

ii. First Floor Area (Block B) – 1240.25 Sq.Ft.

Replacement-Cost-New and similar F.F. structure considering the prevailing material and labour rates is to the tune of around Rs. 180/-.

Therefore,

The Total Replacement-Cost-New of the

$$F.F. = Rs. (180 \times 1240.25)/-$$

$$(i.e. Rs. 2,23,245.00/-)$$

Total Replacement-Value-New of the

$$G.F.F.F. = Rs. (7,30,787.40 + 2,23,245)/-.$$

$$(i.e. Rs. 9,54032.40/-).$$

Computation of Depreciation

Using the Straight-Line-Method of Depreciation (SLD), and assuming the Salvage Value of 10% after the expiry of the useful life span of the building:

$$\text{SLD for 32 spent years} = \frac{0.90 \times 32 \times 9,54,032.40}{(32+43)}$$

i.e. SLD = Rs. 3,66,348.44/-

Therefore,

Total present Value (G.F + F.F) of the investment made by the lessee for the erection of the buildings in question:

= Rs. 5,87,683.96/-   ...(Cost)

PV of Total Outgoings   = Rs. 5,87,683.96/- + Rs. 65,000.00/-

PV of Net Incomings   = Rs. 10,56,125.90/-

VALUE OF LESSEE'S INTEREST　　= Rs. 4,03,441.94/-

= Rs. 4,03,500.00/- (Say)

(Rs. Four Lakhs Three Thousand & Five Hundred Only)

Conclusions

The object of the valuation of leasehold properties is to fairly determine the compensation that a lessee is entitled to if deprived of the otherwise available opportunities under the lease agreement. It is, therefore, more or less a subjective valuation from the lessee's point of view.

The impact of covenants on the property's value is quite obvious. Therefore, a valuer is expected to go through the lease document carefully before ascertaining the lessee's or lessor's interest in the property.

***

Chapter 11

Valuation of Plants and Machinery

Introduction

A professional valuer is frequently called upon to decide the plant and machinery's Present Market Value (PMV). With modern technology producing new machines and drastic changes in the design of old ones, a Valuer or P&M often finds himself confronting a wide variety of unfamiliar equipment. As such, the valuation of plants and machinery is peculiar and unique.

The Valuer needs to understand the basic function of the plant/machine under consideration. This is because the valuation carried out by Current Cost Accounting (CCA) is based on establishing a gross current value and then depreciating it to arrive at a figure that reflects the proportion of the gross value attributable to the remaining economic life. However, it is easier said than done, uncomfortably so. Consider the variety of materials used in machinery manufacturing, having a wide array of diversified properties. Apart from simple basic materials like wood, plastic, steel, aluminum, copper, etc., many alloys are in common use nowadays. The processes and techniques used to manufacture machines are equally diverse and complicated. All industries, including textile, food-processing, chemical, mining, mechanical, etc., heavily depend upon machines of either some kind or the other.

The use and purpose a machine are put to is vast and all-pervasive. The service requirements of almost all the machines are very severe. To undertake the valuation of such a vast variety of machinery, the valuer is required to exercise utmost caution and judgment on his part. He has not only to consider the various factors connected with the machine's operating environment but also has to take into account the materials used, their properties, design, and manufacturing details of the machine, etc., to judge the various tangible and intangible value-laden parameters required for valuation. It becomes imperative for the valuer to depart from the normal procedure - if felt necessary - and adopt a more realistic approach to arrive at a realistic value.

The term "plant" had come up for interpretation in several decisions, and the court has evolved what is known as the functional tests against merely the amenities test for determining what constitutes "plant." In this chapter, an attempt has been made to define "plant" comprehensively.

An adequate discussion of all the methods used to arrive at the correct PMV of plant and machinery property would require at least a good-sized volume: it is beyond this chapter's scope. However, a few principles involved would be considered since they are intimately connected with the subject of depreciation and the effect of inflation or deflation thereon. This chapter ardently attempts to develop and present a modified mathematical simulation model for determining the PMV compatible with various commonly adopted methods of calculating annual depreciation. The proposed simulation model not only accounts for inflation but can also be made compatible with personal computers.

Notation

E = Economical life span of the plant.

C = Capital invested for the plant (i.e., the cost of the plant plus the costs of any additions to it, including installation costs, etc.)

i = Market discount rate, which includes the rate of general price inflation.

I = Project d rate of general price inflation (or deflation).

d = Real discount rate, which does not include the rate of general price inflation.

S = Spent out life of the plant at a particular time "t."

(C-P) = Depreciable value.

K_0 = Depreciation factor (S/E)

K_1 = 1.85/E   [i.e. 1.8 >K_1>()]

K_2 = [(0.9S/E) x *(S + 1) / (E + 1)*]   [i.e. 0.9 > K_2 > 0]

R = Replacement value at the time of study (i.e., or at the end

of the holding period).

L = Expected (residual) future life at the time of study.

P = Scrap value, taken usually as 10% of the Replacement Value

= 0.1 *R*

SLD = The annual amount of depreciation deductions allowed

by the Straight-Line Method.

K = The deterioration factor when 1 > *K* > 0.

SOYD = E (E + 1)/2 = The annual depreciation deduction allowed by the Sum-of-Year- Digits Method.

What is a Plant?

Section 43(3) of the I.T. Act (1961) gives an all-inclusive definition of the term "plant" to include ships, vehicles, books, scientific apparatus, and surgical equipment used for the business or profession.

In the case of IRC Vs. Barclay, Curie and Co. Ltd. (1970) 76 ITR 62 (HL); the question that arose for consideration was whether a dry dock could be construed as a plant for the trade of the company within Section 279 (1) of the English Act. In that case, the dry dock had to be strong and impervious to water so at large vessels could get into it for repairs. In the facts and circumstances of the case, it was held that the entire dry dock and the ancillary structures constituted a plant.

Lord Ried considered the part that a dry dock played in the assessee company's operations and observed (page 67):

"It seems to me that every part of this dry dock plays an essential part. The whole dock is, I think, the means by which, or plant with which, the operation is performed."

The next case is Schofield Vs. R. and H. Hall Ltd. (1974) 49 TC 538 (CA) concerning silos built in the shipyard. The company carried on a trade that consisted of the storage of grains. The question was whether or not the silo is part of the setting in which such trade was carried on. It was found that considering the function of the silos in relation to the assessee's trade, the silos served as an essential part of the overall trading activity. Their function was to hold the grain in a position from which it could be conveniently discharged in varying quantities. Hence, it was held that the silos would rank for capital allowance.

In CIT Vs. Kanodia Cold Storage (1975) 100 ITR 155 (All), the question was whether the building with insulated walls used as a freezing chamber, though it is not machinery or part thereof, is part of the air-conditioning plant of the cold storage of the assessee entitled to special depreciation on its written down value. In the case's specific facts, the whole freezing chamber, including walls and structure, was held to be a plant with which the assessee carried on his business activity.

In the case of Benson Vs. Yard Arm Club Ltd. (1978) 2 All ER 958, 968; (1970) Tax LR 778, 785 (Ch D), the subject matter was a ship that was converted into a restaurant by the assessee. The whole ship was claimed as an apparatus for carrying on their business of a floating restaurant, and as such, it was a plant to claim allowance.

On a review of various earlier decisions, the Chancery Division has held that the vessel is the place or setting where the restaurant business was carried on and was not plant; hence, the expenditure on them did not qualify for capital allowance. In this context, the learned judge has observed that:

"One has only to think of certain large stores, hotels, and restaurants generally, placed in different landscapes and built with different structures to be more attractive. The commercial utility of particular land, it may be, usual premises or places in that way does not, in my judgment, convert them into the plant in the sense of the Income-tax legislation or affect the application of the functional test: they still remain the setting and not the apparatus."

Moreover,

"A word can have many meanings, so to find out the exact connotation of a word in a statute, we must look to the context in which it is used. The context would quite often provide the key to the word's meaning and sense it should carry. Its setting would give color to it and provide a clue to the legislature's intention in using it. As said by Holmes, a word is not a crystal, transparent and unchanged; it is the skin of a living thought and may vary greatly in color and content according to the circumstances and the time it is used."

...(see Manickam and Co. Vs. State of Tamil Nadu [1977] 30 STC 12, 17 (SC).

The classic definition of "plant" is given by Lindley L.J. with reference to the Employees' Liability Act in Yarmouth Vs. France [1887] 19 QBD 647, 658 (CA), reads as hereunder:

"There is no definition of plant in the Act but, in its ordinary sense, it includes whatever apparatus is used by a businessman for carrying on his business - not his stock in trade which he buys or makes for sale; but all goods and chattels, fixed or movable, live or dead, which he keeps for permanent employment in his business."

In Scientific Engineering House P. Ltd. Vs. CIT (1986) 157 ITR 86,96 (SC), after referring to the classic definition of "plant" as stated above, the Supreme Court has observed that:

"... plant would include any article or object, fixed or movable, live or dead, used by a businessman for carrying on his business, and it is not necessarily confined to an apparatus used for mechanical operations or processes or employed in mechanical or industrial business. To qualify as a plant, the article must have some degree of durability; for instance, in Hinton vs. Maden and Ireland Ltd. (1960) 39 ITR 359 (HL), knives having an average life of three years used in manufacturing shoes were held to be plant. In CIT Vs. Taj Mahal Hotel (1971) 83 ITR 44 (SC), the respondent, which ran a hotel, installed sanitary and pipeline fittings in one of its branches in respect whereof it claimed development rebate, and the question was whether the sanitary and pipeline fittings installed fell within the definition of plant given in section 10(5) of the 1922 Act which was similar to the definition given in section 43(3) of the 1961 Act and this court after approving the definition

of plant given by Lindley L.J. In Yarmouth Vs. France [1887] 19 QBD 647, as expounded in Jarrild Vs. John. Good and Sons Ltd. [1962] 40 (CA), held that sanitary and pipeline fittings fell within the definition of plant."

Lord Guest indicated a functional test in these words (page 75 of 76 ITR):

"To decide whether a particular subject is an "apparatus," it seems obvious that an inquiry has to be made as to what operation it performs. The functional test is, therefore, essential at any rate as a preliminary."

In other words, the test would be:

"Does the article fulfill the function of a plant in the assessee's trading activity? Is it a tool of his trade with which he carries on his business? If the answer is in the affirmative, it will be plant."

In CIT Vs. Taj Mahal Hotel [1971] 82 ITR 44, 47, the Supreme Court has observed that:

"Now it is well-settled that where the definition of a word has not been given, it must be construed in its popular sense if it is a word of everyday use. Popular sense means 'that sense which people conversant with the subject matter with which the statute is dealing would attribute to it.' In the present case, Section 10(5) enlarges the definition of the word "plant" by including the word that has already been mentioned before. The word 'include' is often used in phrases occurring in the body of the statute. When used, these words and phrases signify according to their nature and importance, as well as those things the interpretation clause declares that they shall include. The word "include" is also susceptible to other constructions that are unnecessary to go into."

It is, thus, clear that the functional test must be applied to find out if a building or structure or part thereof constitutes 'plant.' It must be seen whether the subject matter involving building, structure, or part thereof constitutes an apparatus or tool of the taxpayer or merely a space where the taxpayer carries out his business. If, as stated above, the building structure or part thereof is something using which the business activities are carried out, it would amount to a plant. On the other hand, where the structure plays no part in carrying on those activities but merely constitutes a place where such activity is carried on, it cannot be regarded as a plant. Viewed from this angle, even if a building has special features, generally speaking, it may remain a building and not a plant.

Purposes of Valuation

The valuation of plant and machinery industries is often required for the following purposes:

i.   Valuation under court orders for liquidation.

ii. Valuation of sick undertakings for the inflow of fresh capital through new partners.

iii. Revaluation of assets to give the shareholders information regarding companies' financial soundness.

iv. Valuation of plant and machinery as a security for release of term loan sanctioned by banks, financial institutions like S.F.C.S., etc.

v.   Valuation under the provisions of Wealth/Income Tax Acts.

vi. Valuation is used to ascertain fixed assets for classification into Cottage/ Tiny/Small Scale/Medium Scale/Large Industry as per norms set by the government; therefore,

vii. Valuation is for insurance purposes.

Inflation: Various Definitions

A very troublesome factor while attempting to arrive at the PMV by using depreciation accounting is the matter of price changes due to inflation and deflation. When considering the effects of inflation on depreciation, it is important to distinguish between general inflation differential escalation and effective annual escalation. All these terms can be defined hereunder:

General Inflation Rate (f)

It is a general measure of a currency's annual decrease in purchasing power. The annual general inflation rate is defined by selected and broadly based indices of price changes. We define T to be the projected annual compound general inflation rate based on the Consumer Price Index (CPI) or the Implicit Price Index (IPI) for the Gross National Product (GNP) for a specified future interval of time. Many organizations have their own indices of general inflation that reflect the business environment in which they work. Despite having general price hikes, for example, the computer industry is observing continuous price drops in microcomputers due to rapid technological advances and expanding competition in this field.

Differential Annual Escalation Rate (f)

It is the annual change in the price of a specific commodity or service "j" which can be more or less than the general inflation. (The subscript "$_j$" labels different commodities, services, or revenue cash-flows). Differential escalation results from technological breakthroughs, increased demand for a commodity or service with restricted supply, and so on, and, can be positive or negative.

Effective Annual Escalation Rate (e)

It is the total annual rate of increase in the price of a commodity or service "j." The effective annual escalation rate includes the effects of general inflation (f) and the applicable differential price change () above or below the general inflation.

Value of Plant and Machinery

PMV estimates the price for which an asset will sell as of date. Methods of estimating PMV include the following:

i.   Base the estimate on the price at which similar, comparably aged property is selling in the commercial market at the time of the study.

ii. Theoretically, a property's PMV should measure the present worth of the future net profits that can be derived through ownership. Such a determination would, of course, necessitate the ability to predict future profits accurately, and some interest rate - to discount future profits - would have to be agreed upon and used.

If the asset generates annual income, estimate PMV, as on the time of resale, as the capitalized value of the future income stream remaining at the time of resale. If the income stream is anticipated over a specific number of years, PMV can be calculated by capitalizing the income stream as per equation (11.1):

$$PMV = \frac{E}{L} \times \frac{Y(t)}{(1+i)^{t}} \qquad \qquad ...(11.1)$$

where, $Y(t)$ = income in year t,

i = the prevailing rate of return on comparable assets at the time of resale.

If the income stream is relatively stable in amount and is anticipated to continue indefinitely, PMV is the capitalized value as per equation (11.2):

$$PMV = Y/i \qquad \qquad ...(11.2)$$

Where, Y= average yearly income.

It is to be noted here that "i" in this case is not the investor's discount rate. Because resale depends on how the market values the future income stream, T is the prevailing market rate of return on comparable assets. Here, the distinction between "real" discount rates "d" (those which exclude purely inflationary or deflationary changes in the general price level) and market discount rates (those which include changes in the general price level) is to be kept in mind. One can use the following equation to derive a market discount rate from a real discount rate by including projected inflation.

$$i = (I + d)\,(1+I) - 1 \qquad \qquad ...(11.3)$$

where:

I = projected rate of general price inflation.

Conversely, using the following equation, one can remove the inflation component from a market discount rate and convert it to a real discount rate:

$$d = [(I + i)/(I +I)] - 1 \qquad \qquad ...(11.4)$$

The guideline for choosing between real and market rates is to choose a real rate if projected cash flows are stated in constant monetary units and a market discount rate if the projected cash flows are stated in current monetary units.

(iii) If one thinks the depreciation schedule accurately reflects the decline in market value, calculated BV at the time of resale may be appropriate as an estimate of PMV. Since BV does not include inflation, it will be adjusted for inflation if the analysis is in current monetary units. If the analysis is in constant monetary units, BV should be stated in the same base-time monetary units used elsewhere in the analysis.

However, such a procedure is difficult to apply. Consequently, several generalized methods are used, each being based upon a certain hypothesis, producing results dependent upon the condition contained in the hypothesis. Therefore, it is necessary to keep in the dictum that there is no single way to determine value.

Historical-Cost Less Depreciation Method of Valuation

In arriving at value by this method, we consider the actual costs incurred in obtaining the property being valued. This historical cost is then reduced by the depreciation that appears to have occurred. This depreciation must be considered in terms of the ability of the present property to render the service. The depreciated historical cost is then taken as the true value.

It is apparent that the historical-cost-less depreciation method neglects many factors, such as:

i. No consideration is given to advances in technological methods that have occurred since the property was acquired. It is obvious that if equivalent plants could be built, using modern methods and equipment, that would render the future service at much less unit cost, the existing plant could never be worth more than the more modern plant in terms of Life Cycle Costs (LCCs), regardless of how much might have been expended in acquiring the old plant.

ii. Although the fact that the depreciation occurs is easily ascertained and recognized, determining its magnitude in advance is not easy. The actual amount of depreciation can never be determined until the asset is retired from service.

Reproduction-Cost-New Less Depreciation

A fictitious equivalent plant or property is usually assumed to be obtained by building it using the most modern methods, according to the most efficient design, so that the weaknesses of the historical-costs methods can be overcome. This theoretical plant is then depreciated until it would render the same amount of future service as the existing plant. Consequently, this method of valuation is often called reproduction-cost-new less depreciation. Technological progress and price level changes are considered by its use. It is, however, also a fact that indications received by the valuer from the market at the time of valuation do not necessarily reflect true replacement cost, as this is subject to negotiations at the time of actual purchase. Such adjustments should be considered while arriving at the new replacement cost.

"Reproduction-Cost-New Less Depreciation method" - as is obvious - can employ different depreciation methods appropriate to the particular case. The term "residual value" is used as an umbrella term to include resale, reuse, salvage, scrap, and unused value remaining at the end of the economical life span of the asset (E), and sometimes, residual value is estimated as a percent of the original cost of the asset. At any given time, "t," residual value is the amount adjusted for inflation, remaining at the end of the holding/study period, and, is a function of the asset's estimated life and the length of the study/holding period.

Residual value at the end of the long residual future life (L) often has little weight in the determination of PMV for three perceptible reasons:

i.   Value declines due to deterioration or obsolescence.

ii. Disposal costs offset residual value, and

iii. Discounting diminishes residual value.

Therefore, when $S > 0$, improving residual value estimates is often less worthwhile.

Reproduction-Cost-New Less Depreciation (Using SLD)

In the Straight-Line Method of Depreciation, the prospective net residual value (P) at the end of the life is estimated and expressed as a percentage of "R" (as P = 0.1R). As per Mukherjee (1993):

$$PMV = 0.9R(1-K_0)K + 0.1R \qquad \qquad \dots(11.5)$$

However, in several cases, using equation (11.5) to determine PMV may not be appropriate if the depreciation schedule using SLD does not accurately reflect the decline in market value. In such cases, other (usually accelerative) methods of calculating depreciation are typically employed. Though it is not true of many industrial and commercial structures and some equipment, this undoubtedly is true in the case of such things as automobiles (where new models and style changes are large factors in the establishment of the PMV), in which case the results of the declining balance method nearly parallel the PMV than those obtained using SLD. This is particularly advantageous from the viewpoint of companies because by taking larger deductions earlier in the depreciation period by using an accelerated depreciation method increases the present value of write-offs.

Reproduction-Cost-New Less Depreciation (Using SOYD)

The formula for PMV may be written as follows (assuming "P'" = 0.1R):

$$PMV = R - (S/E) \times 1.8R + 0.9R \times (S/E) \times [(S + 1)/(E + 1)] \qquad \dots(11.6)$$

$$PMV = R[1- (1.8S/E) + (0.9S/E) \times (S + 1)/(E + 1)]$$

$$PMV = R [1 - K_1 + K_2] \qquad \qquad \dots(11.7)$$

Where,

$$K_1 = f_1(S, E) = 1.8(S/E)$$

$$K_2 = f_2(S,E) = (0.9S/E) \times (S+1)/E+1)$$

So far, the equation (12.7) for PMV ignores the deterioration factor "K," which. in some way or the other, also accounts for inflation (or deflation) as the depreciated amount is to be adjusted for it.

Consider "K" and its effects one gets:

$$PMV = R[1-K_0+K_1]\,K \qquad\qquad …(11.8)$$

For $K=1$,

i. For a new machine $(S = 0)$

$$=> S/E = K_0 = K_1 = 0$$

$$=> PMV = R = \text{New Replacement Value}$$

ii. For a completely depreciated machine $(S = E)$

$$=> K_0 = 1.80 \ \&\ K_1 = 0.90$$

$$=> PMV = 0.\,1\,R = P\ \text{(Scrap Value)}$$

Flowchart of Plant Valuation

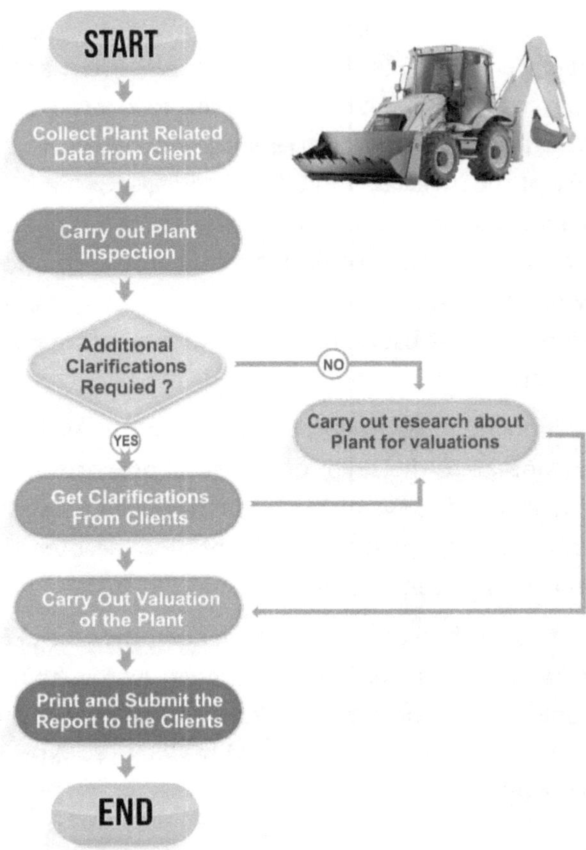

Conclusions

Depreciation accounting is a process of allocation, not of valuation. Depreciation for the year is the portion of the total charge under such a system allocated to the year. Although the allocation may properly account for occurrences during the year, it is not intended to measure the effect of all such occurrences [Accounting Terminology Bulletin No. 1: Review & Resume (para. 56), American Institute of Certified Public Accounts, 1953]. Depreciation accounting is primarily meant for 'Book Value,' which may not necessarily represent PMV due to the following reasons:

i.   As companies may use various depreciation accounting methods that produce different results, book value may have little or no relationship to the actual or market value of the property involved.

ii. Book value does not include inflation. When price levels rise during inflationary periods, even if all the capital invested at the time of the original purchase has been recovered, this recovered capital will not be sufficient to provide an identical replacement. However, there has been a recovery of the invested capital, not the asset, that has depreciated. Inflating annual depreciation to compensate for this phenomenon is not permitted when determining profits for income tax purposes. However, one may need to estimate PMV if he plans to sell an asset, trade it in, convert it to another use, scrap it, or continue using it past the end of the study period,

The "Reproduction-Cost-New Less Depreciation Method" results are of obvious advantage to the seller of industrial property when price levels have risen. The value of constant "AT" (as introduced above in the previous Section), if adopted appropriately, would take into account the effect of all such occurrences while calculating PMV using *"R"* instead of "C."

However, this method does not consider whether the existing property is of the correct size for actual future demand or results from an unwise investment policy. The question also remains as to whether or not the owners should be given full advantage of the increase in price levels that may have occurred.

✳✳✳

Chapter 12

Valuation of Mining Properties

Introduction

The mother earth has an abundant deposit of a fecund variety of mineral resources. Mining assets are very challenging to value. Given the degree of geologic uncertainty around reserves and resources, it's hard to know how much mineral is actually in the ground and exactly how much would be the extraction cost.

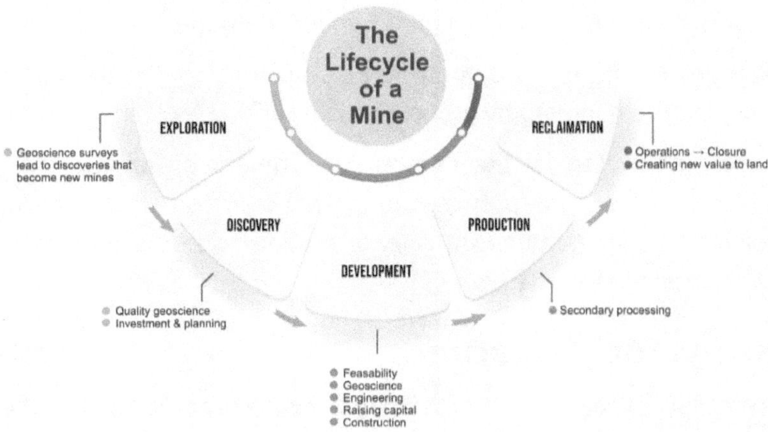

The best way to value a mining asset or company is to build a discounted cash flow (DCF) model that takes into account a mining plan produced in a technical report (like a Feasibility Study). Without such a study, one has to resort to more crude metrics.

This chapter briefly outlines the raison d'etre of valuing diversified mining properties and the state-of-the-art methodology of valuation therefor. This guide to mining valuation will teach you all you need to know to value such assets!

What is a Mine?

As per the Mines Act (1952), 'Mine' means any excavation where any operation to search for or obtain minerals has been or is being carried on, and includes:

i.   every shaft in the course of being sunk;

ii.   every level and inclined plane in the course of being driven;

iii. all shafts, levels, planes, machinery, works, tramways and sidings, whether above or below ground, in or adjacent to, and belonging to, the mine;

iv.   any workshop situated within the precincts of the mine and under the same management and used solely for the purpose connected with that mine or the number of mines under the same management;

v.   any power station for supplying electricity solely for the purpose of working the mine or any group of mines; and

vi.   unless exempted by the Central Government by notification in the official Gazette, any premises or part thereof on which any process ancillary to the getting, dressing, or preparation for sale of mineral or of coke is being carried on.

Reasons for Valuation

A wide variety of reasons exist for valuing mining properties. These reasons may include the following:

i.   Purchase/Sale/Speculation/Mortgage/Leasing of mining properties,

ii.   Acquisition of mining properties,

iii. For the dissolution of partnership or co-operations,

iv. For the purpose of merging different mining companies,

v. To assess value for litigation purposes so as to determine the amount of

vi. court fee stamp in a suit, etc.

vii. For the purpose of listing stock on the exchange,

viii. Estate Valuations,

ix. Bank loans or other financing.

x. Preparation of financial statements,

xi. Feasibility studies so as to support an investment decision.

xii. Competitive analysis

xiii. Auction bidding,

xiv. Income tax requirements.

Factors Affecting the Value

Some of the factors, including that of important non-quantifiable 'intangible' ones, which affect the 'value' of mining properties, especially at the earlier stages of exploitation are:

Assured Recoverable (Extractable) Content of the Ore

The tonnage of metal content of the ore in the deposit is determined by sampling. The gross in-situ value of a mineral deposit in the ground - which is the product of geological reserves, geological grades, and market prices - gives a false impression of the economic value of a deposit because extensive costs must be deducted before a judgment can be made concerning the real value of the deposit. This estimate must be modified according to the percentage of recovery and the amount of dilution to be expected from the proposed method of mining some geological reserves will inevitably be left behind in pillars and remnants, and also, the geological grades are diluted by the mining of the barren or low-grade waste rock material adjacent to the deposit itself.

Cost of Production

This includes the actual cost of mining and metallurgical operations, either modified from the records of past production or estimated if the property is new, freight to markets, selling expenses, administration, and general expenses, including amortization of capital. ' 'The costs of these processes vary between producers because of the natural geologic-geographic circumstances of specific deposits and •Jie economic and political factors in a particular location." Says Leous Kovisars, Manager of Economic Analysis, Cargill Metals/Cargill Inc., New York, U.S.A. An allowance of 10% may be made for contingencies.

Projected Future Price of Mineral Products

Since the life of mine will extend over a number of years, the future price of mineral products must be estimated to calculate the probable profit to be realized.

Life of Mine

The life of a mine depends on the rate at which the ore reserve is mined. A good manager prefers to have a mine yield as steady as possible during its life. Low-grade material can be mined at a profit if prices of mineral products are high. If prices are low, only high-grade ore will yield profit. "Although the financial theory tells us that the theoretical optimum production rate (or optimum mine life) should be chosen, practical experience suggests that this may not always be the case" (Ross Glanville, President of Glanville Management Ltd., Vancouver, British Columbia, Canada).

The Risk of Mining

The risks are higher in mining than in almost any other investment. Many unforeseen contingencies may arise during the operation of the mine,

i.   Remoteness.

ii. Staked, leased, or freehold claims,

iii. Environmental sensitivities.

iv. Proximity to known reserves,

a. Prospects and limitations of the property.

b. General activity in the area,

c. (c)Track Record' of the exploration geologists.

v. any power station for supplying electricity solely for the purpose of working the mine or any group of mines; and

vi. unless exempted by the Central Government by notification in the official Gazette, any premises or part thereof on which any process ancillary to the getting, dressing, or preparation for the sale of mineral or of coke is being carried on.

Reasons for Valuation

A wide variety of reasons exist for valuing mining properties. These reasons may include the following:

i.   Purchase/Sale/Speculation/Mortgage/Leasing of mining properties,

ii.   Acquisition of mining properties,

iii.   For the dissolution of partnerships or co-operations,

iv.   To merge different mining companies,

v.   To assess value for litigation purposes to determine the amount of

vi.   court fee stamp in a suit, etc.

vii.   To list stock on the exchange,

viii. Estate Valuations,

ix.   Bank loans or other financing,

x.   Preparation of financial statements,

xi.   Feasibility studies to support an investment decision,

xii.   Competitive analysis

xiii. Auction bidding,

xiv. Income tax requirements.

Factors Affecting the Value

Some of the factors, including that of important non-quantifiable 'intangible' ones, which affect the 'value' of mining properties, especially at the earlier stages of exploitation, are:

Assured Recoverable (Extractable) Content of the Ore

The tonnage of the metal content of the ore in the deposit is determined by sampling. The gross in-situ value of a mineral deposit in the ground - which is the product of geological reserves, geological grades, and market prices - gives a false impression of the economic value of a deposit because extensive costs must be deducted before a judgment can be made concerning the real value of the deposit. This estimate must be modified according to the percentage of recovery and the amount of dilution to be expected from the proposed method of mining as some geological reserves will inevitably be left behind in pillars and remnants. Also, the geological grades are diluted by the mining of the barren or low-grade waste rock material adjacent to the deposit itself.

Cost of Production

This includes the actual cost of mining and metallurgical operations, either modified from past production records or estimated if the property is new, freight to markets, selling expenses, administration, and general expenses, including amortization of capital. "The costs of these processes vary between producers because of the natural geologic-geographic circumstances of specific deposits and the economic and political factors in a particular location." Says Leous Kovisars, Manager of Economic Analysis, Cargill Metals/Cargill Inc., New York, U.S.A. An allowance of 10% may be made for contingencies.

Projected Future Price of Mineral Products

Since the life of the mine will extend over a number of years, the future price of mineral products must be estimated in order to calculate the probable profit to be realized.

Life of Mine

The life of a mine depends on the rate at which the ore reserve is mined. A good manager prefers to have a mine yield as steady as possible during its life. Low-grade material can be mined at a profit if prices of mineral products are high. If prices are low, only high-grade ore will yield profit. "Although the financial theory tells us that the theoretical optimum production rate (or optimum mine life) should be chosen, practical experience suggests that this may not always be the case" (Ross Glanville, President of Glanville Management Ltd., Vancouver, British Columbia, Canada).

Risk of Mining

The risks are higher in mining than in almost any other investment. Many unforeseen contingencies may arise during the operation of mine.

i.   Remoteness.

ii.   Staked, leased, or freehold claims,

iii. Environmental sensitivities.

iv.   Proximity to known reserves,

v.   Prospects and limitations of the property,

vi.   General activity in the area,

vii. 'Track Record' of the exploration geologists.

viii. General economic and political climate; taxing statute, illegitimate influences (if any), and police protection.

ix.   Supply and cost of labour.

x.   The mining history of the region; profits and difficulties were met.

xi.   Availability - or the lack of it - of infrastructural facilities, including water, power, transportation, fuel, timber, explosives, and miscellaneous materials.

xii. Specific interests of a party bidding for the property,

xiii. Presence of valuable minerals or metals (in situ, stockpiles, lumps, tailings, etc.)

Before the succinct discussion of valuation methods in general, it should be emphasized that the applicability of some methods depends upon the property's status, or stage, from exploration through to production. As per Ross Glanville, some of these stages are:

i.   Hypothetical analysis

ii.   Regional program

iii. Anomalies

iv.   Claims staked (based on anomaly)

v.   Claims staked (based on a 'hot' area)

vi.   Additional geological, geochemical, or geophysical data

vii. Development of a model of a target deposit

viii. One drill hole in a mineralized zone

ix.   Two drill holes in a mineralized zone

x.   Three drill holes to define a plane of mineralization

xi.   More drill holes (establishing indicated reserves)

xii. Preliminary feasibility study

xiii. Enough holes to define proven, probable, and possible ore

xiv. Exploratory development

xv.   Feasibility study

xvi. Construction of Mine/Mill

xvii. Producing mine

Valuation Methods

Some of the valuation methods, that have been used with varying degree of success, are presented below. Some of them are acceptable, some are completely unacceptable, and some should only be used as a 'test of reasonableness' depending on the prevailing circumstances.

Statistical or Probabilistic Method

This method is based on a statistical analysis of the average value of an economic deposit and the chances of discoveries becoming economic and of anomalies (drill targets) becoming discoveries. This method is rather subjective and is better suited to valuing exploration properties at an early stage.

Market Premium or Discount on Share Price

This, again, is a somewhat subjective method that applies a premium or discount to a market price of a share. However, historical premiums and discounts (based on acquisitions) can be used as a guide to value.

Value per Ton of Ore in the Ground

This method is extremely arbitrary since the material in the ground has no value until unless the relationship between grade, recovery, metal prices, costs, etc. are reasonably established.

Price/Earnings Multiple

In this method, earnings are estimated and multiplied thereafter by a Price/ Earnings (P/E) multiple. The method is reasonably acceptable only for producing mines but not as good as the discounted cash flow approach because the P/E multiple is difficult to determine. Also, the method is affected by book items (such as amortization and depreciation), which do not affect the cash flow.

Market Value of Shares

The valuation by this method is based on multiplying the price per share by the number of issued shares. This method is applicable only if the company is listed on a public share exchange and the property to be valued is the company's only major asset. In addition, the price of a few shares sold is not necessarily reflective of what one could sell all the shares for.

Hoskold's Method

The value of the mine is the present value of all the future profits to be derived from the mine. It is common practice to determine the present value of future profits at the rate of interest by the Hoskold formula (Henry Hoskold, "Engineer's Valuing Assistant." 2nd ed., Longman's Green & Company, New York 1905):

Present value of an annuity = $\dfrac{1}{\dfrac{i}{(1+1)^n-1}} + S$

where,

i = interest rate

n = life of annuity

S = salvage value

The Hoskold method involves the creation of a separate, and usually fictitious, conservatively invested sinking fund to provide for recovery of the investment and then solving for the rate of return on the remaining cash flow. Thus, a portion of the positive cash flow from the project is assumed to be reinvested at a conservative interest rate, with the remainder constituting the return on the investment.

More recently, the classical Hoskold method has been reintroduced into some of the literature of capital investment analysis under the name Explicit Reinvestment Rate of Return Method, which could have the interesting acronym ERROR method. Proponents of its use say it has "the advantage of computational ease when there is a single beginning investment, and there are constant receipts and disbursements each year."

Discounted Cash Flow (DCF) Method

Mineral inventory projects are long-term, and the greatest challenge is maintaining the data quality (R.M. Laramee & D.F. Garson, Mineral Resources Division, Geological Survey of Canada, Ottawa, Ontario, Canada). However, suppose cash flows can be estimated or projected with some degree of certainty. In that case, the DCF is the preferred valuation method that considers a mining plan produced in a technical report (like a Feasibility Study). Without such a study, one has to resort to more crude metrics.

The basic concepts of cash flow and time value are combined to evaluate DCF criteria, such as Net Present Value (NPV), Present Value Ratio, and Rate of Return. "Cash flows are initially estimated on a before-tax basis. Taxation considerations may be introduced to convert before-tax cash flow estimates to an after-tax basis. Tax credits and payments and, thus, the determination of after-tax cash flows, are affected by inflation." ...(Michel L. Bilodeau, Deptt. of Mining and Metallurgical Engg., McGill University, Montreal, Canada)." Such cash flows should then be discounted at an appropriate discount rate (considering the risk factors) to obtain a net present value. However, the determination of the appropriate discount rate for mining properties could well be the subject of rigorous discussion.

Some of the requirements, or inputs, for the valuation of a mining property via the DCF approach, are:

i.   Geology and Mineral Inventory

ii. Mineable Ore Reserves (Mining dilution)

iii. Mining Method

iv. Metallurgy-Research

v.   Metallurgy-Design (metallurgical recovery)

vi. Ancillary Services

vii. Capital Costs

viii. Operating Costs

ix. Marketing

x.   Rights, Ownership

xi. Environmental Impact

xii. Socio-Economic Impact

xiii. Financial Analysis

xiv. Orebody Economics

A simplified example of DCF method is presented for illustration (Table 11.1), wherein the net cash flows for each of the years are discounted to the present at a 10% discount rate. The cumulative net present value is + 9.0. However, at a 15% required rate of return, the project shows a negative (-1.0) present value, meaning that if an investor requires a 15% rate of return, the project is unattractive.

Table 11.1

Year	0	1	2	3	4
Gross Revenue Operating Costs Taxes	0 0 0	70 30 00	75 31 04	75. 37 08	70 33 12
Net Cash Flow	-100	+40	+40	+30	+25
Discount Factor	0 0	1	1	1	1
Decimal Factor		1.10.909	$(1.10)^2$.826	$(1.10)^3$.751	$(1.10)^4$.683
Present Value Cumulative NPV	-100 -100	+36.36 -63.64	+33.04 -30.60	+22.53 -08.07	+17.07 +09.00

However, for those mineral properties at varying stages of exploration where reserves are not yet indicated, it is not worthwhile to use the conventional DCF method. It is difficult to quantify revenue and expenditures properly and to judge the appropriate time for initiation of production at the pre-feasibility stage. Consequently, other methods must be employed to value those exploration properties. Some other methods, sometimes rather subjective, are useful when logically derived and pragmatically applied, with a modicum of luck, by experienced mining professionals. As such, subjective valuations are accepted as being reasonable by industry, the financial community, and regulatory bodies. There will always be some elements of subjectivity (or individual preference) in any valuation.

Summary and Conclusions

Experience and information (i.e., data) regarding the geological parameters (such as ore reserve tonnage and grade), engineering plans for mining and processing methods and the capital and operating costs associated with their application, mineral market forecasts of demand and price conditions, provision of physical and social infrastructure, and government policies related to taxation, stringent environmental controls etc. provide the basis of portraying the value of mining properties. In addition, attention must also be given to important non-quantifiable or 'intangible' factors. Economic evaluation techniques are applied to reduce a complex set of parameters to a relatively few indicators of economic value.

Conclusively, the stage or development of a mine influences the method of valuation and the 'certainly' of the valuation. Though there are many valuation methods, including classical Hoskold's method, the preferred valuation method is the DCF approach in the mining industry if cash flows can be projected with some reasonable degree of certainty.

***

Chapter 13

Some Methods of Real Estate Valuation

Comparable sales Methods, Cost Methods, hypothetical building schemes, and development methods of valuation are important methods of valuation. In this chapter, the author has aptly given a comprehensive overview of the pros and cons of these methods by providing explanatory and illustrative examples.

Cost Approach Method of Valuation

The cost approach of valuation is a method used to estimate the value of an asset or property by calculating the cost to replace it with a new one, minus any depreciation. It is commonly applied in real estate and other physical assets.

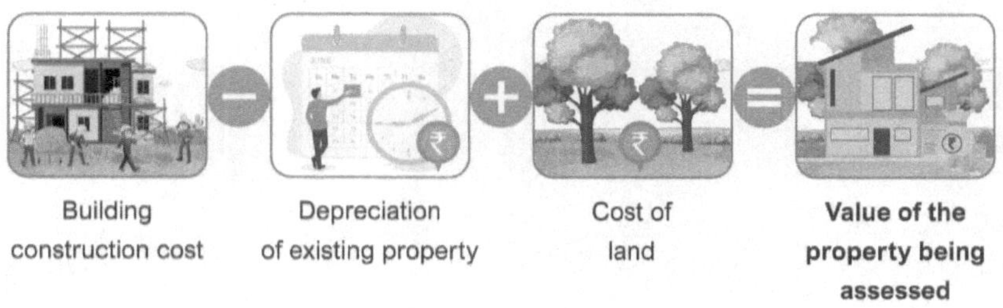

| Building construction cost | Depreciation of existing property | Cost of land | Value of the property being assessed |

Applications:

i.   Real Estate Valuation: For properties like hospitals, schools, or factories with few comparable sales.

ii. Insurance: To estimate the cost of rebuilding or replacing damaged assets.

iii. Machinery and Equipment Valuation: To calculate the current value of machines for resale or financing.

Advantages:

i.   Useful for unique or specialized properties/assets.

ii. Provides a logical and transparent valuation approach.

iii. Accounts for current construction or replacement costs.

Disadvantages:

i.   It may not reflect market value if depreciation is subjective.

ii. Does not consider future income potential (unlike the income approach).

iii. Land value estimation can vary significantly.

iv. This approach is especially relevant when market data or comparable sales are limited.

Comparable Sales Method

The Comparable Sales Method (also known as the Market Approach) is a valuation technique used to estimate the value of an asset, property, or business by comparing it to similar assets that have been recently sold. It is commonly used in real estate, business valuation, and investment analysis.

This method relies on actual sales data of similar assets. It's easy to understand and apply if relevant data is available. It requires a detailed comparison of attributes like size, location, condition, and market conditions.

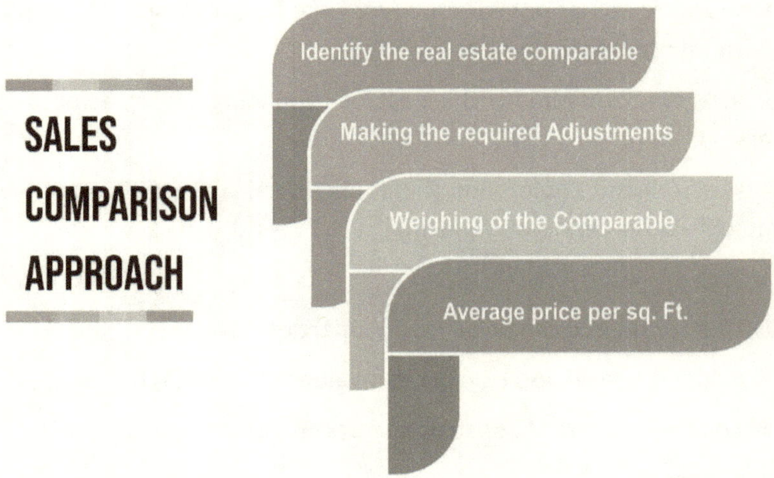

Steps in the Comparable Sales Method:

1. Identify Comparable Assets: Locate recently sold assets similar to those being valued. Ensure the sales are from the same or a comparable market.

2. Analyze the Comparable Data: Assess factors such as price, date of sale, and terms of the sale. Adjust for differences between the comparables and the subject asset (e.g., location, size, or condition).

3. Adjust for Differences: Adjust for variances between the subject asset and comparables. For instance, if a comparable property has a better location, reduce its price for comparison.

4. Calculate the Value: Derive an estimated value by averaging or analyzing the adjusted comparable sales.

SWOT Analysis Related to the Real Estate Valuation

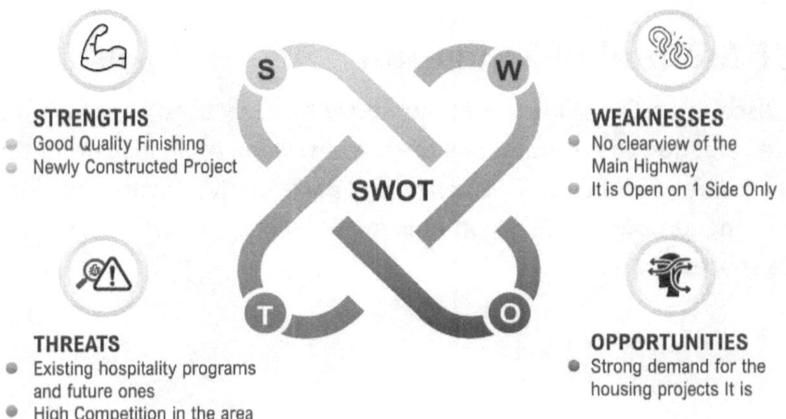

Example:

Suppose a house is being valued, and three similar houses in the neighbourhood were sold recently:

House 1: $300,000 (larger lot)

House 2: $320,000 (similar features)

House 3: $290,000 (needs renovation)

After adjusting for differences, the subject property might be valued at approximately $310,000.

Pros:

1. Reflects Market Trends: Based on actual transactions.

2. Widely Accepted: Frequently used and understood by stakeholders.

3. Data Availability: Easy to access in some markets, especially real estate.

Cons:

1. Requires Recent Comparables: Outdated sales data can distort results.

2. Subjective Adjustments: Adjustments may introduce bias or inaccuracy.

3. Market Volatility: Rapid changes in market conditions may make comparables less relevant.

This method is particularly effective in active markets with ample sales data. However, adjustments may become less reliable in markets with limited comparable sales.

DCF Method of Valuation

The Discounted Cash Flow (DCF) method is a widely used approach for real estate valuation that determines the present value of an investment based on its future cash flows. This method is particularly effective for income-generating properties like commercial buildings, rental apartments, or office spaces.

WHAT IS THE DCF VALUATION USED FOR

- To value a complete business
- To value a project or investment within a company
- To value a bond
- To value shares in a company
- To value an income-producing property
- To value the benefit of a cost-saving initiative
- To value anything that produces cash flow

By definition, the "discount rate" is the interest rate the Federal Reserve charges commercial banks and other financial institutions for short-term loans. The discount rate that is applied at the Fed's lending facility, called the discount window.

Here's how it works step-by-step:

1. Estimate Future Cash Flows: Calculate the expected rental income from the property over the investment period. This includes adjustments for potential vacancies and bad debts. Deduct operating costs, such as maintenance, property management fees, insurance, taxes, and utilities. Calculate the Net Operating Income (NOI): The rental income minus operating expenses.

2. Determine the Holding Period: Decide the time frame for holding the property, typically 5–10 years. This period influences the projected cash flows and terminal value.

3. Forecast the Terminal Value: At the end of the holding period, the property is assumed to be sold. Calculate the terminal value using an appropriate capitalization rate:

4. Select the Discount Rate: The discount rate represents the investor's required rate of return, typically derived from the cost of capital or the weighted average cost of capital (WACC). It accounts for the risk associated with the investment.

5. Calculate the Present Value of Cash Flows: Each year's cash flow and the terminal value are discounted to their present values using the formula:

6. Sum Up the Present Values: Add the present values of all forecasted cash flows and the terminal value to get the total property value.

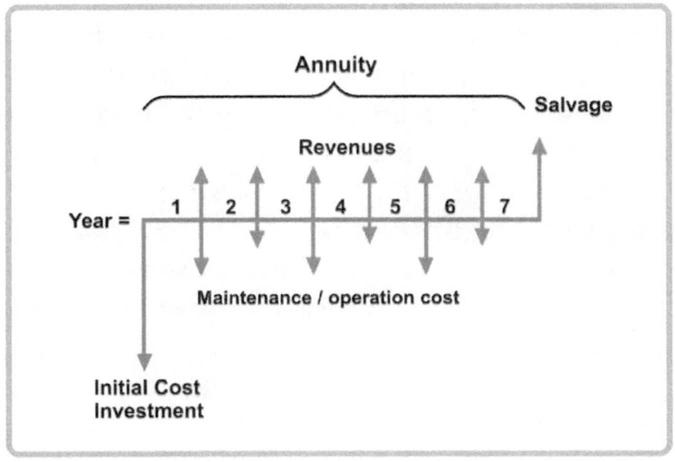

This method is preferred because it accounts for the time value of money, future income potential, and market risks. However, the accuracy depends on the quality of input assumptions, such as rental growth rates, cap rates, and discount rates.

Hypothetical Building Scheme

What would be the value of a building constructed in a commercial area with the potential for future expansion according to the prevailing value of F.S.I. (or F.A.R.) for that area? Would the value be singularly related to its present disposition only? Whether or not this residual F.S.I (or F.A.R.) should justifiably be considered at the time of its valuation. If the answer is affirmative, then how? Though all these appear to be simple questions at their face value, their answer is comprehensively sprawling in hundreds of legal pages of law books and case references, which is not an exaggeration.

The method - which considers the residual potential of land - is known as Land Residual Technique. It is also popularly known as Hypothetical Building Scheme. The jurisdiction of this controversial scheme is not restricted only to the valuation of plots having some construction thereon. A vacant plot can also be considered for its development potential when the development method (or any other method) of valuation - in view of the valuer (or the owner) - does not reflect its true value. In so many ways, it is quite a unique valuation method in itself, unquestionably so.

The very origin or conception of this method is based on the well-defined principle of professional valuation, which states that "the owner is entitled to incorporate in his value assessment the present value of all the future potentialities of his property. In other words, the deferred value of the residual potential for further development of the property in question is also to be accounted for at the time of valuation. In other words, the market value of an asset should be determined not necessarily according to its present disposition but based on the most lucrative and advantageous way in which the owner can pragmatically dispose of it in the open market, either in one singular block or in lots."

Steps of Valuation

Valuation by the method of the Hypothetical Building Scheme (H.B.S.) involves the following general steps:

i.   Comprehensive preparation of a H.B.S. based on factual data. This is the very first and the most important step of this method. Despite the use of the word "Hypothetical" in the method, building schemes should be prepared in exact accordance with the prevailing standards and norms.

ii. Compute the total cost of the scheme, including all direct and indirect costs involved, after its contemplated completion.

iii. Compute the expected net annual return after the scheme's completion (i.e., expected gross annual return - expected gross outgoings).

iv. Compute the capitalized value by capitalizing the expected net annual return using an appropriate capitalization factor.

v.   Find the present value of the expected net annual return using the prevailing rate of interest deferred for the construction period.

vi. Calculate the net present value of the property in question using the following relationship:

Net present value = present value of expected net annual return as calculated in step (v)

Minus

total scheme cost as calculated in step (ii) deferred for half the completion period.

Following the worked-out example will clarify all these valuation steps to perceptive readers.

illustrative Example

Work out the value of 10,000 Sq.m. of land based on the Hypothetical Building Scheme with the base foundation as rent. Following are the given data:

Area of land to be used for recreation purposes   10%

Cost of development of recreation area (per Sq.m)   Rs. 80/-

Area of land to be used for the means of access roads,
and for other ancillaries, etc.   15%

Cost of construction of access roads,
storm water drains, and for other ancillaries (per Sq.m.) Rs. 165/-

Floor Space Index (F.S.I.):   20.00

Balcony and otla area permissible
20%

Carpet area (as a percentage of total construction area)   80%

Rate of capitalization   10.00%

The expected time required for the completion of the scheme   2.5 years

The expected rent after the completion of the scheme   Rs. 60/-
per Sq.m of the carpet area per month

Gross outgoings (municipal and other
taxes, insurance, watch & ward,
maintenance, collection of rent, etc.)   28% of gross rent

Cost of construction of the building, including
all direct and indirect costs (per Sq.m.)

(a) Ground floor (including foundation)   Rs. 3000/-

(b) First floor (66% of G.F. cost)   Rs. 2000/-

(xiii) Architect's/Engineer's fees for architectural
planning, structural designing, and
technical supervision   3.0% of the cost of
construction

Rate of interest   8.50%

(Note: These approximate data have been given in the problem solely for illustration. A valuer is required to explore them all quite comprehensively for their actual values at the time of valuation.)

Solution

(i) Computation of carpet area

Area of land	= 10,000 Sq.m.

Deduct:

Area required for approach roads, recreation facilities, stormwater drains, and other ancillaries etc., (i.e., 25% of the total area of land) = 2,500 Sq.m

Area available for actual construction (Sq.m.) Sq.m. = (10,000 – 2,500)

Permissible F.S.I. =2.00

Therefore, the Permissible floor area = 15,000 sq.m.

Add:

Balcony & otla area

(i.e. 10% of the permissible floor area) = 1,500 Sq.m

Total area   16,500 Sq.m.

Carpet area (80% of the total area) = 0.80 x 16,500 Sq.m

= 13,200 Sq.m

(ii) Computation of capitalized net return

Expected gross return per month after the completion of the scheme = Rs. 60 x 13,200

=Rs. 7,92,000/-

Expected net return (per month) after the completion of the scheme

(i.e., gross return - gross outgoings) =Rs.7,92,000x(1 – 0.28)

= Rs. 5,70,240/-

Net return (per annum)	= 12 x Rs. 5,70,240/-
	= Rs. 68,42,880/-

Capitalised net annual return and hence	
the value of the property after the construction	
is over (@ 10% in perpetuity)	= 10 x Rs. 68,42,880/-
	= Rs. 6,84,28,800/-

Therefore,

Present value of the property, excluding the	
cost of construction	
(deferred @ 8.50% for the period of	
construction i.e., 2.50 years	= SPPWF x Rs. 6,84,28,800/-
	= 0.8155031 x Rs. 6,84,28,800/-
	= Rs. 5,57,71,593/- ...(13.1.1)

Note: Single Payment Present Worth Factor (SPPWF) can directly be calculated from the following formula:

$$\text{SPPWF} = \frac{1}{(1+i)^n]} = 0.8155031$$

where,

i = interest rate (i.e., 0.085), and

n = number of years after which the future payment will be made (i.e., 2.5 years).

(iii) Cost of scheme

Cost of development of recreation area	= Rs. (80x1,000)/-
(@Rs. 80/-per Sq.m.)	= Rs. 80,000/-
Cost of development of access roads,	
stormwater drains, and other ancillaries,	= Rs. (165x 1,500)/-
etc, (@Rs. 165/- per Sq.m.)	= Rs. 2,47,500/-
Cost of construction	

(@ Rs. 3,000/- per Sq.m. for the Ground Floor0	= Rs. (3000 x 7,500)/-
	= Rs. 2,25,00000/-
(@ Rs. 2,000/- per Sq.m. for the First Floor)	= Rs. (2,000 x 7,500)/-
	= Rs. 1,50,00000/-

Total cost of construction

(G.F. Cost + F.F. Cost + Development Cost)   = Rs. 3,78,27,500/-

----

Cost of construction deferred @8.50% for

half the period of construction (i.e., years)

$$= \text{SPPWF x Rs. } 3,78,27,500/-$$

$$= \frac{1}{(1+0.085)^{1.25}} \times \text{Rs. } 3,78,27,500$$

$$= 0.9030521 \times \text{Rs.} 3,78,27,500/-$$

$$= \text{Rs.} 3,41,60,205/- \qquad\qquad ...(13.1.2)$$

(iv) Present value

Present value of land in an undeveloped stage

[i.e. (13.1.1) - (13.1.2)] = Rs. (5,57,71,593-3,41,60,205)/- = + Rs.2,16,11,388/-

Therefore, the value of the land in question is calculated to be Rs. 2,16,11,380/-, using the Hypothetical Building Scheme. In other words, the average land value is Rs. 2161/- per Sq.m. (or Rs. 200.77/- per Sq. Ft.).

Note: If one gets a negative answer at last, it clearly indicates that the property in question has no prospective development potential and that applying the H.B.S. is a complete failure in all such cases. Hence, such properties are to be valued based on their present disposition, using only other valuation methods that the incumbent valuer feels are appropriate.

Whether Such Schemes Are Admissible as Evidence?

Although this method has received approval from the court in several cases, the admissibility of this method in all cases is doubtful. Available case references show that Lord Shaw, Lord Macnaghten, etc., are among the several prominent proponents of the use of this method in the case of building land. In an interesting case, hon'ble Justice Batty aptly observed that:

"The hypothetical method appears to me open to no reproach if the hypothesis is based on inferences from ascertained facts."

...Govt. of Bombay Vs. M.M. Cama, 9, B.L.R. 1232; M.M. Cama Vs. Govt. of Bombay, 16 B.L.R. P.C. 55 Appeal No. 103.

However, the list of strong opponents (in specific cases) is much larger. The admissibility of this method solely depends upon the professional skill of the valuer not only in preparing an appropriate scheme but also in his ability to justify his assumptions before the adversaries.

This method conceptually depends upon a series of assumptions. These assumptions - even when made with honest intentions - grant even to adversaries the possibility of partial truth and oneself the possibility of error. An adamant adversary can always claim that the hypothesis is based on feats of imagination and not on the genuine inference drawn from ascertained facts. An accusing finger of reasonable doubt can always be raised as this method eventually grants abundant liberty to the valuer. Factual information can cleverly be manipulated for the owner's advantage if some "desk-top valuer" (term invoked by Mr. B.K. Sabapathy) maliciously wishes to do so.

i.   As the name suggests, this method solely depends upon a series of hypothetical assumptions. If at all the very first assumption goes wrong, the subsequent ones inevitably go wrong. Anyone can come up with a series of hypothetical assumptions to support his claim, especially in the case of compulsory land acquisition. It was argued in all such cases that the potential value of the property under acquisition was far more than the market value despite instances of the sale of comparable open lands available in the neighborhood.

ii. Expected cost of construction, estimated rents, and probable outgoings are very uncertain in nature. It gives a lot of liberty to the valuer to make manipulative assumptions to arrive at some predetermined pseudo-valuations. Valuations, in other words, can easily be cooked.

iii. Assessed value, using the H.B.S., includes the builder's profit and largely depends upon the skill, available capital, and professional experience of the (hypothetical) builder.

It can, therefore, be concluded that the H.B.S. is a reasonably good method for ascertaining the residual development potential of property if all the other methods fail to represent the true value potential of the property in question. Valuation carried out by this method can also be made admissible as evidence before the Court of Law if practiced judiciously and without any prejudice by the valuer. Comprehensive detailing based on factual inferences is of utmost importance for its success.

Developer's Method of Valuation

The method - which ingeniously considers the development potential of a large piece of land - is known as the Developer's Method of Valuation. Does this method deal with the overall development of a large piece of land by forming the maximum possible number of well-planned smaller plots with the best of the requisite amenities, and that too? t the least possible development expenses. At the time of its valuation, a large vacant plot can always be considered for its development potential when any other valuation method - in view of the valuer (or the owner) - does not reflect its true market potential. In so many ways, it is a unique valuation method in itself, unquestionably so.

The developer's method of valuation may obligatorily or voluntarily be needed for the valuation of larger plots due to the following reasons:

i.   For compulsory land acquisition proceedings.

ii. To evaluate unsecured ground rent.

iii. To advise a developer/builder/speculator on the price of a large undeveloped piece of land.

iv. To advise, on the other hand, a small investor as to the purchase price of developed land.

Need of the Method

A building plot of land of smaller size cannot be compared with a large tract or block of land for several cardinal reasons. Large pieces of land are not to be valued similarly to smaller plots as comparable sales instances are often not available for larger ones.

It is therefore advisable to value large piece of land based on any one of the following methods (not necessarily in that order of preference):

i.   Developer's method of valuation

ii. Hypothetical Building Scheme

iii. Valuation by belting

Valuation by the "method of belting" has already been discussed in Chapter 6 of this book.

How Does the Development Method Differ from the Hypothetical Building Scheme?

It is now an established fact that a large piece of land can not be compared with small lands situated in a similar locality. For several diversified reasons, small lands fetch more value per unit area.

One way of valuing such lands is by using the method of belting. H.B.S. is yet another method used for the valuation of large plots, which can not be valued by the belting method due to some reason. Very large plots can only be valued appropriately by the Developer's method of valuation, though distinct demarcating lines among the jurisdictions of all these methods (in terms of plot area) can neither be easily drawn nor is it the subject of discussion in this chapter.

There may be some confusion between the Developer's method of valuation and the H.B.S. These valuation methods use certain processes and principles, and they develop their ideology to explain reality and justify their existence and sustenance. Once we clearly understand how these processes and principles are interrelated, and how they transform one another, we gain a much clearer understanding of them.

Hypothetical Building Schemes & Developer's Method of Valuation

Despite several differences, there is an unambiguous, striking, and hidden connection between the characteristic attributes of these valuation systems (or techniques).

The following may be cardinal points under which the striking differences and unobtrusive similarities between the Developer's method of valuation and H.B.S. may broadly be categorized:

i. The whole concept of H.B.S. revolves around developing large plots of land by imaginary buildings along with requisite infrastructural facilities such as recreation areas, approach roads, stormwater drains, and other ancillaries. In the Developer's method, on the other hand, the whole valuation exercise is restricted only to carving out small building plots with provisions for necessary infrastructures and approach roads thereon. The developer's method is only associated with the development of a "building site."

ii. The characteristic attribute of the developer's method of valuation enjoys a lesser degree of liberty and, hence, is more justifiable, as compared to that of H.B.S. Developer's method, as such, may be considered a two-dimensional aspect. It is only the abundant degree of liberty associated with the H.B.S. that makes its acceptability a highly controversial affair before the court of law in most cases.

iii. The Developer's method deals with the overall development of a large piece of land by forming the maximum possible number of well-planned smaller plots with the best of the requisite amenities and that too at the least possible development expenses. The jurisdiction of H.B.S. - on the other hand - is not restricted only to the valuation of vacant plots having no construction at all. A plot having some construction thereon can also be considered for its residual building potential when any other valuation method - in view of the valuer (or the owner) - does not reflect its true value.

iv. Both these methods are based on massive evidence (legal & otherwise). However, their admissibility in all the cases is doubtful.

Steps of Valuation

Development potential, in principle, is estimated by first calculating the deferred value of the gross sum capable of realization from the sale of small plots and then deducting therefrom the present worth of the estimated overall cost of development. Valuation by the Developer's method involves the following general steps:

i. Comprehensive preparation of an economical development scheme based on factual data by employing a qualified architect/engineer. This is the very first and the most important step of this method. Development scheme should be prepared to make appropriate provisions for open spaces, etc., In exact accordance with the prevailing standards and norms. On the other hand, leaving open spaces in excess of prevailing norms would reduce the net area available for sale.

ii. Compute the total cost of the development scheme, including all direct and indirect costs involved, after its contemplated completion. Direct & indirect development costs would include the following:

(a) Cost of recreation area development,

(b) Earthwork (cutting and/or filling),

(c) Means of access,

(d) Power sub-station and street light,

(e) Provision of stormwater drains,

(f) Municipal taxes on open plots, etc.

(g) Architect's or engineer's fees, legal charges, brokerage, stamps, advertisement, management and office expenses, etc.

(h) Developer's profit (including interest on blocked-up capital).

iii. Compute the expected cumulative sale value (gross) of all the small plots so developed after the completion of the development scheme.

iv. Calculation of the present worth of the expected sale value using the prevailing interest rate deferred for half the period of the sale of the last plot.

v.   Calculation of the net present value of the undeveloped property in question using the following relationship:

Net present value of the undeveloped property = present value of expected sale value as calculated in step (iv)

Minus

the total cost of the development scheme (as calculated in step (ii) deferred for half the completion period.

The following example would make these steps very clear to the perceptive readers.

Illustration

What would be the value of a large plot admeasuring 40,000 Sq.m if the plot is to be valued by the Developer's Method of Valuation based on the following data:

Available Data

(i) Area of land for recreation purposes, means of access, storm-water drains,

power sub-station (if needed), and for other ancillaries
15% of the plot area

(ii) The average price of small plots in the locality   Rs.   875/- per Sq.m.

(iii) Expected period of land development   1.50 Years

(iv) Architect's and/or engineers' fee   3% of the cost of development work

(v) Development cost on the effective area

available for sale   Rs. 92/- per sq. m.

(vi) Legal charges, brokerage, registration, stamps, etc.   8%

(vii) Developer's profit (including the risk and

also the interest on blocked-up capital)   15%

Valuation

The total area of land to be developed	40,000 sq. m.

Deduct

Area of land needed for recreational purposes,

means of access, power sub-station, and

other essential amenities @ 25% of the

total land area (Approx.)	10,000 Sq.m.
Net available area for sale	30,000 Sq.m

This area of 30,000 Sq.m. will fetch an average price of Rs. 875/- per Sq.m. or Rs. 2,62,50,000/-. All the plots so developed will not be sold simultaneously even after offering an attractive brokerage to the local real estate brokers. The total time period required to sell all the plots would largely depend upon the prevailing market conditions. Assuming that the last plot will be sold after 3.50 years from the date of purchase:

$$SPPWF = \frac{1}{(1+i)^n]}$$

or

$$SPPWF = \frac{1}{(1+0.09)^{1.75}]}$$

i.e.,

$$SPPWF = 0.8600$$

and

present value of Rs. 2,62,50,000/- for

the average period of 1.75 years at 9%	Rs. 2,62,50,000/- x SPPWF
or,	Rs. 2,62,50,000/- x 0.8600
i.e.,	Rs. 2,25,75,269/-

Deduct

Cost of development of recreation area,

means of access, power sub-station, etc., at

the rate of Rs. 92/- per Sq.m. of effective

area of 30,000 Sq.m.   Rs. 27,60,000/-

If the overall development period is taken
as 1.50 years (approx.), this amount will
not be paid in full right at the time of commencement, but will be paid in instalments.
Hence, the present value of Rs. 27,60,000/-
deferred for the period of 0.75 year
(being the average period) @ 9%   Rs. 27,60,000/-x SPPWF

                                                 Rs. 27,60,000/- x 0.93741

                                                 Rs. 25,87,254.80/-

Where; SPPWF (Single Payment Present Worth Factor) can be calculated as
follows:

$$SPPWF = \frac{1}{(1+0.09)^{0.75]}}$$

   i.e.,

$$SPPWF = 0.93741$$

Architect's or engineer's fees at 3% of Rs. 27,60,000/-   Rs. 82,800/-

Legal charges, brokerage, stamps, advertisement,
etc. @ 8% of Rs. 2,25,75,269/-   Rs. 18,06,021,50/-

Developer's or investor's profit at 15%
of Rs. 2,25,75,269/-   Rs. 33,86,290.40/-

                                                         Rs. 78,62,366.70/-

----

Therefore,

   value of plot in an undeveloped stage Rs. 2,25,75,269.0/-

   Less Rs. 78,62,366.70/-

   Rs. 1,47,12,902.30/-

The market value of the undeveloped plot in question, therefore, has been worked out to be Rs. 1,47,12,902.30/- or Rs. 367.82/- per Sq.m. Developer's profit in the above illustrative example has been assumed to be 15%. It may, however, vary from as low as 10% to as high as 25% of deferred sale proceeds. A reasonable idea would be to limit it between 15% to 20%, as 10% would be too low and 25% would be too high. These extreme values can nevertheless be adopted in special cases if an acceptable justification can be given for the same. It should also be noted that the Flat Rate Technique is nothing but an offshoot of the Developer's Valuation Method.

Flat Rate Technique For The Valuation of Large Lands

Flat Rate Technique - as applied for the valuation of large plots - is not an ingenious method of its own but can merely be described as an offshoot of Developer's Method. There is an unambiguous, striking, and hidden connection between these two. A characteristic attribute of this system (or technique) of valuation as well, very similar to the Developer's Method, allows comparables of small plots to be adopted for evaluating larger plots when the sale instances of comparable large-sized plots - as reference "benchmarks" - are not available for the valuer. Flat Rate Technique can also serve as a check on the Developer's Method of Valuation as both of them have the shared objective, i.e., to evaluate large lands based on instances of large plots after making necessary deductions for requisite infrastructure.

However, comparables of small-sized plots, as they are, can not directly form the real base of valuation of large plots unless they are suitably adjusted by applying the appropriate Reduction Factor - for the area of land needed for infra-structural development, cost of infra-structures (such as approach roads, stormwater drains, power sub-station, playgrounds, gardens, etc.), and for other relevant reductions (as appropriate) including that of the discounting of future payment receipts (using an appropriate discounting factor, of course).

As will soon become apparent, this method is based on massive evidence (legal and otherwise) and on what might be called a semi-systematic model of the Developer's Method. It is - if one wishes to express it in the most literal sense - a simplified, generalized, and compressed version of the Developer's method. The only difference between these two methods is that in the case of the Developer's Method, the cost of each and every item of infrastructure is estimated, and allowances are made for other relevant factors, which are deducted from the sale value of small plots. In the case of the flat rate technique, appropriate flat-rate deductions are made to account for two factors, namely the area of land needed for infrastructural development and its deferred cost.

Illustration

As the name suggests, the flat rate technique applies the flat rate to the whole land in question. The basic ideology behind this method (or technique) can easily be explained to the perceptive viewers by the following typical illustration:

i.   Area of land under valuation = 30,000 Sq.m

ii.   Comparable sale instances are available for the value of small plots situated in the = Rs. 2,000/- per Sq.m. in the same locality. Hence,

Value of land = 30,000 x Rs. 2000/- x Reduction Factor

If the overall value of the Reduction Factor (R.F) is taken as 0.30 for this particular case, then,

Value of land = Rs. 1,80,00,000/-

As has already been stated heretofore, the flat-rate deductions are made to account for two factors, namely;

i.   area of land needed for infrastructural development, and

ii.   its deferred cost.

In some cases, therefore, Reduction Factors can be applied separately for these two aspects. For example, an R.F. of 0.10 can be applied in the above illustration for the land needed for infrastructural development. To account for the cost of infrastructural facilities to be provided, an R.F. of 0.20 (or any other value as deemed fit by the valuer as per the prevailing conditions) will have to be applied.

Legal Admissibility of Flat Rate Technique

Several questions would pragmatically crop up in the minds of inquisitive readers in the context of the Flat Rate Technique. Can the value of adjacent and similar small plots be applied to the land covering a large extent?... and how? What would be the legal admissibility of this method before the court of law?... and so on. There are several instances when Hon'ble judges have explored this situation from a proper perspective and expressed their wise views thereafter to set illuminating guidelines for this particular context. In the case of Bombay, improvement for this particular context. In the case of Bombay Improvement Trust Vs. Merwanji (A.I.R. 1926 Bombay 420), it was observed that...

"... method of valuing land wholesale from retail price is to take anything between one half and one third, according to the circumstances of the expected cross valuation as the wholesale price."

However, to use this tool (or technique) quite effectively, one must be able to adopt an appropriate value of R. F. since this method's success (or failure) solely depends upon the selection of the same depending upon the prevailing conditions. Although no dearth of legal references is available in this context for guidance, selecting an appropriate R.F. would starkly be a matter of profound professional judgment on the part of the valuer.

***

Chapter 14

Failure of Valuations - Causes & Remedies

Valuations of immovable/movable properties provide information to several financial decisions (such as sale/purchase/mortgage/renting/ lease taxation/partition etc.) based thereupon. As such, a good valuation must quintessentially be a fairly accurate reflection of reality. Any value assessment that considerably deviates from the actual value beyond the reasonable tolerance limits is proverbially labelled bad valuation. In this chapter, routine raisons d'etre that might contribute to such frivolous value deviations are identified and examined, their economic consequences are considered, and recommendations are made as to how this common problem might significantly be minimized. A prescriptive argument is made for the early development of a consummately realistic valuation system so that more accurate valuations may be made and subsequent financial uncertainties - commonly manifested by such deviations - may be avoided or at least minimized to the point of utmost triviality.

This chapter has been written to open up a debate among professional valuers toward developing a conceptual framework of a justifiably balanced, fair, accurate, credible, and unambiguous valuation approach.

Introduction

The characteristic attribute of a competent professional valuer is his functional ability to synthesize/operate upon subjective valuation systems to assess values objectively by judiciously transforming observable information, visual events, and intangible intuitions/sensing into some interactive and (monetary-wise) quantifiable value parameters. This ability distinguishes him distinctly from - scientists who methodically pursue themselves in making the natural phenomena explicable, painters who consummate spectral abstracts on stretched canvas for aesthetic enrichment, virtuosi who create works of fine arts, writers who explore reality for literary enhancement, and commonplace individuals (proverbially known as men on streets) who utilize the output of both art and science for their functional and spiritual needs.

Valuers use scientific methods and tools for analysis but are not scientists; they are concerned with economic evaluation but are not economists; they utilize cash-flow diagrams but are not accountants. In professional practice, valuation dovetails the rigorous endeavour of scientific inquiry with the visual, intuitive, and personal attributes of an innately creative artist (not as a source and sequel, but as complementary parts of a much larger whole), thus bringing together valuation devices and systems which are functional, efficient, reliable as well as logically befitting within the time-established framework of mandatory, discretionary and obligatory valuation rules and axioms.

With the passage of time, early human species learned the art of transaction (barter) by mutually exchanging their could-be-spared and should-be-spared commodities in accordance with their adjudged values in terms of strength, quality, ease of availability (or scarcity), etc. - all basic valuation concepts albeit they did not formally have any scientific training for the quantification of the same. Primitive intuitive solutions were first discovered for their tribal exchange-rate quantification requirements and later improvised to keep pace with fast-growing societal needs. Most of these activities would today be classified as valuation, and some would be considered highly innovative vintage work. Although neither an exact science (Viscount Simon) nor an absolute art (Byrlic Abbin), valuation is indisputably practiced by every individual in his day-to-day life, sparing only those who have solitarily retired in the snow-laden solitude of Himalayan caves, for the singular purpose of spiritual enlightenment of their souls.

Valuations provide similar information to some decisions, such as estimating or financial accounting information, to others. Financial statements -which are prepared on the basis of historical data - are required to comply with generally accepted accounting principles (GAAP) described in accounting literature to ensure that the information they provide is accurate and useful for decisions. Selecting estimating and accounting methods is as much an art as a science, to meet practical situations of reality.

Though valuation and estimating have strong similarities, they are basically different. To estimate is to produce a systematically documented statement of the approximate quantity of material, time, or cost required to perform the construction/erection/renovation of a contemplated facility within a stipulated duration using certain given specifications. As such, estimating is fundamentally futuristic, projecting probabilistic financial activity over the future depending primarily upon the "Scope -definition" of the project. Though there are some applications of estimating to valuation, some estimating principles have no such application to valuation, and others conflict directly with good valuation practice.

No abstract mathematical model can possibly be simulated for its universal acceptance in the field of valuation. Value is an oscillating function of human conduct and idealists do not accept the possibility of developing a set of universal laws that can explain and predict human conduct because the very act of obtaining data is dependent on who the data gatherer is. According to this philosophy, it is impossible to separate facts from values. It is worthwhile to note here that all the legislative/taxing statutes and other factors which, either directly or indirectly, affect "value" in one way or the other are nothing but the manifestations of human conduct at large. As the reliability of valuation is identified with the state of knowledge, a difficult question is frequently raised about whether the "discipline of definitive valuation" should be considered an art or a science.

Valuation is thought of an art most often a proverbial bad valuation has been made. This label implies a system employing a whole range of approximations as a surrogate of (or substitute for) missing information, which tends to produce errors and inaccuracies (discreet and/or cumulative) by forcing the incumbent valuer to perform valuation by making a series of guesses, which are usually informed extrapolations based upon whatever relevant information he has at that time. Often, bad valuations result, although the valuer followed the procedure with a minimally prejudiced description of what was known to him and being maximally vague about what was not.

Had he tried to "guess-valuate," he probably, with a modicum of luck, could have come much closer. Very likely tough, he had no justifiable reason to embark on such "blue-sky" speculation. Valuers are pragmatic, logical, sensible, and systematic and believe people are rational. Their decisions are predictable and reasonable, and in the decisions, the outcome matters and not the individual act. While these are necessary and useful attributes for solving valuation problems, human and societal responses are often irrational, emotional, and unsystematic. Valuers are often irrational, emotional, and unsystematic. Valuers are thus often frustrated when their logical approach does not result in an acceptable resolution of value-laden problems.

Why Valuations Fail?

Though valuations fail frequently, a dearth of literature exists on this common phenomenon. Value assessment deviates come in various packages, rather rarely arising from a single isolated fact but usually from juxtapositions or combinations of several.

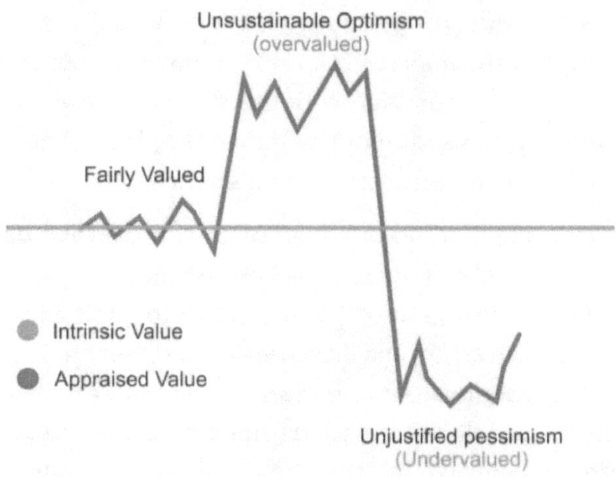

The raisons d'etre as to why valuations fail can be listed as hereunder:

Poor Efforts

Any valuation may stumble due to the poor efforts made by the incumbent valuer. Such a result may come about because the valuer is professionally inexperienced or inept in his field. Also, the inadequacy of monetary remuneration, a prime motivating force for a professional valuer, may not only lessen his interest in the profession but also compel him to cut short his otherwise would-be whole-hearted efforts toward a reliable value assessment. Good valuation practices using the defense of adopted rates and adequate remuneration will minimize this source of bad valuations to the point of utmost triviality.

Cooked/Pseudo Valuations

On even rare occasions, a valuation might get unrighteously "cooked" to favor a potential client or to seduce a donor/funding agency or taxing authority, which might seem to be an exceptional deal from the viewpoint of the associated individuals. The professional valuers, though, would not be involved in such chicanery.

Use of Unreal Data

Anyone can come up with a set of numbers/data. A challenge to the professional valuer is to produce a valuation that is an accurate reflection of reality. This is first a question of professional experience, and second a matter of relevant historical data. All too often, a valuer uses numbers/data that are handy or from a source that would seem to release the valuer from his personal, professional responsibility, safeguarding him thereby against his so-called professional indemnity. This may be data from past experience or published in government (or otherwise) guides. Using such data without knowing its similarity to the job at hand may produce an inaccurate valuation report. For example, broad guideline values of lands as issued by the Registrar of Deeds may not truly represent the actual value of the land in question. It is particularly important that the valuer not select information simply for its convenient availability or apparent objectivity.

The availability of requisite stochastic data for the reliability analysis of valuation systems, at least in the context of real estate, is questionable.

Lack of Academic Training

Valuation, quite ironically, is not considered a basic ingredient of the formal educational process, and even the students of civil engineering/ architecture are not sufficiently exposed to the concepts of valuation, although they are given a fair dose of basic sciences right from the primary stage. Valuation, unlike other conventional professions, is a different and comprehensive field as it creates many variations from one case to another depending upon the context of that particular case. Still, quite ironically, it has produced very few wholesome personalities whose life and work could be regarded as worthy of emulation.

Lack of GAVP

No die has yet been cast as available valuation literature does not provide generally accepted valuation principles (GAVP) against which valuation practice can adequately be judged, though the literature's primary focus is on valuation formats, procedures, and processes for particular applications thereof. It gives little attention towards establishing a fundamental base or foundation to valuation decisions so that the formats, procedures, and processes will satisfactorily provide properly documented valuation - reports that are fairly accurate and useful for financial decisions to be taken thereupon as several among these decisions are far from being merely useful - they are crucial.

Furthermore, proper documentation implies a systematic and not necessarily a cosmetic presentation. The lack of GAVP leaves a particular void in teaching valuation, whether in academia or professional practice. Professional valuers need to understand its fundamentals in the same manner that engineers in design need to understand design fundamentals.

Lack of Information

Today's valuation system has leaped to higher stages of differentiation and complexity than the old one and needs more information and other resources to sustain itself. However, as new materials, products, and technologies are constantly entering the market, keeping oneself abreast of all these changes, including those of relevant legal and taxing statutes, is difficult.

Sometimes, it may also be difficult to transform observable information, visual events, and intangible sensing into some interactive and quantifiable value parameter (monetary wise).

Attitudes & Misconceptions

Attitudes are susceptible to roadblocks and play a vital part in our decision-making process by supporting the continuation of existing habits. The most comprehensive description of attitude is that "They are a set of motivations, emotions, and perceptions held by a person about the world" (Benjamin, 1986), which are formed by complex processes. Attitudes can also make us obsolete.

Engineers and architects, in general, are creatures of habit and attitude just like other individuals, and their instinct is to take the first convenient solution that comes to mind, develop it, put it into the design, and cast it in concrete. Attitudes are difficult to deal with and even more difficult to change. Imagine, for instance, being the inventor of a new construction method and then having to overcome people's attitudes when they viciously attack your new idea. For example, when patents were taken out for the steel-frame skyscrapers in 1988, the "Architectural News" predicted that the expansion of iron would crack all the plaster, and all that would be left would be a shell. We all know that the idea worked remarkably well and revolutionized the construction industry.

It would not be inconsequential here to point out that an issue is an issue in the real world. It is often labeled engineering, economic, valuation, social, or legal, depending upon an individual's discipline, experience, and ways and means of approaching it. Valuers, often due to their disciplinary orientation, expertise, and past experiences, may tend to concentrate on specific issues at the cost of other issues that may be of similar importance.

You have heard the expression, "Twenty years of experience tells me my valuation is reliable." How often is that one year of experience multiplied twenty times? All have honest misconceptions and valuers are no exceptions. As such, misconceptions can alienate the valuers from reality. Experience sometimes gives us an honest misconception because we were not exposed to subsequent development that would change the truth we believe from our earlier experience. Our best efforts can end up being incorrect. We have to judge the facts while deciding whether to "stick to our conviction or be convicted by our stickiness," says R. Waldo Emerson.

Human Errors & Negligence

Evaluation and prediction of human error is the most perplexing, pervasive, and evasive problem. System reliability cannot be assessed by consideration of hardware alone. An ability has been developed to quantitatively evaluate hardware deviations (and probably apply control and correction thereto). Still, developing a similar capability relative to the human component has lagged.

"… a valuer is liable for negligence," says Er. J.P. Shrivastava (1993). Therefore, his expert opinion on value matters may or may not be accepted by the concerned authorities as its reliability can be questioned based on suspected negligence.

Intangible Assets

As mentioned in Chapter 2, valuation is the measurement of wealth (or the wealth-producing capacity of an asset). Hence, both are related to each other in some way or another. Efficient use of productive factors ushers the growth process of a wealth-producing organization, undoubtedly so. Today, a revolutionary new economy is arising on the horizons based on knowledge, rather than conventional factors of wealth-production.

Given the appropriate data, information, and/or knowledge, reducing all the other inputs used to create wealth is possible. The right knowledge inputs can reduce labour requirements, cut inventory, save energy and raw materials, and reduce the time, space, and money needed for wealth production. All these savings will have positive reflections on the cash flows. What makes the Third Wave economy truly revolutionary is that while land, labor, raw materials, and perhaps even capital can be regarded as finite resources, knowledge is inexhaustible for all intents.

Unlike a single blast furnace or assembly line, knowledge can be used by two companies simultaneously. And they can still use it to generate more knowledge. Conventional economists and accountants still have trouble with this idea because it is hard to quantify. Still, knowledge is now the most versatile and most important of all the factors of production, whether it can quantitatively be measured or not.

The real values of giant companies like Microsoft or IBM, Sony or Intel, depend more on the ideas, insights, and information in the heads of their employees and in the data banks and patents these companies control than on the trucks, assembly units, and other physical assets they may own. Thus, capital itself is now increasingly based on intangibles.

Catastrophic Changes

In some cases, valuers are expected to find out the futuristic value of a property after the expiry of a stipulated lease period. Although an honest attempt is made to do so, catastrophic changes may negate such projected values. All such projections are made based on past data, assuming that the prevailing trend would continue indefinitely. Prediction of a futuristic event that may dramatically disturb the trend is beyond the capability of an ordinary human being unless he has developed what is known as the sixth sense as well.

Miscellaneous

Lack of time, professional expertise, and requisite knowledge on the part of valuer, measurement errors, catastrophic changes in the operating environment, and perplexing parlance of legal and taxing statutes may also contribute to the development of bad valuations.

Although having received much lip service and earsplitting clamor in the present decade, reliability monitoring has paradoxically been a neglected subject. Still, it must play a more important role in the future if the valuation of complex systems is to be improved. It is identified with a state of knowledge and not with a state of things. In other words, it is not an objective to succeed, valuers should maintain certainty with a minimally prejudiced description of what is known and being maximally vague about what is incognito. The degree of certainty (or uncertainty) is related to the quantum of information available to the valuer. The specialized knowledge of each and all of the interrelated components in a valuation system gives a descriptive picture, which is purely qualitative of the word "reliability."

The movement to quantify reliability is a twentieth-century phenomenon, and the reason thereof is the proliferation of more complex systems with their worldwide impact on each and every aspect of life. The field of valuation is no exception. The reliability of a valuation system depends on numerous external uncontrollable variables, which may be continuous or discrete, fixed or probabilistic, accurately known or assigned values only by guess. Valuers seldom have complete information, i.e., all relevant facts, and hence, cannot be sure of the conclusions arrived at.

Probability is a substitute for certainty, thereby the starting point for the quantitative reliability analysis. While the visible results of the prediction procedure is to quantify the reliability numbers, the prediction process is often equally important. This is so because prediction cannot be made without acquiring rather detailed information, which, in turn, often gives the valuer new knowledge previously unavailable to him. Even if he cannot secure the information needed therein, this inability nevertheless identifies for him the expanse of ignorance in which he is forced to work.

Down Valuations of Assets

Down valuation, also called undervaluation of assets, refers to assessing the value of assets at a level lower than their fair market value. This can occur intentionally or unintentionally and has several implications:

1. Financial Reporting: Companies may undervalue assets on their balance sheets to reduce tax liabilities or create hidden reserves. This practice, however, can mislead investors about the company's true financial health.

2. Investment Opportunities: Investors might seek out undervalued assets as potential investment opportunities. They believe that the market will eventually recognize the true value of the assets, leading to significant returns.

3. Tax Implications: Undervaluing assets can reduce property taxes or other taxes based on asset value. However, it can also lead to legal consequences if discovered by tax authorities.

4. Mergers and Acquisitions: Undervaluation can be a strategy to acquire assets at a lower cost in the context of mergers and acquisitions. This might involve underreporting the value of assets during negotiations.

5. Impact on Shareholders: For publicly traded companies, undervaluation of assets can affect stock prices and shareholder value. If investors believe the company's assets are worth more than reported, it can influence their investment decisions.

6. Legal and Regulatory Issues: Intentional undervaluation of assets can lead to legal issues, including charges of fraud or manipulation. Companies must adhere to accounting standards and regulations to ensure accurate asset valuation.

While undervaluation might offer short-term benefits, it can have long-term negative consequences, including loss of credibility, legal penalties, and financial instability.

Following are the two classical cases of down valuations:

Case I: Google

Google founders Larry Page and Sergey Brin approached Excite CEO George Bell in 1999, to sell their search engine at $1 million. After rejecting the initial offering, the pair dropped to $750,000, but Bell still rejected it. Today, Google is valued at around $498 billion.

Case II: United Kingdom

There was an interesting piece of news on BBC in July 2018. There has been a "significant" rise in homes valued less by the mortgagee than buyers have agreed to pay.

Emoov, one of the UK's largest digital estate agents, said one in five of its sales resulted in a down valuation. Such down valuations by lenders forced buyers to pay thousands of pounds extra upfront to avoid the sale collapsing.

Why did it happen? Valuers - who carry out the property valuations for the mortgage providers - "simply cover their backs" when they anticipate a downward trend in the real estate market.

Overall, a down valuation is just as negligent as an overvaluation. All fellow professionals should conduct a thorough analysis to avoid down valuations so that prospective buyers can negotiate better loan terms and seek other advantages.

Overvaluation of Assets: Some Interesting Case Studies

Despite all said and done in the books of ethical standards to be observed by professional valuers, deliberate overvaluation is a stark reality. Following are some examples of over-valuations:

Case I: Enron

The Enron Corporation was an American energy company based in Houston, Texas. When news of widespread fraud within the company became public in October 2001, the company declared bankruptcy.

As per the Fair Accounting Standards Board (FASB), Fair-Value Measurements, of companies should be determined by reference to the following:

1. Market prices on the same assets (Level 1)

2. Market prices of similar assets (Level 2) and,

3. Where these prices are not available or appropriate, present value and other internally generated estimated values (Level 3).

Enron extensively used Level 3 estimates and, in some instances, Level 2 estimates, for its external and internal reporting.

Enron's accountants used accounting devices to report cash flow to cover up fair-value overstatements of projects undertaken.

Enron's use of fair-value accounting is substantially responsible for its demise. Unrealized discounted future profits from the contracts won were inflated in the present profits in accounting books.

Though it was largely an accounting fraud, it also involved an overvaluation component. Enron confessed that the value of its assets might have been overstated by as much as $24 billion. Those who want to know how Enron did it are advised to read the book "POWER FAILURE: The Inside Story of The Collapse of ENRON" by Mimi Schwartz and Sheron Watkins.

Case II: Trump Tower

One such overvaluation was the 10,966-square-foot Trump Tower apartment triplex where Trump lived for decades. Between 2012 and 2016, the ruling said Trump submitted statements falsely claiming the triplex was 30,000 square feet, which resulted in an overvaluation of between $114 million and 207 million dollars for the benefit of negotiating better loan terms. Engoron, the judge, wrote that the defendants suggested the square footage calculation was subjective. "Well yes, perhaps, if the area is rounded or oddly shaped, it is possible measurements of square footage could come to slightly differing results due to user error," he wrote. However, the judge continued, a "discrepancy of this order of magnitude, by a real estate developer sizing up his own living space of decades, can only be considered fraud."

Case III: Waste Management

Waste Management Inc., the Houston-based publicly traded company, allegedly reported a whopping $1.7 billion in false earnings, falsely increasing the depreciation length for their property, plant, and equipment on the balance sheets.

Case IV: HDIL

At one point, Hindustan Development & Infrastructure Limited (HDIL) was India's third-largest real estate company. To seek more loans it deserved, they got their 7 properties overvalued between 2012 and 2015 by two valuers.

These overvalued properties were mortgaged to Punjab and Maharashtra Co-operative Bank to secure loans. The total scam was to the tune of INR 66,700 million. The bank collapsed, and many went to jail.

Case V: WorldCom

WorldCom was the USA's second-largest long-distance telephone company. The fraud was uncovered in June 2002 when the company's internal audit unit led by unit vice president Cynthia Cooper discovered fraudulent entries. Eventually, WorldCom was forced to admit that it had overstated its assets by over $11 billion. About a year later, the company went bankrupt.

In all the above examples of over-valuations, it is evident that unfair practices in professional valuers never pay. They are eventually exposed. All fellow professionals should abstain from such practices and keep their hands clean. Overreliance on financial data may sometimes lend a valuer in trouble.

Summary And Conclusions

As often as not, valuations proverbially fail due to one reason or the involuntary combination of several possible reasons, as discussed heretofore. For a fairly definitive valuation, an even greater amount of professional indemnity must be developed within the system. The adoption of unreal data by the valuers is highly deplorable. Neglect of formal valuation training in university curricula, especially for engineers/architects, demonstrates gullibility beyond belief.

***

References

1. Anantharajan, T.; "Trade-off Games in Planning for Residential Areas," International Journal for Housing Science and its Applications, Vol. 2, 1984, pp. 197-208.

2. Balaguruswamy, E.; "Reliability Engineering," Tata McGraw Hill Publishing Company Limited, New Delhi.

3. Biswas, A.K.; "Monitoring and Evaluation of Irrigation Projects," Journal of Irrigation & Drainage Engg. (ASCE), Vol. 116, No. 2, March/April, 1990.

4. Das, P.L.; "Valuation of Prospective Ownership Apartments at Premises in Ballygunge Gardens, Calcutta," (J.) Indian Valuer, January, 1993.

5. Davda, P.K.; "Factors Contributing to Indirect Cost of Residential Flats at Bombay," (J.) Indian Valuer, April, 1992.

6. DeGramo, E.P.; Sullivan, W.G.; Cansada, J. R.; "Engineering Economy," Macmillan Publishing Company, New York, 1984.

7. Draper, N.R. & Smith, H.; "Applied Regression Analysis," 2nd Edition, John Wiley & Sons, New York, 1981.

8. Ganguly, S.K. (Guide); "To Develop Software for Depreciation Cost & Replacement Model," B.E. Thesis by Y.M. Tidke et al. submitted to Nagpur University, 1993.

9. Garden F.C.; "Enough Scope Yields Better Estimates," Journal of Construction Engg. & Management (ASCE), Vol. 113, No. 2, June, 1987.

10. Grant, E.L.; Ireson, W.G.; Leavenworth, R.S.; "Principles of Engineering Economy," John Wiley & Sons, New York, 1982.

11. Grewal, B.S.; "Higher Engineering Mathematics," Khanna Publishers, 1993.

12. Income Tax Act - 1961.

13. IS: 3861-1975 (First Revision), "Method of Measurement of Plinth, Carpet & Rentable Areas of Buildings."

14. Jag Mohan; "Mortgage: What it Means to a Valuer," (J.) Indian Valuer, Vol. XXVIII, No. 8, August, 1996.

15. Khanna, I.; "Demolition Derby," Business India, December 21 (1992) -January 2 (1993).

16. Mittal, M.P.; "Effect on Valuation of Size of Land in Acquisition," Proceedings for Compensation Purposes," (J.) Indian Valuer, Vol. XXIV, February, 1992.

17. Modi, M.G.; "Approach to Valuation of Land, Building, and Plant & Machinery,"(J.) Indian Valuer, Vol. XXVI, Dec., 1994.

18. Mukherji, P.K.; "Valuation of Plant & Machinery with the help of Mathematical Model and its Extensions," Proc. National Seminar on the Valuation of Movable/Immovable Assets and Annual Convention of the Institution of Valuers, Lucknow, Dec. 1993.

19. Nain Ashok; "Professional Valuation Practice," Tata Mc-Graw Hill Publishing Company Limited, New Delhi.

20. Namavati, R.H.; "Professional Practice (Estimating & Valuation)," Lakhani Book Depot, Bombay, 1988.

21. Namavati, R.H. "Theory and Practice of Valuation," Lakhani Book Depot, Girgaum, Bombay, 1991.

22. Namavati, R.H.; "Valuation Relating to Standard Rent."

23. Namavati, R.H.; "Valuation in Court," Lakhani Book Depot, Bombay.

24. Nowlay, K.B.; "Valuation for Mortgage of Real Properties," Proc National Seminar on the Valuation of Movable/Immovable Assets and Annual Convention of the Institution of Valuers, Jaipur, Dec., 1995.

25. Rangwala, S.C.; "Valuation of Real Properties," Charotar Publishing House, Anand (Gujarat), 1984.

26. Rathore, S.S.; "Format of Questionnaire for the Valuation of Agricultural Lands," (J.) Indian Valuer, Vol. XXIII, April, 1991.

27. Rathore, S.S. (Guide); "Valuation of Immovable Properties," B.E. Thesis Submitted by A.K. Vidyarthi et al. to the Nagpur University, 1991.

28. Rathore, S.S.; "Complexities Involved in the Valuation of Agricultural Lands," Proc. National Seminar on the Valuation of Movable/Immovable Assets and Annual Convention of the Institution of Valuers, Goa, Dec. 1992.

29. **Rathore, S.S.; "Valuation of an Orange Farm in Malegaon (M.S.)," (J.) Indian Valuer, Vol. XXV, May, 1993. For this paper, the Author received a "Silver Medal" from the Hon'ble Governor of U.P. in the Ravindrayalaya Auditorium (Lucknow) on 28.12.1993 for the best paper of the year 1993 (Category II).**

30. Rathore, S.S.; "Value of Agricultural Lands in India - Changing Scenario," Proc. National Seminar on the Valuation of Movable/Immovable Assets and Annual Convention of the Institution of Valuers, Lucknow, Dec. 1993.

31. Rathore S.S.; "Valuation of Ownership Apartments," Proc. National Seminar on the Valuation of Movable/Immovable Assets and Annual Convention of the Institution of Valuers, Lucknow, Dec. 1993.

32. Rathore, S.S.; "Value Engineering in Construction Industry - Growing Concern," Proc. National Seminar on the Valuation of Movable/Immovable Assets, and Annual Convention of the Institution of Valuers, Lucknow, Dec. 1993.

33. Rathore, S.S.; "Commercial Land Use and Land Values," Proc. National Seminar on the Valuation of Movable/Immovable Assets and Annual Convention of the Institution of Valuers, Lucknow, Dec. 1993.

34. Rathore, S.S.; "Reliability Monitoring of Valuation Systems," Proc. National Seminar on the Valuation of Movable/Immovable Assets and Annual Convention of the Institution of Valuers, Lucknow, Dec. 1993.

35. Rathore, S.S.; "Philosophy of Value," Proc. National Seminar on the Valuation of Movable/Immovable Assets and Annual Convention of the Institution of Valuers, Jaipur, Dec. 1995.

36. Rathore, S.S.; Shekhar, S.; "Valuation of Leasehold Properties," Proc. National Seminar on the Valuation of Movable/Immovable Assets and Annual Convention of the Institution of Valuers, Jaipur, Dec. 1995

37. Rathore, S.S.; "Gazing the Crystal Ball - Effect of NEP on Urban and Rural Land Values," Proc. National Seminar on the Valuation of Movable/Immovable Assets and Annual Convention of the Institution of Valuers, Jaipur, Dec. 1995.

38. Rathore, S.S.; "Social Determinants of Land Use and Land Values," Proc. National Seminar on the Valuation of Movable/Immovable Assets and Annual Convention of the Institution of Valuers, Jaipur, Dec. 1995.

39. Rathore, S.S.; "Complexities Involved in the Valuation of Agricultural Lands," (J.) Indian Valuer, Vol. XXV, July, 1993.

40. Rathore, S.S.; "Factors Affecting the Value of an Agricultural Land," (J.) Indian Valuer, Vol. XXV, Feb., 1993.

41. Rathore, S.S. & Asati S.R.; "Valuation of Building - A Review and Recapitulation," (J.) Indian Valuer, Vol. XXV, March, 1993.

42. Rathore, S.S. (Guide); "Valuation of Immovable Properties with Special Reference to Agricultural Lands," B.E. Thesis Submitted by A.J. Khan et al. to Nagpur University, 1993.

43. Rathore, S.S.; "Teak Wood Plantation - An Information Brochure for Valuers and Investors," (J.) Indian Valuer, Vol. XXV, Sept., 1993.

44. Rathore, S.S.; "Quality Circle Concept for Valuer," (J.) Indian Valuer, Vol. XXV, October 1993.

45. Rathore, S.S.; "Tax Planning for Engineers & Architects," (J.) Indian Valuer, Vol. XXV. Oct., 1993.

46. Rathore, S.S.; "Computer Compatibility of Valuation System," (J.) Indian Valuer, Vol. XXV, Feb., !994.

47. Rathore, S.S; ' Tax Planning in Respect of Income from Immovable Properties," (J.) Indian Valuer, Vol. XXVI, No. 4, April, 1994.

48. Rathore, S.S.; "Reliability Monitoring of Valuation Systems," (J.) Indian Valuer, Vol. XXVI, May, 1994.

49. Rathore, S.S.; Why Valuations Fail" (J.) Indian Valuer, Vol. XXVI, July. 1994.

50. Rathore, S.S.; "Value of Agricultural Lands in India - Changing Scenario," (J.) Indian Valuer, Vol. XXVI, July, 1994.

51. Rathore, S.S. & Pandey, D.; "Valuation of Mining Properties," (J.) Indian Valuer, Vol. XXVI, Nov., 1994.

52. Rathore, S.S.; "Commercial Land Use and Land Values," (J.) Indian Valuer, Vol. XXVI, Nov., 1994.

53. Rathore, S.S.; "Value - A Multifaceted Word." (J.) Indian Valuer, Vol. XXVII, March, 1995.

54. Rathore, S.S.; "Reliability Monitoring of Valuation Systems," (J.) Indian Valuer, Vol. XXVII, No. 4, April, 1995.

55. Rathore, S.S.; "Modified Mathematical Simulation Model for the Determination of PMV." (J.) Indian Valuer, Vol. XXVII, May 1995.

56. Rathore, S.S.; "Depreciation; An Effective Tool of Valuation," (J.) Indian Valuer, Vol. XXVII, No. 6, June, 1995.

57. Rathore, S.S.; "A Brief Commentary on Capitalisation Factor," (J.) Indian Valuer, Vol. XXVII, July, 1995.

58. Rathore, S.S.; "Value Engineering in Construction Industry - Growing Concern," (J.) Indian Valuer, Vol. XXVII, August, 1995.

59. Rathore, S.S. & Singh H.; "Issues and Strategies Related to Unauthorised Construction," (J.) Indian Valuer, Vol. XXVII, August, 1995.

60. Rathore, S.S.; "Building Economics - An Effective Tool for Reducing Cost and Increasing Value," (J.) Indian Valuer, Vol. XXVII, No. 9 Sept., 1995.

61. Rathore, S.S.; "Complexities Involved in the Valuation of Immovable Properties," (J.) Indian Valuer, Vol. XXVII, Oct., 1995.

62. Rathore, S.S.; "Why Construction Estimates Fail?" (J.) Indian Valuer, Vol. XXVII, December, 1995.

63. Rathore, S.S.; "Value: Why Does it Oscillate?" (J.) Indian Valuer, Vol. XXVIII, January, 1996.

64. Rathore, S.S.; "What is Valuation?" (J.) Indian Valuer, Vol. XXVIII, May, 1996.

65. Rathore, S.S.; "Practice of Valuation - A Unique Profession," (J.) Indian Valuer, Vol. XXVIII, August, 1996.

66. Rathore, S.S.; "Gazing the Crystal Ball: Effect of NEP on Urban and Rural Land Values," (J.) Indian Valuer, Vol. XXVIII, August, 1996.

67. Rathore, S.S.; "Social Determinants of Land Use and Land Values," (J.) Indian Valuer, Vol. XXVIII, September, 1996.

68. Rathore, S.S.; "Failure of Estimates - Causes and Remedies," (J.) Indian Valuer, Vol. XXVIII, November, 1996.

69. Rathore, S.S.; "Philosophy of Valuation," Vol. XXVIII, December, 1996.

70. Rathore, S.S.; "Futuristic Scope of Valuation," Editorial, (J.) Indian Valuer, Vol. XXVIII, December, 1996.

71. Rathore, S.S.; "Multi-Dimensional World of Value: A Comprehensive Purview," Proc. National Seminar on the Valuation of Movable/ Immovable Assets and Annual Convention of the Institution of Valuers, Jabalpur, Dec. 1996.

72. Rathore, S.S.; "Effect of Inflation on the Overall Depreciation of Plant & Machinery," Proc. National Seminar on the Valuation of Movable/ Immovable Assets and Annual Convention of the Institution of Valuers, Jabalpur, Dec. 1996.

73. Rathore, S.S.; "Valuation of Compulsory Land Acquisition," Proc. National Seminar on the Valuation of Movable/Immovable Assets and Annual Convention of the Institution of Valuers, Jabalpur, Dec. 1996.

74. Rathore, S.S.; "Land Value Projections Using Regression Techniques," Proc. National Seminar on the Valuation of Movable/Immovable Assets and Annual Convention of the Institution of Valuers, Jabalpur, Dec. 1996.

75. Rathore, S.S.; "Depreciation Versus Depletion," Proc. National Seminar on the Valuation of Movable/Immovable Assets and Annual Convention of the Institution of Valuers, Jabalpur, Dec. 1996.

76. Rathore, S.S. & Singh, M.; "Value: Does it Differ?" Proc. National Seminar on the Valuation of Movable/Immovable Assets and Annual Convention of the Institution of Valuers, Jabalpur, Dec. 1996.

77. Rathore, S.S.; "Complexities Involved in the Professional Practice of Valuation," Proc. National Seminar on the Valuation of Movable/ Immovable Assets and Annual Convention of the Institution of Valuers, Jabalpur, Dec. 1996.

78. Rathore, S.S.; "Improper Placement of Valuation (As a Subject) in University Curriculum." Editorial, (J.) Indian Valuer, Vol. XXIX, January, 1997.

79. Rathore, S.S.; "Covenants of Lease: Do They Affect Value?" (J.) Indian Valuer, Vol. XXIX, May, 1997.

80. Rathore, S.S.; "Valuation at the Dawn of the 21st Century," (J.) Indian Valuer, Vol. XXX, March, 1998,

81. Rathore, S.S.; ' 'Diversified Purposes of Valuation of Real Estates and the Role of Valuer: A Comprehensive Purview". (J.) Indian Valuer, Vol. XXX, No. 6, June, 1998.

82. Rathore, S.S.; "What is Market?" Editorial, (J.) Indian Valuer, Vol. XXX, No. 8, June, 1998.

83. Rathore, S.S.; "Valuation of Insurance Losses," (J.) Indian Valuer, Vol. XXX, No. 8, August, 1998.

84. Rathore, S.S.; "Can Reliable Value-Projections be Made by the Use of Scientific Methods?," Editorial, (J.) Indian Valuer, Vol. XXX, No. 8, August, 1998.

85. Rathore, S.S.; "Hypothetical Building Scheme: A Controversial Method of Valuation," (J.) Indian Valuer, Vol. XXX, No. 8, August, 1998.

86. Rathore, S.S.; "Practice of Valuation: Academic & Contextual Concerns," Editorial, (J.) Indian Valuer, Vol. XXX, No. 9, September, 1998.

87. Rathore, S.S.; "Developer's Method of Valuation," (J.) Indian Valuer, Vol. XXX, No. 9, September, 1998.

88. Rathore, S.S.; "Diversified Purposes of Valuation of P & M: A Brief Review," (J.) Indian Valuer, Vol. XXX, No. 10, October, 1998.

89. Rathore, S.S.; "Valuation of Plant & Machineries," Editorial, (J.) Indian Valuer, Vol. XXX, No. 11, November, 1998.

90. Rathore, S.S.; "A Comparative Study of Hypothetical Building Scheme & Developer's Method of Valuation," Proc. 29th National Seminar on the Valuation of Movable/Immovable Assets and Annual Convention of the Institution of Valuers, Bhubaneshwar, Dec. 1998.

91. Rathore, S.S.; "Can a Property Have Zero Market Value?" Editorial (J.) Indian Valuer, Vol. XXX, No. 12 December, 1998.

92. Rathore, S.S.; "Object Orientated Programming: Philosophy & Valuation Modelling," Proc. 29th National Seminar on the Valuation of Movable/Immovable Assets and Annual Convention of the Institution of Valuers, Bhubaneshwar, Dec. 1998.

93. Rathore, S.S.; "Artificial Intelligence: Can it be Developed in Computers for Valuation?" Proc. 29th National Seminar on the Valuation of Movable/Immovable Assets and Annual Convention of the Institution of Valuers, Bhubaneshwar, Dec. 1998.

94. Rathore, S.S.; "Value of Computer Software," (J.) Indian Valuer, Vol. XXX, No. 12, December, 1998.

95. Rathore, S.S.; "Valuation - An Art or Science?" (J.) Indian Valuer, Vol. XXXI, No. 1, January, 1999.

96. Rathore, S.S.; "Valuation Versus Estimation: An Academic Overview," (J.) Indian Valuer, Vol. XXXI, No. 8, August, 1999.

97. Rathore, S.S.; "Format of Questionnaire for the Valuation of Personal Computers," Accepted for publication to the (J.) Indian Valuer.

98. Rathore, S.S.; ' 'Flat Rate Technique for the Valuation of Large Lands: An Overview," Submitted for publication to the (J.) Indian Valuer.

99. Rathore, S.S.; "Complexities involved in the Professional Practice of Valuation," Submitted for Publication to the (J.) Indian Valuer.

100. Rathore, S.S.; "Can Computers Replace Valuers?" Submitted for Publication in the (J.) Indian Valuer.

101. Rathore, S.S.; "Valuation for Mortgage of Properties," Submitted for Publication to the (J.) Indian Valuer.

102. Rathore, S.S.; "Growth & Scope of Market: A Sweeping Synthesis," (J.) Indian Valuer, Vol. XXXI, No. 8, August, 1999.

103. Rathore, S.S.; "Land Value in Reversion: A Brief Review," Submitted for publication to the (J.) Indian Valuer.

104. Rathore, S.S.; "Gazing the Crystal Ball: Friction-Free Market of the Future," Editorial, (J.) Indian Valuer, Vol.1, January 1999.

105. Rathore, S.S.; "Engineering Economy: An Important Tool of Valuation," Submitted for Publication to the (J.) Indian Valuer.

106. Rathore, S.S.; "Value Projections Using Multiple Regression Techniques," Submitted for Publication to the (J.) Indian Valuer.

107. Rathore, S.S.; "Land Valuation by Belting Method," (J.) Indian Valuer, Vol. XXIX, No. 3, March, 1997.

108. Rathore, S.S.; 'Valuation Modelling in Visual Basic," (J.) Indian Valuer, Vol. XXXI, No. 2, February, 1999.

109. Rathore, S.S.; "What is a Mining property?" (J.) Indian Valuer, Vol. XXXI, No. 3, March, 1999.

110. Rathore, S.S.; "Philosophy & Practice of Valuation," ISBN 81-7764-162-X, Allied Publishers Limited, New Delhi, India, 2001.

111. Rathore, S.S.; "Philosophy & Practice of Valuation," Guest Lecture delivered in the University of East London, Dockland Campus, United Kingdom, 20th June, 2024.

112. Rathore, S.S.; "Evolution of The Indian Valuation System Since 1858," ISSN 2583-3553, Vol. 56, Issue 07, (J.) Indian Valuer, July 2024, PP. 39-41.

113. Rathore, S.S.; "Overvaluation of Assets: Some Interesting Case Studies," ISSN 2583-3553, Vol.56, Issue 09, (J.) Indian Valuer, September, 2024.

114. Rathore, S.S.; "Why Book Value Differs from Market Value?" ISSN 2583-3553, (J.) Indian Valuer, September, 2024.

115. Rathore, S.S.; "The Land Compensation Acts of India and UK: A Comparative Study," (J.) Indian Valuer, ISSN 2583-3553, November, 2024.

116. Rathore, S.S.; "Real Estate Taxation in Union Budget 2024," Submitted for Publication, (J.) Indian Valuer, ISSN 2583-3553, July, 2024.

117. Rathore, S.S.; "The Scope of AI in Real Estate Valuation in India," Submitted for Publication, (J.) Indian Valuer, ISSN 2583-3553, August, 2024.

118. Rathore, S.S.; "Can Economic Theories Explain the Trends in Real Estate Market?" Submitted for Publication, (J.) Indian Valuer, ISSN 2583-3553, August, 2024.

119. Rathore, S.S.; "The Land Compensation Acts of India and UK: A Comparative Study," (J.) Indian Valuer, ISSN 2583-3553, November, 2024.

120. Rathore, S.S.; "Caveats, Limitations, and Disclosures in Valuation Reports," Submitted for Publication, (J.) Indian Valuer, ISSN 2583-3553, September, 2024.

121. Rathore, S.S.; "What is Planned Obsolescence?" Submitted for Publication, (J.) Indian Valuer, ISSN 2583-3553, December, 2024.

122. Pranav Hemant Ambaselkar, "Depreciation & Obsolescence of Property – A Comprehensive Guide Based on IVS Standards," Indian Valuer Journal, ISSN 2583-3553, November 2024, PP 90-98.

123. Sane, Y.S.; "Valuation for Mortgage," (J.) Indian Valuer, Vol. XXVI, May, 1994.

124. Sabapathy, B.K.; "Practical Valuation (Immovable Property)," Tiruchirappalli (TN).

125. Sabapathy, B.K.; "Formula to Find Out the Future Value of the Property in the Year 2000," (J.) Indian Valuer, Vol. XXIII, No. 6, 1991.

126. Sabapathy, B.K.; "How to Estimate the Value at the End of 60th Year - A Case Study," (J.) Indian Valuer, Vol. XXVII, No. 6, 1995.

127. Sabapathy, B.K.; Format for Valuation of Flats,'' (J.) Indian Valuer, Vol. XXVII, June, 1995.

128. Shrinath, L.S.; "Reliability Engineering," Affiliated East-West Press Pvt. Ltd., New Delhi.

129. Shrivastava, J.P.; "Valuation of Land By Belting Method," (J.) Indian Valuer, Vol. XXIII, July 1991.

130. Shrivastava, J.P.; "A Valuer is Liable for Negligence," (J.) Indian Valuer, Vol. XXV, August, 1993.

131. Smith, C.O.; "Introduction to Reliability in Design," McGraw-Hill.

132. Swartz. Mimi & Watkins, Sharon; "POWER FAILURE: The Inside Story of The Collapse of ENRON," A Currency Book Publication, March 2003.

133. Tandon, B.D.; "Ownership Flats in Multi-storeyed Buildings," National Seminar on "Valuation of Movable & Immovable Assets," New Delhi. December, 1991.

134. The Transfer of Property Act, 1882.

135. The Land Acquisition Act, 1894.

136. The Right to Fair Compensation and Transparency in Land Acquisition, Rehabilitation and Resettlement Act, 2013.

137. Toffler, A.; "Future Shock," Bantam Books, New York, 1971.

138. Toffler, A.; "The Third Wave," Bantam Books, New York, 1981.

139. Toffler, A. & Toffler H.; "War and Anti-War," Warner Books, UK, 1993.

140. Verma,' K.S.; "Consideration in Valuation of Plant & Machinery," (J.) Indian Valuer, Vol. XXV, January, 1993.

141. Zimmerman, L.W. & Hart, G.D.; "Value Engineering," CBS Publishers & Distributors, Delhi.

* * *

Index

***